Public Finance

Principles, Policies and Practices

Public Finance
Principles, Policies and Practices

Arjun Y. Pangannavar

ATLANTIC
PUBLISHERS & DISTRIBUTORS (P) LTD

Published by

ATLANTIC

PUBLISHERS & DISTRIBUTORS (P) LTD

7/22, Ansari Road, Darya Ganj,
New Delhi-110002
Phones : +91-11-40775252, 23273880, 23275880, 23280451
Fax : +91-11-23285873
Web : www.atlanticbooks.com
E-mail : orders@atlanticbooks.com

Branch Office
5, Nallathambi Street, Wallajah Road,
Chennai-600002
Phones : +91-44-64611085, 32413319
E-mail : chennai@atlanticbooks.com

Printed in India at Nice Printing Press, A-33/3A, Site-IV,
Industrial Area, Sahibabad, Ghaziabad, U.P.

Dedicated to

My Sisters
Late Smt Satyavva
Late Smt Balhavva
Late Smt Yallavva
Late Ms Mahalingavva
Late Ms Parvati
and
Ms Sushila

Foreword

Public budget policy is an interesting topic, so the public is keenly interested to know government's stance on taxation, tax-reliefs, tax-structure, public spending, borrowing and deficit financing. All types of governments are eager to have their intervention in economic transactions—internal and external, through budget policy inspite of strong objection by economists like Milton Friedman against social control operated economic system. Making social justice depend on effective budgetary policy is an experiment of Indian government. The students of economics must know about the operation of public funds by government and its policy decisions. The awareness of public economics is the need of the hour; atleast tax-payers should know the purpose and logic behind taxation.

Dr. Arjun Y. Pangannavar has written this book on the major aspects of public finance under the title *Public Finance: Principles, Policies and Practices* so as to meet the needs of undergraduate and postgraduate students of public economics in various colleges and universities. The book consists of six modules that cover major aspects of the subject, including policies and practices. It will also be useful for the candidates preparing for various competitive examinations. It is based on a new technique of self-learning of economics, and is also teacher-friendly.

S.D. Naik

Preface

Being an important branch of economics, public finance occupies a significant place in decision-making in the light of development of modern economies. Public finance is popularly known as public economics. It is the science of management of public funds that is the basic necessity of the modern government functioning, irrespective of the type of the country's economy—democratic, socialist or communist.

Every government has to perform three basic functions, viz. protection from external aggression, maintaining internal law and order, and organizing the activities to place the people of its country at higher level of satisfaction. The governments undertake a number of public projects for the benefit of the society, including social security, protection and other public utilities like roads, railways, supply of electricity, irrigation, etc.

Public finance is a matter of universal concern, because every citizen enjoys some advantage from the services of governments and also contributes towards the revenue of the government. To produce public services, the government needs money which it collects from varied sources such as taxes, tariffs, duties, borrowing, and deficit financing. The government prepares budget every year and gets approval from the Parliament. It has widened the role of government in controlling economic activities of the State.

Public finance deals with governments' operation in public fund such as public revenue, public expenditure and public debts. This operation is based on the fiscal policy of the country. The government has to select right type of taxation system because the burden of tax should not hurt tax-payers and disturb the economic condition of the country; public expenditure should be based on the principle of maximum social advantage.

The excessive public borrowing and spending have been raising the burden of tax on both present and future generations; sometimes, they derailed the economy. Indian economy has of late been disturbed by such activities. It all depends upon the fiscal policy and its effects. Deficit financing through issue of new money may be desirable today but it creates discontentment among people due to decrease in the value of currency. The pleasure or discontentment of the people depends on the way in which the government operates public fund.

The book consists of six chapters. The first chapter covers the meaning, definitions, subject-matter and scope of public finance. The importance of its study and the role of government in modern economy are also dealt with. The analogy between private and public finance and principle of maximum social advantage are discussed in a precise way. The second chapter covers the entire discussion on the various aspects of public revenue. Taxation systems, types and canons are presented in a lucid way. The theories on distribution of tax burden have been examined. Effects of taxation on economy and taxable capacity have also been discussed.

The third chapter deals with public expenditure, covering its field of study, types and principles. Wagner's Law and causes for increasing public spending and its effects are part of this chapter. The fourth chapter throws light on various aspects of public debt. Types of public debt, its sources, its merits and demerits have been discussed. The theories on burden of public borrowing, effects of borrowing on the economy, public debt management and public debt redemption methods are main parts of this chapter.

The fifth chapter explains in detail the budgeting and fiscal policy. Due coverage has been given to budgetary techniques, rules and norms, principles, theories, good qualities and components of budgeting. Fiscal policy has been discussed in detail. Deficit financing has also been dealt with in detail.

The sixth chapter discusses exclusively the government public finance, explaining theory and practice.

It is hoped that the book will cater to the needs of students of the subject at undergraduate and postgraduate levels as it covers various issues and problems of public fund operations. It will also be useful for the candidates preparing for various competitive examinations.

I am grateful to the authorities on the subject whose works have been an inspiration for me to bring out this book; and the teachers who extended their helpful suggestions.

I thank the teachers of economics and also M/s Atlantic Publishers and Distributors (P) Ltd.; my family and relatives for their co-operation in the completion of this book.

Arjun Y. Pangannavar

Contents

1

Introduction to Public Finance

1.1 PUBLIC FINANCE

Public finance is another important branch of economics. Public finance is a matter of universal concern, because every citizen of a country enjoys some advantage from the services of governments and also contributes towards the revenue of the government. The governments undertake a number of public projects such as social security, protection and other public utilities like roads, railways, supply of electricity, irrigation, etc. for the benefit of the society. The modern governments are spending a lot on such programmes in the recent years. The public expenditure is increasing at a rapid rate due to expansion of government functions. Therefore, it is equally important to know the sources of public revenue, principles of taxation and the reasons for increase in government expenditure and public debt. In brief, it deals with operation of public funds and government policies like budget and fiscal policies.

1.1.1 Meaning and Definitions

Public finance deals with the operation of public funds that includes public revenue, public expenditure and public debts. The word public means government or State. Public finance deals with the finances of the governments such as Central, State and Local. It deals with the income and expenditure of these public authorities or the government. Public finance has been defined by many economists but some important definitions are discussed as under:

(i) Prof. Dalton: Prof. Dalton has defined public finance as it is "concerned with income and expenditure of public authorities and with the adjustment of one to another".

(ii) Prof. Bastable: Prof. Bastable defines "Public finance deals with expenditure and income of public authorities of the state and their mutual relation as also with the financial administration and control".

(iii) Prof. Harold Groves: Prof. Harold Groves defines public finance as "a field of enquiry that treats on income and outgo of governments (Federal, State and Local). In modern times, this includes four major divisions: public revenue, public expenditure, public debt and certain problems of fiscal system as whole such as fiscal administration and fiscal policy".

These definitions have taken into account only the income and expenditure aspects but they failed to throw light on the effects of fiscal operations of the government authorities on social and economic policy.

Thus, according to these economists, public finance is concerned with how public authorities collect revenue and how revenue expenditure process was administered. It was not concerned with how the revenue and expenditures of the government will affect the economic and social aspects of the economy. Thus, according to them, the scope of public finance was narrow and it was a positive science.

However, with the publication of *General Theory of Employment, Interest and Money* by J.M. Keynes in 1936 the influence of government fiscal operations on the overall level of economic activity and the level of employment became an integral part of the study of Public Finance. Thus, the objective of public finance in the late 1930s changed to know the influence of government financial policies upon the affairs of the people.

(iv) Prof. B.P. Herber: By taking into all aspects of public finance Prof. Herber has defined public finance as "The government means of allocation is accomplished through the budgetary practices of taxing and spending.... In addition to allocation function, public finance is also concerned with the three other major areas of economic activity—distribution, stabilization and economic growth.... Thus, public sector economic decision-making, just as private sector decision-making, necessarily influences allocation, stabilization and economic growth".

Public finance, thus, studies and analyses the effects of government taxation and expenditure policies on four major aspects: (a) allocation of scarce productive resources, (b) distribution of income and wealth, (c) economic stability and level of employment, and (d) economic growth.

The above definitions have widened the meaning of public finance. It now includes not only the revenue and expenditure of the governments but also the effects of fiscal operations upon the economic and social aspects of the economy. Besides, government also exercises value judgment while undertaking operations like taxation, expenditure debt, budget, etc. Thus, the scope of public finance is widened under modern context so it is both positive science and normative science.

1.1.2 Scope of Public Finance

The scope of public finance can be discussed under three heads: (a) functions of the State, (b) fiscal operations, and (c) subject matter of public finance.

(a) Functions of the State: The term State refers to government—Central, State, Local. Adam Smith has discussed three types of State duties in his book *Wealth of Nations* (1776). They are: (i) defending the society from external aggressions, (ii) securing internal justice or law and order, and (iii) erecting and maintaining public institutions and works. Since classical economists were the advocates of 'laissez-faire policy' (free-trade policy), they limit the functions of the State to external defence and internal law and order so it was police state. But during the course of time socialists advocate 'socialization of means of production' meanwhile J.M. Keynes, through his General Theory of Employment, emphasized on governments' participation in socio-economic life of the country. So the modern states became 'Welfare States' the scope of functions of modern state became wide. The main functions of the State are:

(i) Internal and external security—defence-force, police force, civil administration, etc.

(ii) Justice-judiciary.

(iii) Control and regulation of economic organizations and their activities.

(iv) Propagation of social and cultural activities such as social security, education, public health, etc.

(v) Regulation and control of anti-social practices like gambling, illicit alcohol trade, immoral activities, etc.

(vi) Conservation of natural resources.

(vii) Control of transportation and communication for integration of State.

(viii) The administration of government financial system, expenditure, revenue and fiscal control.

(ix) Occasional control of religion and religious rights.

In brief, the functions and responsibilities of state increased much in modern context.

(b) Fiscal Operations: Fiscal operations refer to operations of public finance. It has close impact on investment and consumption in the economy. Thereby, it successfully controls aggregate demand and stabilizes the economy. Hence, Prof. Musgrave says that "Although particular tax and expenditure measures affect the economy in many ways and may be designed to serve a variety of purposes, several more or less distinct policy objectives may be set forth". According to Prof. Musgrave, the fiscal operations of government consist of taxation and public expenditure and they effect on economy in many ways. Further, he contends that the objectives of fiscal operations are:

(i) ***To Secure Adjustment in Allocation of Resources***: According to Prof. Musgrave, market mechanism alone cannot perform all functions of the economy thus the government should also perform some functions of the economy through its public sector. Therefore, there is need for production of social goods and services by public sector such as defence, justice, social and cultural welfare, public utilities, transports, etc. So resources should be allocated between social goods and private goods through budgetary policy.

(ii) *To Redistribute Income and Wealth*: Prof. Musgrave says that the taxation and public expenditure measures are used to redistribute income and wealth among the people of the country. It is being done through imposing taxes of high income group households (rich people) and so collected revenue is being spent for betterment or uplift of the poor.

(iii) *To Secure Economic Stabilization*: The revenue and public expenditure process of the government helps to control economic fluctuations like inflation, deflation, depression, etc. The overall employment level and price-situations are mainly depending on aggregate demand. So the fiscal operations could be used to control unemployment and price instability. For instance, if the country is suffering from unemployment, government could generate employment opportunities by the establishment of public sector industries.

(iv) *To Accelerate Economic Development*: Actually, fiscal operation is boon to poor or underdeveloped countries. The poor countries always suffer with capital deficient problem, vicious circle of poverty and low productivity problem. The fiscal instruments like taxation, borrowing, deficit finance and public expenditure, are being used for mobilization of resources to achieve accelerated rate of economic growth with stability and redistribution of income and wealth among people in underdeveloped countries. It is called 'Activating Finance'.

(v) *To Secure Social and Economic Justice*: The fiscal operations are being used to reduce the social and economic inequalities among the people of the country. Taxation helps to collect income from rich and so collected income could be spent on upliftment of poor through public expenditure programm. It reduces socio-economic inequalities or provides socio-economic justice in the country.

(c) **Subject Matter of Public Finance:** Public finance is a science which deals with the income and expenditure of government. It includes four major divisions:

(i) ***Public Revenue***: It includes methods of raising public revenue, principles of taxation and revenue related other problems are also discussed in this branch.

(ii) ***Public Expenditure***: It deals with heads of public expenditure, principles of public expenditure and its effects on economic life of the country.

(iii) ***Public Debt***: It deals with the study of methods of raising various types of public debts, repayment-methods, causes of public borrowing, public debt policy and effects of public debt dealings on economy.

(iv) ***Fiscal Administration***: It deals with budget, budgetary policy and reforms. It exclusively includes study on methods of administration, control and regulation of operations in public funds.

Since the functions of State and economic problems are continuously changing, the scope and subject-matter of public finance is widening. So the scope and subject-matter of public finance is not static but dynamic in nature.

Besides, public finance is a positive science as well as normative science. It is a positive science because it studies collection of revenue, spending of revenue and its administration as they are. Since value judgment is involved in taxation and public expenditure operations, public finance is also a normative science.

1.2 DISTINCTION BETWEEN PUBLIC FINANCE AND PRIVATE FINANCE

Generally, public finance refers to government finance whereas the private finance refers to finance of private individuals. There are some similarities and dissimilarities between the finance of private individuals and the government finance.

(I) Similarities: The similarities between private finance and public finance are: Both the individuals and the government have to (a) balance their incomes and expenditures; (b) derive the maximum benefit with the minimum use of resources; (c) borrow to bridge the gap between their revenue and expenditure; and (d) can increase their income by increasing their investment expenditure.

(II) Dissimilarities: There are some significant differences between government finance and individual finance. They are:

(i) ***Income and Expenditure Adjustment*:** There is a real difference in approach of the private finance and government finance. The individual ordinarily knows his income and he must arrange his scheme of expenditure accordingly. A government, on the other hand, first calls for an estimate of expenditure from the various departments, settles the total expenditure and then levies the taxes accordingly. The government generally adjusts its income according to its expenditure. In brief, individuals know their income so they adjust their expenditure to their income whereas government first estimates the expenditure then raises income to adjust with expenditures.

(ii) ***Budget-Period*:** The government always prepares the budget for one year. Private individuals do not have specific budgets for specific period. Private individuals do not have any fixed period in defining their income and expenditure. The individuals do not balance their budget by a particular date or during a given period. Whereas a government must have budget for specific period, say one year.

(iii) ***Loan-Option*:** The individuals do not have the option of internal loans. The government on the other hand has the option of both internal and external borrowing facilities. The individuals have to borrow only from the external sources.

(iv) ***Deficit-Correction*:** Deficit financing is an important source which helps to correct the deficit in budget. The government can opt for printing currency notes. Majority of the governments at present print currency notes to meet their excess expenditure. This measure is adopted when the government feels that its citizens are over taxed. But this is not possible for the individuals. Private individuals have no option to print their own currency notes.

(v) ***Differ in Objects*:** The objectives of the government and the individuals differ. The individuals try to maximize their personal satisfaction but on the other hand the government is interested in the maximum social benefit. The government always tries to provide the maximum benefit by spending wisely on the projects benefiting the society and not on the projects which benefit few individuals. Further, the government seeks to achieve full employment, an equitable distribution of income and rapid economic growth and economic stability through its fiscal operations. On the other hand, these are not subject-matter of the individual finance.

(vi) ***Changes in Finance*:** The governments can always think of making deliberate and big changes in their finance. It is not possible for private individuals to bring major changes in their finance. He can do it once or twice but not always. Private individuals have to experience a lot of pains to adjust excess expenditure and sometimes they may not succeed in doing so. On the other hand, governments are in a much better position to make big and fundamental changes in the scheme of public income and public expenditure. The individuals lack elasticity in their personal finance.

(vii) ***Future Provisions*:** The government finance makes provisions for the future. Governments spend large amount of money on schemes of irrigation projects, a forestation, public works or social security schemes for which either there may be no monetary return or the return may be delayed for generations. The individual, on the other hand, is anxious to reap quick returns. He spends generally for immediate benefits.

(viii) ***Differ in Types*:** The modern governments generally prepare deficit budgets. Generally, modern governments follow deficit budget policy to achieve economic goals like full-employment, price stability, etc. It means their expenditures are more than revenue. On the other hand, the individuals always prepare surplus budgets. The individuals spend less than what they earn. For an individual surplus budget is considered a virtue. But for a State it need not be so. Modern governments have to go for deficit budget to increase income and employment opportunities. J.M. Keynes advocated deficit budget to combat depression.

(ix) ***Publicity***: Individuals generally do not disclose the details regarding their income and expenditure. Secrecy is maintained in individual finance. But publicity, on the other hand, is the essence of public finance. Budgets are published and the widest publicity is given to them. Publicity to the budget proposals strengthens the fiscal policy.

1.3 PRINCIPLE OF MAXIMUM SOCIAL ADVANTAGE

The principle of public finance is also popularly known as 'Principle of Maximum Social Advantage'. It governs the operation of public finance to maximize the economic welfare of the society as a whole.

Public revenue and public expenditure are the two fundamental operations of the government so they should be governed by the fundamental principle. Prof. A.C. Pigou and Prof. Dalton have formulated and popularized the fundamental principle of public finance. Prof. A.C. Pigou called it 'Principle of Maximum Aggregate Welfare' and Prof. Dalton called it 'Principle of Maximum Social Advantage'.

1.3.1 Statement and Explanation

The principle states that the state or government should collect revenue and spend the same money so as to maximize the welfare of the people. When a government imposes tax on the people, it creates some disutility and, on the other hand, when a government spends money there is gain in utility. Therefore, a government should so adjust the revenue and expenditure that the surplus of utility is maximized and disutility is minimized. It should be noted that the public spending should not maximize individual welfare but it should maximize the welfare of society as a whole. Hence, Prof. Dalton states the principle as "As a result of these operations of public finance (revenue and expenditure), changes take place in the amount and in nature of wealth which is produced, and in the distribution of that wealth among individuals and classes. Are these changes in their aggregate effects socially advantageous? If so, the operations are justified, if no, not". In brief, according to the principle, the operations of public finance should secure maximum social advantage. It is explained in detail as under:

(a) Extent of Public Revenue and Expenditure: Prof. Dalton has pointed out the manner and the extent of public revenue to be collected and public expenditure to be incurred. Thus, he says "Public expenditure in every direction should be carried just so far, that the advantage to the community of a further small increase in any direction is just counter balance by the disadvantage of a corresponding small increase in taxation or in receipts from any other source of public income". It means with every additional unit of tax raised, the burden of sacrifice will increase and the amount of benefit will decrease. So the government should undertake such extent of public revenue and expenditure where the benefit derived from additional unit of money spent is just equal to the sacrifice imposed by raising additional unit of tax. In other words, the public expenditure should be incurred up to the point where the marginal utility derived from it is just equal to the marginal disutility incurred by imposing tax. It is illustrated in Fig. 1.1.

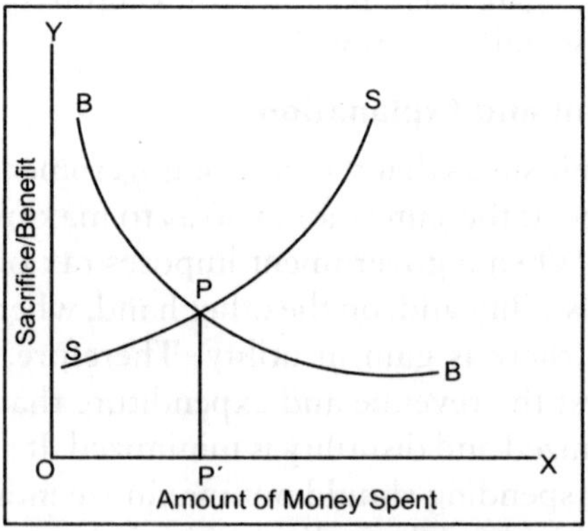

Figure 1.1: Extent of Public Revenue and Expenditure

The amount of money spent is measured along 'OX' axis and the sacrifice involved and benefit derived are measured along 'OY' axis. 'BB' curve shows the benefit derived from amount of money spent as public expenditure. 'SS' curve shows the sacrifice involved due to tax. Both curves are intersected each other at point 'P' which explains that the benefit derived from additional unit of money as public expenditure 'OP' is just equal to the marginal sacrifice or disutility incurred due to imposition of tax. 'OP' should be the extent of public revenue and expenditure.

(b) Distribution of Resources: The principle further says that the distribution of public expenditure among different heads should be that the last rupee spent on each head should yield same amount of satisfaction or benefit. In other words, a rupee spent on poor-relief item should yield the same amount of satisfaction that derives from a rupee spent on war-item. It is application of law of equi-marginal utility to public finance. Further, if the marginal utility of poor-relief item is greater than the marginal utility of war-item, the resources should be transferred from war-item to poor-relief item till the marginal utilities from both items become equal or same.

(c) Distribution of Burden of Taxation: Prof. A.C. Pigou advocated that the burden of taxation on different sources should be distributed according to the principle of least aggregate sacrifice. It means the burden of taxation should be distributed on different sources in such a way that the marginal sacrifice of each source should be equal or same. For example, if the marginal burden of taxation on agriculture is ₹ 10, then, the marginal burden of taxation on industry should also be ₹ 10. Prof. Pigou put it in his words as "In order to secure least aggregate sacrifice, tax should be distributed that the marginal utility of the money paid in taxation is equal to all the tax payers".

(d) Richard A. Musgrave's View: Prof. A.C. Pigou and Prof. Dalton have proposed two principles of budget policy. They are (i) the resources should be distributed among the different public uses so as to equalize the marginal return of satisfaction for each type of outlay, and (ii) the public expenditures should be pushed to the point where the satisfaction lost from the last rupee taken in tax and thereby the marginal satisfaction derived in public and private sectors is equalized. Prof. Musgrave by using these two principles has explained the principle of maximum social advantage on the basis of valuation of individual preferences. It is illustrated in Fig. 1.2.

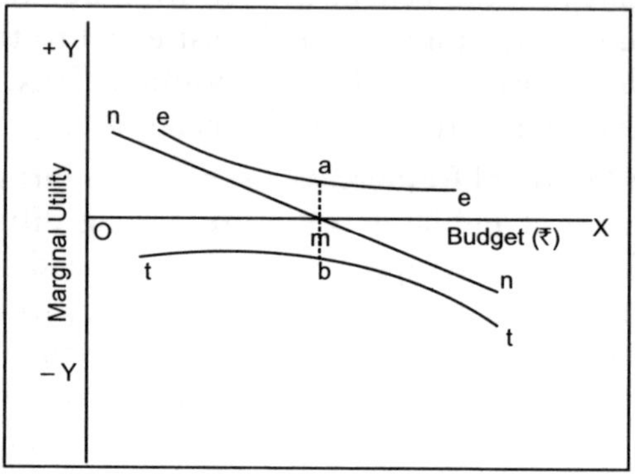

Figure 1.2: Principle of Maximum Social Advantage

The amount of budget is measured along with 'OX' axis and 'OY' axis measured marginal utility (+) or disutility or sacrifice (–). Utility derives due to public expenditure and disutility occurs due to taxation. The marginal utility of public expenditure is shown by 'ee' curve that shows the marginal utility declines for every increment in public expenditure. The disutility or sacrifice due to taxation is shown by 'tt' curve that increases due to increase in taxation. The difference between utility (ee) and disutility (tt) is 'net benefit' that is shown by 'nn' curve. According to Musgrave's approach, the optimum size of budget is determined at 'm' where the net benefit is zero (am–bm=0). It means that the satisfaction derived from additional rupee spent on public expenditure should be equal to the disutility or dissatisfaction occurred due to additional rupee collected as tax from public. Thus, the minimum sacrifice approach to the allocation of taxes is trade-off by the maximum benefit approach to the determination of public expenditure. Generally, these two approaches are combined in general theory of budget planning.

Summary

It is concluded from the above discussion that there are three fundamental principles of public financial operations that help the government or state to achieve the objective of maximum social advantage. They are:

(i) The public expenditure should be continued till the last rupee spent on it must be equal to the sacrifice made in form of paying a rupee as tax.

(ii) The resources or money of the government should be allocated on the basis of principle of equi-marginal utility. It means the marginal satisfaction or benefit of the public expenditure-heads should be same or equal, for example, the benefit derived from an additional rupee spent on defense should be equal to the benefit derived from an additional rupee spent on education.

(iii) The tax burden or taxes should be so distributed that the marginal utility of money paid as taxes should be same to all tax payers.

1.3.2 Prof. Dalton's Test of Social Advantage

The operations of public finance have certain objectives. These objectives enhance the social advantage or welfare of the people of the country or community. Prof. Dalton has suggested the following tests to ascertain the achievement of these objectives:

(i) Public Protection: The protection or preservation of people or community from internally and externally is the main objective of the government. Defence from external attack and maintenance of internal law and order ensures the security and promotion of socio-economic life of the citizens. It enhances economic and non-economic welfare of the people. So there must be strong defense-force, police force, administration, etc.

(ii) Improvements in Production: According to Prof. Dalton, improvements in production means (a) increase in productivity of per worker, (b) improvements in production organization like the minimization of waste of resources, and (c) improvement in pattern of production so as to meet the need of the community or people. The improvements in production enhance the economic welfare of the people.

(iii) Improvements in Distribution: It is the third important objective of the state policy. Whatever is produced should be properly distributed among the different groups of the community so as to reduce inequalities like income, wealth, etc. in the country.

The fluctuations and inequalities of income and wealth of individuals and families should be reduced by proper distribution of income and wealth in the country.

(iv) Economic Stability and Full-Employment: The social advantages of the people depend upon the economic stability and full-employment conditions of the country. So the fiscal operations should reduce the fluctuations in business conditions like inflation, depression, recession, etc. and provide employment opportunities to unemployed in the country.

(v) Provisions of Future: In the words of Prof. Dalton, "The statesman is a trustee for the future, no less than the present. The individuals die, but the community, of which they form part, lives on. The statesman, therefore, should prefer a large social advantage in the future to smaller one of today." So the state has double responsibility of looking after the interest of both present and future generations, more the future and lesser the present.

1.3.3 Limitations and Difficulties or Criticisms

Of course, the principle of maximum social advantage is the fundamental principle of public fund operations and it is guiding principle of the government financial activities. But there are certain limitations and difficulties in its practical operation. They are:

(i) It is difficult to balance between marginal utility from public expenditure and disutility due to taxation: Even at individual level it is difficult to balance between utility derived from income and disutility of sacrifice of income paid as tax. This difficulty is much greater to the government because it collects different taxes from different individuals from different places and spends on different heads at different places.

(ii) It is difficult to estimate the future yields of present public expenditure: It is not possible to the state to balance between utility will be derived in future from present public expenditure and the disutility of present sacrifice money paid as tax. For, it is difficult to the state to estimate the future yields of the present public expenditure, for example: it is difficult to say that the tax-revenue spent today on the development of roads will give equal amount of benefit to the society in future.

However, Prof. Musgrave also admitted these difficulties and limitations. Further, he said that there is no concrete standard to measure efficiencies of public expenditure programmes. Hence, the principle of maximum social advantage is criticized because of these limitations and difficulties.

1.4 IMPORTANCE OF PUBLIC FINANCE

There was no much importance to public finance before 20th century. The classical economists like Adam Smith, David Ricardo and others were advocating free-trade policy so they were opposing government interference in regulating economic activities. They had the strong opinion that the government activities should be limited to defence affairs and maintaining of internal law and order, i.e. police force. But during 20th century all police states became welfare states so the government activities became manifold. It enhances the importance of public finance. The following are the main importance or role of public finance.

(i) Expansion of State Activities: The modern states became welfare states so the functions and activities of the government are increased much. The governments have undertaken social, economic, political and general services so the public expenditure increased much. A proper taxation policy should be formulated to raise public revenue to meet the growing public expenditure.

(ii) Increase in Use of Money: The modern economies are monetary economies. The use of legal tender money and bank money increased much in the every sectors of the economy. The governments have to carryout its transactions with the help of money. This has enhanced the significance of public finance.

(iii) Emergence of General Services: The modern governments have to perform general services like education, public health, social security, etc. The governments have to carryout these general services to improve the welfare of the community so it has increased the importance of public budget.

(iv) Reduction in Income Inequalities: The redistribution of income and wealth is necessary to reduce the gap between rich and poor. Otherwise, it leads to class conflict and unrest in the civil society. Under public finance, the taxes are being imposed on rich according to their ability to pay and so collected revenue is being spent on the welfare activities for poor. Public finance helps the government to undertake income and wealth redistribution activities.

(v) **Increase in Employment:** Generation of employment opportunities in the economy is one of the main responsibilities of the modern governments. All types of economies have been facing unemployment problem. It is an obstacle to the economic development process. Market-operated economic systems fail to generate more employment opportunities but the social control operated economic systems create more employment opportunities by undertaking public works. It has increased the importance of public finance in modern context, for example in India; the government has implemented various wage-employment and self-employment schemes to generate employment opportunities in the country.

(vi) **Importance in Social Sector:** Public finance plays a vital role in organization of social services like public health, education, social security schemes, etc. They help to provide social justice (equality) to the poor people.

(vii) **Role in Underdeveloped Economy:** There is deficiency of capital, lack of entrepreneurship and skill labours, technical backwardness, etc. in underdeveloped countries. These gaps could be filled by government so public finance plays a vital role in development of these countries.

1.5 THE ROLE OF GOVERNMENT IN MODERN ECONOMY

The failures of market-operated economy supported need for social control-operated economy during the post-World War I period. The various opinions of various economic thoughts about the role of government interventions in regulation of economic activities, in the context of rise of welfare-state political system, came into limelight. Modern governments mainly follow mixed economic system wherein both private and public sectors function side by side, for instance India, USA and other countries too practice mixed economy model. Like private, government entered in production and distribution activities through its establishments and institutions. Social or public wants are being supplied by these government organizations. In modern context, governments are generally argued to have four main macroeconomic goals, viz. (i) to maintain full employment, (ii) to ensure price stability, (iii) to achieve high level of economic growth, and (iv) to keep exports and imports in balance. In other words, government has the responsibility of maintaining internal and external balance with growth and stability. To discharge this responsibility government has formulated economic policies through which it regulates entire economic system. These are discussed as under:

(a) **Fiscal Policy:** Modern governments using budget as instrument to achieve macroeconomic goals along with public services. Government attempts to manipulate its budget deficit or surplus to achieve economic goals through its policy, called fiscal policy. In other words, it is generally any government decision about spending, taxation, borrowing and deficit financing. By using this policy, government can easily influence aggregate demand thereby all economic activities. Fiscal policy has the following instruments to achieve macroeconomic goals:

(i) ***Automatic or Built-in Stabilizers*:** The taxation and public spending are built-in so that automatically they work to control economic problems or situations. For instance, taxes will go down and public spending will increase when the economy is going into a recession. On the contrary, they automatically work in reverse. Generally, automatic stabilizers include the measures like progressive income tax, unemployment insurance, subsidies to agricultural products, government purchase of excessive agricultural products, etc.

(ii) ***Active-discretionary Fiscal Policy*:** It is unlike built-in stabilizer. It is the deliberate manipulation of the government spending and taxes to influence the economy, for example, changes in tax rates, changes in government expenditure structure, etc.

(iii) ***Crowding-out Effect*:** To prevent excess flow of fund to private sector, government sells its bonds and treasury bills to the public that leads to crowding-out of money to the public sector. It is the negative effect of the fiscal policy because the decline in supply of fund to private sector increases interest-rate thereby reducing private investment.

(iv) *Laffer's Curve*: The curve shows that the relationship between the tax rates and the tax revenue. It shows that the highest tax revenue can be collected by fixing the tax rate to 50 per cent. The same income from taxes is collected at the rates of 25 per cent as well as 75 per cent. However, the tax rate should not be higher than 50 per cent because tax-evasion takes place. Government has a key role to play while formulating tax-structure.

(v) *Expansionary or Inflationary Fiscal Policy*: Fiscal policy is used to encourage increase in aggregate demand when the economy is facing depression in both short-run and long-run. Short-run expansive fiscal policy is used to increase the real output and employment when the resources are not used to produce maximum potential output. Long-run expansive fiscal policy is used to increase the price level or create inflation to increase real output, but the real output remains the same because of crowding-out effect.

(vi) *Restrictive or Deflationary Fiscal Policy*: Fiscal policy is used to restrict the aggregate demand during short-run and long-run when the economy is facing boom. Short-run restrictive fiscal policy reduces excess aggregate demand and reduces under-utilization resources thereby reducing the price level. Long-run restrictive fiscal policy is used to decrease in price level and nominal and real interest rate. The level of real output and unemployment will be maintained intact if private investment replaces government expenditures.

(b) **Monetary Policy:** Monetary policy is the instrument used by the government or its monetary authority, central bank of the country, to control the money supply, the supply of credit, interest rates, or any other monetary variables for achieving the economic goals such as price stability. It is used along with fiscal policy. There are two types of tools or instruments of monetary policy:

(i) *Direct Control*: Government or central bank has direct control over loans. The government institutions directly regulates loans or credits on consumer goods.

(ii) *Indirect Control*: Central bank regulates supply of money and credit by using its three main tools, viz. cash reserve ratio, discount or bank rate and open market operations. There are two types of monetary policies in practice; these are:

(a) ***Expansionary or Inflationary Monetary Policy***: It helps to increase the supply of money in the economy during depression and recession to recover output, income, employment, etc. economic variables; underdeveloped countries use it as instrument of development.

(b) ***Restrictive or Deflationary Monetary Policy***: It helps to reduce excess supply of money in the economy to control inflationary situation.

Government through its monetary policy regulates demand and supply of money and credit in the economy to achieve price stability.

(c) **Income Policy:** Government regulates income through policy-measures like wage-rate control and control on income of various forms. Income policy is the policy designed to limit the growth of incomes directly to help to reduce inflation caused by supply-side factors. By imposing maximum ceiling on increase in size of income, the government controls cost push inflationary spiral and helps the economy return to price level stability. Fixation of wage and salary, rent, interest, distribution of dividend, etc. by the government policy keep the income growth within limit.

(d) **Social Policy:** There is no specific social policy by the government, however, government through its policy-measures want to achieve certain social goals such as re-distribution of income and wealth. It is usually some kind of monetary or fiscal policy. Taxation is an example to reduce income inequality in the country. Public spending helps to improve socio-economic conditions of the poor. When the government wants to improve the level of education, it can increase its spending on it; when it wants to improve the living standard of low paid workers, it can impose minimum wage. These are considered to be social policies but in origin they are fiscal measures. Government produces goods and services to meet the public wants.

(e) **Environment Policy:** Modern governments are aware of sustainable development issues. They have environmental protection policies. Protection of natural resources such as forests, mines, air, water, soil, fuels, etc. are the main concern of the governments.

(f) Trade Policy: Government regulates both domestic and foreign trade through its policies. Domestic price-policy helps to control internal prices of all goods and services. Agricultural price-policy, industrial goods' price-policy, etc. protect the interest of both producers and consumers. Public distribution system supplies essential goods to poor at fair price. Buffer-stock operations maintain price-stability through controlling demand and supply conditions in the market.

To regulate foreign trade government has its export and import policy. For protection of home-economy, all countries choose to adopt protectionist policies. These protectionist policies are called trade barriers such as tariffs and quotas. Similarly, government regulates foreign exchange transactions to maintain external equilibrium and stability of exchange rate.

In brief, modern governments regulate, directly and indirectly almost all economic transactions through their various policies. Modern governments are engines of economic growth with stability.

1.6 MODEL QUESTIONS

(a) Questions each needs answer in 2-3 sentences (2 Marks each)

1. What is public finance?
2. What do you mean by scope of public finance?
3. Give the statement of Principle of Maximum Social Advantage.
4. Name any two main functions of the State.
5. Name any two limitations of public finance.
6. Give any two similarities between public finance and private finance.
7. Name any two policies of the government.

(b) Questions each needs short-note type answer (5 Marks each)

1. Give a brief account of the difference between public finance and private finance.

2. Write a note on the scope of public finance.
3. Discuss in brief the criticisms on Principle of Maximum Social Advantage.
4. Write a short-note on importance of public finance.
5. Write a note on Prof. Dalton's Test of Social Advantage.
6. Explain in brief the main functions of the State.
7. Discuss in brief Prof. Musgrave's view on Principle of Maximum Social Advantage.
8. Write a short-note on the role of government in modern economy.

(c) Questions each needs essay type/long answer

1. Define public finance, explain its scope.
2. Define public finance, explain its importance.
3. Explain the similarities and dissimilarities between public finance and private finance.
4. Discuss in detail the Principle of Maximum Social Advantage.
5. Examine the role of government in modern economy.

2

Public Revenue

2.1 PUBLIC REVENUE

2.1.1 Meaning

The functions of the modern government are expanding continuously and as a result of it their expenditures are also increasing. To meet all these expenditures, the modern government collects revenue in the form of taxes, fees, prices, etc., from the citizens and from other sources. In other words, 'public revenue' means the income of government.

Hence, Dr. Dalton has defined public revenue as "public income in a broad and narrow sense, i.e. in terms of 'Public Receipts' and 'Public Revenue'." Public revenue consists of government income from taxes, prices of goods and services supplied by government undertakings, income from administrative activities like fees, fines, etc. and gifts and grants. Public receipts include public revenue plus income from all other sources like government borrowing from individuals, banks, etc.

2.1.2 Sources of Public Revenue

Government collects its income from the various sources. The two important sources of revenue of the modern states are (i) Tax Revenue, and (ii) Non-Tax Revenue. Tax revenue means the income of the government which is being collected from the public by imposing on them the various taxes. The tax revenue is derived from the (a) Direct Taxes, e.g. income tax, wealth tax, gift tax, expenditure tax, etc. and (b) Indirect taxes, e.g. customs duties, excise duties, sales tax, etc. The income being collected by the government from the sources other than taxes is called 'non-tax revenue'. Non-tax revenue is derived from fees, prices, penalties and other miscellaneous receipts. The modern governments also raise loans to augment their revenues. However, the sources of public revenue can be classified and studied as under:

(i) Sources Tax Revenue: Tax is a very good source of revenue of the modern government. It is discussed as follows:

(a) ***Taxes:*** The most important source of public revenue is tax. P.E. Taylor defines tax as "compulsory payments to governments without expectation of direct return or benefit to tax payer". Prof. Tausig has defined tax as "the essence of a tax, as distinguished from other charges by government, is the absence of a direct *quid pro quo* between the tax payer and the public authority". Thus, it is obvious that tax is (a) a compulsory contribution made by individuals and institutions to the government and (b) it is meant for the general purposes of the government. The individual cannot expect that the government should provide him specific services in return for the tax paid by him. For instance, if an individual pays income-tax, he cannot claim in return that the government should post a policeman at his door-step to protect his property. But on the other hand the State carries on the general administration and provides lot of benefits to the community at large. But these are *common benefits* meant for all the citizens of the state not any special benefit meant for a particular taxpayer. There is *no direct quid pro quo*. The taxes are used to meet the general expenses of the government which yield common benefits.

Generally, government collects tax revenue from two sources, (i) Direct taxes like income tax, wealth tax, etc. and (ii) Indirect taxes like taxes on goods and services. The revenue collected by government by way of taxation is called 'tax revenue'.

On the basis of above analysis the main *characteristics of tax* can be drawn as:

(i) Tax is a compulsory contribution so on cannot avoid its payment. It is a legal collection.

(ii) Taxes are imposed by the government only.

(iii) Taxes are being paid for general interest of the people.

(iv) Tax is the sacrifice of income by tax payer.

(v) There is no relation between the tax paid to the government by person and the benefit received from the government by the person.

(vi) Tax can be imposed on income, wealth, property, goods, services, etc.

(ii) Sources of Non-Tax Revenue: The modern governments have developed the various other sources of their income, in addition to taxes. They are studied as under:

(a) ***Price or Commercial Revenues*****:** The public sector has an important place in the development of the modern economies. The public enterprises are successfully functioning along with the private enterprises. The governments generally launch public enterprises when private sector is either unwilling or unable to enter certain fields where the returns are either uncertain or long term in nature such as multipurpose project, railways, hydroelectric works, water works, etc. The government does not supply these services or goods manufactured in government undertakings free but charge a price. Thus, when the public enterprises sell a commodity or render a service, the charges imposed on the consumer, who avails of the service or buys a commodity, is called a price. Prices charged by the government for the goods and services supplied by the post offices, price on telephone services, railway and bus fare, etc., are few examples of price.

(b) ***Administrative Revenues*****:** Government renders various services to public through its various departments. These departments generate income to the government called administrative revenue. They are discussed as under:

(i) *Fee*: Fee is also a compulsory payment made by those who obtain a definite service in return from the government. The fee is imposed to cover a part of the cost of the service provided by the government. It is generally does not exceed the cost of the service. The modern governments have the welfare objective in mind while charging the fees. The educational fee is an ideal example. In the words of Plehn, "A fee may be defined as a compulsory contribution of wealth made by a person, natural or corporate, under the authority of public power to defray a part or all of the expenses involved in some action of the government which while creating a common benefit, also confers a special benefit, or one that is arbitrarily so regarded." Thus, a fee is charged for a specific service which is provided by the government.

The fee charged to issue a license is another example for fee. Interest of the general public is kept in mind while charging fee.

The difference between a fee and a price is that in a fee public interest is prominent, whereas a price is a payment for a service of business character, e.g., charges for traveling on State railways. You can escape the price by not purchasing a service. Price also differs from a tax. A tax is paid for a common benefit, whereas both fees and prices are paid for specific benefits.

(ii) *Special Assessment*: Special assessment is levied by the government or semi government organizations like city municipal corporations. Prof. Seligman defines special assessment as "a compulsory contribution levied in proportion to the special benefit derived to defray the cost of the specific improvement to property undertaken in the public interest." When the government builds a road, public garden, marketing mal, etc., all the property in the neighbourhood will appreciate in value. In such cases the government has a right to appropriate a part of the appreciated value of the property. It is collected by the governments in the form of special assessment. Special assessment is compulsory like a tax. But the tax imposed for a special purpose is called special assessment. These assessments are intended to cover a part of the expenditure incurred by the government bodies in creating the facilities for the benefit of the people.

According to Seligman, the essence of a special assessment is that (a) there is the element of special purpose, (b) the special benefit is measurable, (c) these assessments are not progressive but proportional to the benefit received, (d) they are for specific local improvements, and (e) they are intended to provide facilities to the community.

(iii) *Rates*: Rates are levied by local bodies, i.e. panchayats, municipalities, city municipal corporations, etc., for local purposes. They are generally levied on immovable property of the residents but not necessarily for any special improvements effected or special benefits conferred. The rates generally vary from locality to locality.

(iv) *Fines and Penalties*: Fines are imposed as a penalty for breaking the law. A fine is compulsory like a tax but it is imposed more as a deterrent of crime than as a source of revenue. For example, fines charged by government libraries for having delay in the return of books. Government departments like judicial, revenue, police, forest, etc. impose fines and penalties on persons, organizations and others who violate rules, orders, etc.

(v) *Forfeitures*: The surety or bond will be given by the person or organization involved in contract or facing criminal charges in the court of law. If an under trial fails to appear before court or a party to contract fails to carry his part of the contract, the money deposited as surety or bond is forfeited. The money so forfeited goes to the State. It is, however, a minor source.

(vi) *Escheat*: When a person dies heirless or without a successor or leaves no will behind, his property or assets will go to the State. This claim of the State to the assets of the diseased person is called escheat.

(vii) *Tributes and Indemnities*: These are paid by foreign countries. Tributes are paid by conquered countries and indemnities for any damage done to the country either by war or aggression or otherwise.

(c) ***Grants and Gifts***: Grants and gifts are other important sources of public revenue and they are voluntary contributions by individuals or nations. They are discussed as under:

(i) *Grants*: Grants are given by a government at a higher level to that at the lower level, e.g. from the Central Government to the State Government or from the State Government to a Municipality, Corporations or Panchayats. Such grant systems are mainly found in federal countries like India, USA, etc. The grants are given for a specific purpose, e.g. to carryout development activities, for undertaking public works programmes, for public health or for general education.

Governments also receive grants from foreign countries called 'foreign grants'. Such grants may be military aid, technical aid, economic aid, etc.

(ii) *Gifts*: Gifts are received either from governments or some private bodies or individuals. Gifts are also received from foreign government for relief in natural calamities like earth quake, floods, droughts, cyclones, etc. The individuals also give donations to the government bodies for specific purposes such as building a hospital, construction of a bund across a river to provide drinking water to the village, construction of community hall in a town or a village, etc.

2.2 CANONS OF TAXATION OR CHARACTERISTICS OF A GOOD TAX SYSTEM

Since the activities and responsibilities of modern state have become many more, the public expenditure has been increasing continuously. So the government should develop a good tax system to collect its revenue in more scientific and feasible way. The tax system which governs by the definite principles or canons is called a good tax system.

Adam Smith made a significant contribution to the canons of taxation. His contribution to public economics is still regarded as classic. His statement of the canons of taxation has hardly been surpassed in clarity and simplicity. Adam Smith's canons still constitute the foundation of all discussions on the principles of taxation.

In addition to Adam Smith's canons, according to modern economists, still more principles have to be considered to develop a good tax system. The main characteristics of a good tax system are discussed as under.

2.2.1 Canons of Taxation by Adam Smith

Adam Smith has suggested the canons of taxation as follows:

(i) Canon of Equality: The canon of equity means "the citizens of every state ought to contribute towards the support of the government, as nearly as possible, in proportion to their respective abilities, that is, in proportion to the revenue which they respectively enjoy under the protection of the state".

This canon strongly supports the principle of equity or justice. This is the most important canon of taxation. This canon lays the moral foundation of the tax system. The canon of equality does not mean that every tax payer should pay the same amount of the tax to the government. If every taxpayer pays the same amount of the tax, the poor will pay more than the rich. Such tax system will be unjust. It also does not mean that the tax payer has to pay the tax at the same rate. This is proportional tax system, and a proportional tax is also not a just tax.

The canon of equality advocate the principle of equality of sacrifice. The amount of the tax paid is to be in proportion to the respective abilities of the tax payers. It means the tax system should be progressive. Hence, Adam Smith rightly says: "It is not very unreasonable that the rich should contribute to the public expense not only in proportion to their revenue but something more than that proportion." This will naturally result in the equity in the payment of the tax where the poor are protected from high tax rates.

(ii) Canon of Certainty: The tax which each individual is expected to pay ought to be certain, and not arbitrary. It means the taxpayer should the time of payment, the manner of payment and amount of the tax to be paid to the government. The rate of tax and method of payment ought to be clear and plain to the tax payers. There should not be any confusion and uncertainty in the payment of any tax. Otherwise every person subject to the tax is put more or less in the power of the tax collectors. The tax collector may exploit the ignorance of the taxpayers and may charge more for some and less for others. This leads to exploitation of the taxpayers which may lead to corruption and also the revenue of the government may decrease. Therefore, Adam Smith has clearly stated that the uncertainty in taxation encourages corruption.

Thus, certainty is the most fundamental canon of taxation because all attempts at equality will prove illusory without the taxes being certain. There should be no element of arbitrariness in a tax. This is a fundamental requirement of the canon of certainty. The tax system should not to be left to the caprice or the sweet will of the income-tax department. The taxpayer should be able to understand for himself why he is called upon to pay a particular amount of tax. Therefore, the modern governments have been giving wide publicity to the budget proposals and discussions thereon. The passing of the budget is a guarantee of certainty. "An old tax is no tax" is a maxim of taxation. If the tax is well known all the taxpayers are certain about the payment of the tax, its rate, mode, method and time of payment. An old tax being well known, the reactions of the people are certain and they are supposed to have made the necessary adjustments in the payment of the tax. The tax is not felt. It causes the least disturbance in the economic arrangements of the taxpayer. There is little inconvenience from an old tax.

Further, certainty is necessary not only from the point of view of the taxpayer but also from that of the State. The government should be able to estimate roughly the revenue expected from the various taxes proposed to be levied and the time when they are expected to flow in. On this basis, the governments will be able to plan their developmental and welfare programmes.

(iii) Canon of Convenience: Another important canon of tax is canon of convenience. According to Adam Smith, every tax ought to be levied at the time or in the manner in which it is most likely to be convenient for the tax payer. The canon of certainty says that the time and the manner of payment should be certain. But the canon of convenience says that the time of payment and the manner of payment should be convenient to the taxpayers. The tax on land or house need to be collected at a time when rent is expected by the landlord. This method is convenient to the taxpayer. The tax need not be paid personally to the tax authorities but may be paid by cheque. Otherwise there will be a lot of inconvenience and harassment.

Taxes on consumers are very convenient. The consumer pays the tax when he purchases goods and services. Further, he purchases the goods only when he has the money to buy and he chooses his own time to purchase. The method of payment of the tax is also very convenient because the consumer makes no special arrangement for paying a tax. He pays it when he buys the commodity. The tax is wrapped up in the price of the commodity.

The land revenue collection method in India is convenient to the taxpayers because it is paid in installments and after the harvest time. Income tax, on the other hand, is against the principle of convenience. The income tax assesses have to produce all his documents to the income-tax authorities in order to satisfy them about the documents and accounts. The taxpayer has to make regular visits to the tax departments which may consume his lot of precious time also. The taxpayers thus may undergo lot of trouble and oppression.

(iv) Canon of Economy: According to Adam Smith, "Every tax ought to be so contributed as both to tax out and to keep out of pockets of the people as little as possible, over and above what it brings into the public treasury of the State." It means the cost involved in the collection of the tax should not be more than the amount of the tax collected by the government. The tax becomes is economical if the cost of collecting the tax is very small. If, on the other hand, the salaries of the officers engaged in collecting the tax take away a big portion of the tax revenue, the tax is certainly uneconomical. The tax revenue should be more than the amount spent in the collection of the tax. There should not be any evaporation or leakages when the tax is collected. Further, if the taxpayers face any inconvenience or suffering in the payment of tax then also the canon of economy will not be satisfied. Therefore, the tax system needs to be free from corruption and harassment.

The canon of economy is also discussed in the broader sense. The taxes levied by the government should not retard the development of trade and industry. High income-tax rates will adversely affect savings and capital formation which form important ingredients of economic growth. High tax rates affect the productive capacities of the economy and the rate of economic growth will slow down. Fall in production and income of the community thus would obviously be uneconomical. A tax is economical if it does not hamper in any manner the economic progress of a country.

Taxes on harmful drugs and intoxicants are regarded as economical, because they not only bring income to the State, but also discourage unproductive expenditure. But taxes on raw materials are uneconomical because they raise the price of the manufactured goods and weaken the competitive power of the industry.

The first canon of Adam Smith is ethical and the other three are administrative in character.

2.2.2 Other Canons

In addition to Adam Smith's canons, the modern economists like Sir J. Stamp, Prof. Musgrave and others have suggested few more canons or characteristics of a good taxation. They are discussed as follows:

(i) Fiscal Adequacy or Productivity: The revenue received by the government should be sufficient to meet expenditures of its administrative, developmental and welfare functions. The tax revenue should not be less than the expenditure of the government. The government should be free from financial embarrassments. It is necessary that the tax proceeds should adequately cover the government expenditures and the government does not run into a deficit. But at the same time the government should collect more tax than what it needs. Excess collection of the tax is expected to harm the productive capacities of the community and the progress of a country. This may also lead to mis-utilization of the resources of the community.

The canon of productivity would indicate that a few taxes bringing large revenue are better than many taxes bringing very small revenue. Multiple tax system need to be avoided as it is likely to cause some inconvenience to the citizens. At the same time the government should not depend on few taxes which may affect its revenue.

(ii) Elasticity: The canon of elasticity and fiscal adequacy are closely related. The canon of elasticity advocates that the requirements of the government increase, the revenue should also increase. If the revenue falls short of the expenditure the developmental activities will badly suffer. The governments should always be in a position to raise additional revenue at times of an emergency or a period of stress and strain. The tax structure should be such that somc of the taxes should be capable of yielding more revenue at times of emergency. Income tax is a very good example of an elastic tax, particularly in India. The governments in the last few years are successful in raising more revenue by levying surcharge on income tax. There should also be provision to raise the tax rates which augments the revenue of the governments.

(iii) Flexibility: The canon of flexibility and canon of elasticity are alike. There a significant difference between the two. Flexibility means that there should be no rigidity in the tax system. The tax system should be able to adjust to new conditions according to the revenue requirements of the government. On the other hand, elasticity means that the revenues can be increased and decreased according to the needs of the government. The flexibility in the tax system helps in making alterations in the tax system to augment resource base. This in turn helps in changing the tax rates also. Thus, presence of flexibility is a condition of elasticity.

(iv) Simplicity: The tax system should be simple, plain and intelligible to the common man's understanding. A complicated tax system will lead to corruption and the taxpayer will be harassed by the tax authorities. This will distort a good tax system. In a complicated tax system, the taxpayer may not understand how much he is to pay and why he is to pay the tax. The tax gatherers will have the opportunity to exploit the taxpayers. This will naturally result in corruption and oppression.

(v) Diversity: Diversity in the tax system is another important principle of taxation. This canon advocates the introduction of a large variety of taxes which helps the citizens to contribute to the revenue of the government according to their capacity or ability. Therefore, presence of a single tax or only a few taxes will not do. The taxpayers should be approached in a variety of ways. There should be a wise admixture of direct and indirect taxes. In this manner, the canons of fiscal adequacy and equality may be better satisfied. But too great a multiplicity will be bad and uneconomical. Too many taxes may not bring the required revenue to the government.

(vi) Achievement of Social and Economic Objectives: The modern governments have set some social and economic objectives which need to be satisfied by spending tax revenue. Therefore, the effects of taxation should be compatible with the economic and social objectives of the State. The institutions and methods adopted should be effectively used for attainment of these objectives. The neutrality principle followed in the olden days no longer is applicable to the modern governments. The modern governments need to be more active and they need to function according to the growing needs of the people.

Moreover, in conclusion, the good tax system should be designed so as to meet the requirements of equity, efficiency and convenience of taxpayer and administration both. The characteristics of good tax system do not end with these canons but it should be also influenced by the factors like (a) the tax policy should bring about economic stability and development besides the attainment of other political and social goals, (b) the tax policy should be used effectively along with the monetary and economic policies of the government to combat threats to economic instability and stagnation, (c) the tax policy should also help in reducing the economic inequalities, (d) it should minimize government interference with economic decisions, and (e) it should facilitate the fiscal policy to achieve its objectives.

2.3 TYPES OF TAXES

The taxes can be classified on the basis of nature, aim and methods of taxation. The modern system of taxation is generally classified and studied as under:

2.3.1 Direct and Indirect Taxes

Taxes are classified as the direct and indirect taxes which are studied as follows:

I. Meaning and Distinction: Dalton has made the distinction between direct and indirect tax as, "a direct tax is really paid by a person on whom it is legally imposed, while an indirect tax is imposed on one person, but paid partly or wholly by another." In other words, direct tax is one the impact or immediate money burden and the incidence or the ultimate money burden of it is on the same person whereas indirect tax is one which can be shifted or passed on to another person. In brief, in the case of direct tax the impact and incidence of tax are on same person but in case of indirect tax the impact and incidence of a tax are on different persons. A direct tax cannot be shifted to another person but an indirect tax is shifted to another person. For example, tax on income and property can be called direct taxes wherein the impact and incidence on same person whereas taxes on commodities are generally called indirect taxes wherein the impact is on one person and incidence is on another person. Excise duty and customs duties are also the best examples of indirect taxes. These taxes are first collected from the dealers or producers and later they are paid by the consumers.

Prof. J.S. Mill remarks on the difference between direct-indirect taxes as "when it is the intention of the government that a person, who legally pays the tax, must bear it; it is a direct tax. But when government intends that a tax collected from one should be passed on to others, it should be called an indirect tax."

When a tax is levied on monopoly, if he does not shift it to his customer it will be direct tax or if he shifts it to his customer it will be indirect tax. The death duty is commonly considered a direct tax because it falls on the successor and it tends to stay there.

The distinction between the direct and the indirect tax is thus settled by whether the tax has been shifted or not. If tax is shifted, it is indirect tax, otherwise it is direct tax.

II. Merits and Demerits of Direct and Indirect Taxation: The finance minister generally relies on both the types of taxes to collect revenue. No finance minister relies exclusively on one type. Both direct and indirect taxes are needed to make up an equitable and adequate tax system. The following are the merits and demerits of both the tax systems.

(a) ***Merits of Direct Taxation***: Some economists advocate the practice of direct tax system because it has following advantages.

(i) Equitable: Direct taxes are considered to be just and equitable, because they are generally based on the principles of progression. The direct taxes are based on the principle of ability to pay. These taxes fall more on the rich and less on the poor.

(ii) Economical: The direct taxes are economical because the cost of collection is small. There is no intermediary between the taxpayer and the government, no part of the tax evaporates in transit. Each rupee taken from the taxpayers is deposited in the State's treasury.

(iii) Certainty: The direct taxes satisfy the canon of certainty. The yield of direct taxes can be calculated with a fair degree of precision. The taxpayer is certain about how much he is expected to pay and, similarly, the State is also certain about how much it has to receive as income from direct taxes.

(iv) Elasticity: Direct taxes have a high degree of elasticity. They satisfy the canon of elasticity. The revenue of the government can be raised by rates of taxes. In addition to this, the revenue of the government increases with the increase in the income of the people.

(v) Civic Consciousness: The direct taxes create a civic consciousness among the taxpayers. The taxpayers take intelligent and keen interest in the method of public expenditure. They are interested in knowing whether the revenue raised is properly utilized or not. The person who pays direct taxes feels that they are contributing towards the State expenditure. The civic consciousness checks the wastage in the public expenditure.

(vi) Reduction of Inequalities: Direct taxes are progressive. Rich pay a high rate of taxes and the poor pay a lesser rate of taxes. This helps in the reduction of income inequalities. This helps in bridging the gulf between the rich and the poor people. However, economic inequalities cannot be reduced by taxes alone.

Public expenditure should be directed in such way that it benefits the poor.

(b) ***Demerits of Direct Taxation***: There are several disadvantages of direct tax system in spite of its merits. They are discussed as under:

(i) Inconvenient: Direct taxes are very inconvenient to pay. Every taxpayer has to submit the statement of his total income along with the source of income from which it is derived. Further, the tax has to be paid in a lump sum; the filling of tax returns is a complicated affair; and there is possibility of a lot of harassment to the taxpayers.

(ii) Unpopular: Direct taxes are very unpopular. Nobody likes to pay them. The direct taxes generally are not shiftable. The taxpayer feels the pinch of the tax. To part with money is not an easy thing especially when there is no direct benefit enjoyed by the taxpayer.

(iii) Possibility of Tax Evasion: A direct tax is said to be tax on honesty. All the taxpayers are not honest. They try to evade the payment of taxes in one or the other way. The taxpayers adopt fraudulent methods to avoid tax.

(iv) Arbitrary: The direct tax rates are fixed arbitrary by the government. The rates are not determined on any scientific principle. Changes in the government sometimes also lead to fixation of different rates. Thus, the direct taxes are arbitrary.

(c) ***Merits of Indirect Taxation***: Some other economists advocate indirect tax system because it has the following merits:

(i) Equitable: The principle of equity through indirect taxes can also be satisfied by imposing the taxes on those goods generally consumed by the rich. That is why luxuries are generally taxed at a higher rate.

(ii) Convenient: An indirect tax is convenient. These taxes are paid in small amounts and at intervals instead of in one lump sum. They are generally included in the price of the commodity and hence the burden of these taxes is not felt by the taxpayers. Many people do not desire know how much tax they are paying. They prefer to be taxed in the dark. The indirect taxes are

convenient from the point of view of the government also as it is directly collected from the manufacturer.

(iii) Elastic: The indirect taxes can be elastic. The revenue from the indirect taxes can be increased or decreased. When the government wants to raise more revenue, the indirect taxes can be imposed on those goods for which the demand is relatively inelastic. They can, therefore, be varied according to the State needs.

(iv) No Tax Evasion: It is very difficult to evade an indirect tax, because it is included in the price of the commodity. This tax can be avoided only if the consumer avoids the purchase of a commodity. However, the people who maintain false accounts and the smugglers may avoid the payment of indirect taxes.

(v) Productive: The indirect taxes may be made progressive by imposing few taxes yielding a large amount of revenue to the government. If the taxes are imposed on those goods for which the demand is relatively inelastic then naturally few taxes help in bringing more amount of revenue. In the case of India the Union excise duties and customs duties have yielded substantial amount of revenue and the governments are able to effectively using these taxes to bring more revenue.

(vi) Social Benefits: If the government desire to reduce the consumption of harmful and intoxicant drugs, heavy taxes may be imposed on such items. Increase in taxes may discourage the consumption of these goods and thus it will have a beneficial social effect.

(vii) Re-allocation of Resources: Imposing taxes on some of the commodities such as alcoholic drinks, will discourage their production. The resources used in their production may be utilized in the production of those commodities which are essential from the point of view of the society. Thus, the government will be in a position to divert resources to the production of social goods.

(viii) Wide Coverage: Indirect taxes are imposed on a large number of commodities. Thus, almost all the sections of the society are made to contribute to the government exchequer, which helps in financing of public utility services. Thus, the indirect taxes are broad based.

(d) *Demerits of Indirect Taxation*: Though the indirect taxation has several merits, it has also certain demerits that are discussed as under:

(i) Uncertain: Indirect taxes are uncertain. It is not always possible to the tax authorities to accurately estimate the revenue from different taxes. Since the tax collection depends upon the amount of goods bought by the consumers, the estimation of exact revenue from it is very difficult.

(ii) Regressive: The indirect taxes are regressive in nature. All the consumers whether rich or poor have to pay the same rate tax on commodities, for example, tax on match box. It is not possible to avoid these taxes. The poor are forced to pay these taxes because they purchase all these necessities of life. The poor spend a large size of their income on necessaries of life. Hence, the poor pay more percentage of the tax compared to the rich. The rich people spend only a small portion of their income on the necessaries so they pay relatively less tax. Thus, the indirect taxes are regressive.

(iii) No Civic Consciousness: Indirect taxes do not develop any civic consciousness in the taxpayer because nobody feels that he is paying a tax. Because the tax is included in the price of the commodity and it is paid in small amounts.

(iv) Administrative Cost: The administrative cost of collecting the indirect taxes is generally more. The indirect tax department has a large size of staff, their salaries are higher and administration expenses are more. So it resulted into high cost of the tax collection.

(v) Inflationary: Generally, indirect tax raises price. When the indirect taxes are imposed on the commodities, every increase rate of tax leads to increase in the price of those commodities. It creates inflationary situation in the country. Thus, indirect taxes are always inflationary.

(vi) Tax Evasion: The indirect taxes can be easily avoided by maintaining fictitious accounts for the goods produced and sold. For example, a retailer or wholesaler may not issue receipts to the customers which avoid sale tax. Similarly, if a tax is imposed on the agricultural produces the portion of the output consumed by the grower escapes from paying of tax.

(vii) Discourage Savings: As the indirect tax comes along with the price of a commodity, it is compulsory for every consumer to pay the tax. Since the common man spends a larger portion of his income on the essential goods, the indirect tax takes away some parts of his income in form of rise in price thereby his savings will naturally decrease.

(e) ***Comparison of Direct and Indirect Taxes***: Both the types of taxes are different in nature and effect. However, both are compared on the basis of three aspects which are discussed as under:

(i) Allocation Effect: When a tax is levied, it will effect on resource or income allocation of the taxpayer. If government wants to collect a given sum of income by imposing tax on consumer, it may impose direct tax like income tax or indirect tax like sale tax. The sacrifice incurs due to tax is more in indirect tax than direct tax. It means the indirect tax affects more adversely than direct tax on consumer. It is illustrated with example in Fig. 2.1.

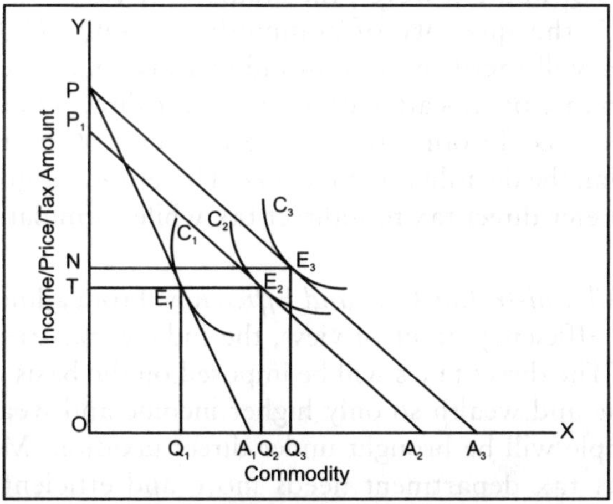

Figure 2.1: Allocation Effect of Direct and Indirect Taxes

Income of the consumer, price of commodity-x and tax-amount are measured along 'OY' axis and quantity of commodity-x along 'OX' axis. C_1, C_2 and C_3 are indifference curves which represent the level of satisfaction of the consumer. PA_1, P_1A_2 and PA_3 are price line or budget line.

Before Tax: The consumer has 'ON' size income so the price or budget line is 'PA_3' and he is equilibrium at 'E_3' which is on higher level indifference curve 'C_3'. The quantity of commodity-x purchased is 'OQ_3'.

After Tax: When government decides to take away 'TN' size of income in form of tax, (i) if it decides to impose sale tax (indirect tax) as a result of it the price of commodity-x will increase and so also the price or budget line will shift to 'PA_1'. As a result of it the consumer will be placed at 'E_1' equilibrium point which is at low level of satisfaction shown by 'C_1' indifference curve, the quantity of commodity-x purchased will be 'OQ_1', or (ii) if it decides to impose income tax (direct tax) on income of the consumer as a result of it the consumer's income will be reduced by 'NT' and so also the price or budget line will shift to 'P_1A_2' which is parallel to 'PA_3'. As a result of it the consumer will be placed at 'E_2' equilibrium point which is at low level of satisfaction shown by 'C_2' indifference curve, the quantity of commodity-x purchased will be 'OQ_2'. But, however, the indifference curve 'C_2' is higher than 'C_1'; the quantity of commodity-x '$OQ_2 > OQ_1$' so the consumer will sacrifice more in indirect tax than in direct tax. Hence, in case of allocation of resources the direct tax is superior to indirect tax. In other words, the disutility of indirect tax is higher than the disutility of direct tax. Therefore, the government should prefer direct tax to indirect tax while formulating its tax policy.

(ii) Administrative Cost and Efficiency: From administration cost and efficiency point of view, the indirect taxation is more suitable. The direct taxes will be imposed on the basis of the size of income and wealth so only higher income and wealth group class people will be brought under direct taxation. Meanwhile, the direct tax department needs more and efficient staff for collection of tax so it leads to most costly operations. Moreover, it is difficult to approach every person for direct taxation.

But indirect taxation, according to Prof. Prest, is more suitable and convenient from cost and administrative points of view. It approaches everybody like small independent producers, illiterate people who are unable to keep accounts, unorganized sectors, big and organized sectors, etc. So indirect taxation is more suitable to underdeveloped or backward economies.

(iii) Distribution of Income and Wealth: Economic justice or equality is the main objective of the modern welfare state. Direct taxation is more suitable method to impose tax on rich people according to their ability to pay capacity. Since direct tax like income tax is progressive tax, rich people pay more tax thereby it reduces the gap between rich and poor; poor are exempted from direct taxes. On contrary, indirect taxation is a general measure; it falls on both rich and poor equally. The indirect tax burden falls more on poor so it is regressive taxation. Hence, direct taxation is considered as an important measure to reduce inequalities of income and wealth.

However, the finance minister should maintain a proper balance between the two types of taxes as both these taxes are considered as financial virtue of tax authorities. We cannot assume that the entire burden of direct taxation falls on the rich and that of indirect taxation on the poor. Indirect taxes, like taxes on luxuries, fall on the rich and not on the poor. And the direct taxes like tax on income, tax on property fall on the rich. In a good tax system, there should be a proper balance between direct and indirect taxation. Indirect taxation makes the system of taxation broad based. The two tax systems are complementary. According to Gladstone, the direct and indirect taxes should be viewed as equally attractive sisters, neither of whom should be persuaded too ardently. The government should maintain the balance between the two with proper and appropriate grace.

2.3.2 Proportional and Progressive Tax

The taxes are also classified as 'proportional tax and progressive tax' the principles of proportional tax and progressive tax are studied as under:

(a) Proportional Tax: A proportional tax is one which is imposed at same rate on all people irrespective of their size of income. The rate of the tax for all the taxpayers remains the same. If all the taxpayers have to pay, say, ten per cent of their income as tax to the government, it is case of proportional taxation. It is explained in Table 2.1 with an example:

Table 2.1: Proportional Tax

Size of Income (₹)	Tax Rate (%)	Tax Amount (₹)
50,000	10	5,000
1,00,000	10	10,000
2,50,000	10	25,000

Thus, from the above example, it is clear that the percentage of the tax remains the same in respect of proportional tax. But the tax amount paid by the individuals is more for higher income and low for lower income. It means the rich pay more and poor pay less under the proportional taxation system. However, the burden of proportional tax on each unit of income, say each rupee, is same on all size of income groups. It is explained as:

$$PRTB = \frac{TA}{TB} = \frac{5000}{50000} = \frac{10000}{100000} = \frac{25000}{250000} = 0.1$$

PRTB = Proportional Tax Burden

TA = Tax Amount

TB = Taxable Income or Tax Base

Since tax rate is same on all income base, the burden of proportional tax is same, i.e. 0.1 on all persons. It is also illustrated in Fig. 2.2.

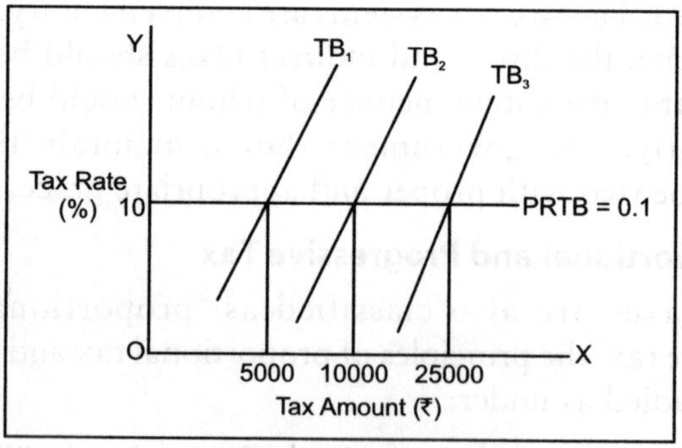

Figure 2.2: Proportional Tax

Tax rate (10%) is measured along 'OY' axis; the tax amount or proceedings is measured along 'OX' axis. PRTB line measures the burden of proportional tax on each tax base or taxable income. TB_1, TB_2 and TB_3 curves represent tax base or different level of taxable income. The proportional tax rate is same, i.e. 10 per cent on all level of income ₹ 50000 (TB_1), ₹ 100000 (TB_2) and ₹ 250000 (TB_3) respectively. But the burden of tax on each rupee is 0.1 (PRTB).

Merits and Demerits of Proportional Taxation: Classical economists advocate the proportional taxation. Adam Smith says "The subject of every state ought to contribute towards the support of the government, as nearly as possible, in proportion to their respective abilities, that in proportion to the revenue which they respectively enjoy under the protection of the State." In other words, every person should pay tax to the government in proportion to their income. However, the proportional taxation has both merits and demerits. They are discussed as under:

(i) ***Merits or Argument in Favour of Proportional Tax:*** The following are the main merits of the proportional taxation.

(a) *It does not affect the relative position of the taxpayer*: The main objective of taxation is that it should not alter the relative position of the taxpayer.

(b) *It is uniform and simple in nature and effect*: The proportional tax rate is uniform or same to all taxpayers and it is simple to estimate and calculate tax amount.

(c) *It does not affect adversely on the willing to work and save nature of the taxpayer*: If the tax rate is progressive, it will kill the willingness to work and save of the taxpayers.

(d) *Its burden is justifiable*: The burden of tax falls evenly on all taxpayers and it also increases as income increases.

(ii) ***Demerits or Argument against Proportional Tax:*** The advocates of progressive taxation criticize the proportional taxation because it has the following demerits.

(a) *It falls more heavily on small income groups (poor) than on high income groups (rich)*: Since the burden of proportional tax is same on all taxpayers, it will be felt more on poor; for example, 10 paisa tax burden on one rupee income is felt more burdensome by poor than rich.

(b) *It is not based on ability to pay principle*: Since proportional tax rate is same to all income groups, the tax amount collected from rich would be less than their ability to pay the tax, for example, a rich is capable to pay government ₹ 10 lac as tax amount but under proportional tax rate government collected from him only ₹ 1 lac.

(c) *It is inelastic in nature*: Since its burden is same on poor and rich both, during the time of need for additional financial resources government could not raise the tax rate because already poor are feeling more tax burden.

(b) Progressive Tax: On the other hand, progressive tax means the rate or percentage of the tax rises as the size of taxable income increases. The principle of a progressive tax is "higher the income, higher the rate or percentage of tax". It is explained in Table 2.2 with an example:

Table 2.2: Progressive Tax

Size of Income (₹)	Tax Rate (%)	Tax Amount (₹)
50,000	10	5000
1,00,000	20	20,000
2,50,000	30	75,000

Thus, from the above example, it is clear that the percentage of the tax or tax rate does not remain same in respect of progressive tax. The tax amount paid by the individuals is more for higher income and low for lower income. It means the rich pay more and poor pay less under the progressive taxation system. However, the burden of progressive tax on each unit of income, say each rupee, is not same on all size of income groups. It is explained as:

$$PGTB = \frac{TA}{TB} = \frac{5000}{50000} < \frac{20000}{100000} < \frac{75000}{250000}$$

$$\therefore PGTB = \frac{TA}{TB} = \frac{1}{10} < \frac{2}{10} < \frac{3}{10}$$

$$\therefore PGTB = 0.1 < 0.2 < 0.3$$

PGTB = Progressive Tax Burden

TA = Tax Amount

TB = Taxable Income or Tax Base

Since tax rate is not same on all income base, the burden of progressive tax is also not same, i.e. 0.1, 0.2 and 0.3, so it is differ from income group to income group on all persons. It is also illustrated in Fig. 2.3.

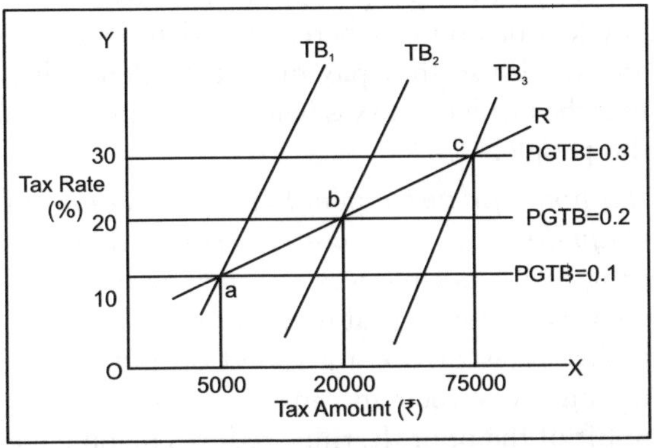

Figure 2.3: Progressive Tax

Tax rate is measured along 'OY' axis; the tax amount or proceedings is measured along 'OX' axis. PGTB line measures the burden of progressive tax on each tax base or taxable income. TB_1, TB_2 and TB_3 curves represent tax base or different level of taxable income. The progressive tax rate is not same on all levels of income, ₹ 50000 (TB_1), ₹ 100000 (TB_2) and ₹ 250000 (TB_3). It is 10 per cent on ₹ 50000, 20 per cent on ₹ 100000 and 30 per cent on ₹ 250000, thus, the burden of tax on each rupee is not same, i.e. 0.1, 0.2 and 0.3 (PGTB). It shows that the burden of progressive tax is less on low income and more and more on higher and higher income levels. Hence, R curve (we by joining a, b and c points) shows the progressive tax rate, it increases or rises upward from left to right as the level or slab of income increases.

Merits and Demerits of Progressive Taxation: Generally, the modern economists have advocated progressive taxation as it is based on the principle of ability to pay and suitable to modern democratic countries. However, its merits and demerits are discussed as under:

(i) ***Merits or Arguments in Favour of Progressive Tax*:** Prof. Taylor, Prof. Kaldor and the advocates of progressive taxation have argued in favour of progressive tax as it has following merits:

(a) *It assures equal distribution of tax burden among the people*: Since it is based on principle of ability to pay, the people pay tax according to their ability to pay tax. The income and wealth determine the taxpaying capacity of the people: poor have low income so they pay less or no tax whereas the rich have more income and wealth so they pay more tax. Hence, it is justified that the burden of tax is being distributed equally among the people.

(b) *It is powerful instrument to reduce income or economic inequalities in the country*: Prof. Kaldor argued that progressive tax reduces the income inequalities in the country. It means that under progressive tax higher and higher rates of tax are levied on rich people thereby taking away their income for public expenditures on uplift of the poor. It, thus, reduces income inequalities.

(c) *It is economical in character*: Government can raise more tax revenue by raising tax rate with same efforts or cost of collection.

(d) *It is more elastic*: Government can raise its tax revenue by raising tax rate to meets its growing financial needs. On contrary, it may reduce tax revenue by declining tax rate when financial needs decline. So it is more elastic in nature. It is suitable to developing countries like India.

(e) *It is more linked with economic activities*: Production, income, employment, investment, demand, etc. are the economic activities. Since progressive tax is graduating in nature, tax rate increases as the level on income or income slab increases, on contrary, it declines automatically as income and other economic activities decline; so it works like built-in stabilizer automatically.

(f) *It controls inflation*: Particularly, when there is demand push inflation in the country it needs control of consumption. Under such situation the progressive taxation helps the government to raise existing tax rates and imposing new tax rates thereby to take away income from the people so as to reduce their demands for goods and services in the economy. Similarly, the investment activities can be encouraged through reducing tax rates on income of the corporate bodies which, eventually, results in to increase in production for controlling of inflation. Thus, it acts as instrument of economic growth and stability.

(ii) ***Demerits or Argument against Progressive Tax***: The advocates of proportional taxation like J.S. Mill, McCulloch and other classical economists condemn the progressive tax system. J.S. Mill says: "a graduated income tax was an entirely unjust mode of taxation and in fact, a graduated robbery." These critics criticized progressive taxation because it has following demerits:

(a) *It is not based on any scientific principle*: Fixation of tax rates is entirely arbitrary, based on no guiding principles. Of course, 'ability to pay' is taken into account but there is no base for fixation of tax rates and income slabs to be fixed for them.

(b) *It is based on unrealistic assumption*: It is based on the assumption that the marginal utility of money is less to rich and more to poor. Since utility is subjective phenomena and difficult to measure, it difficult to compare the marginal utility of money between rich and poor. In brief, it is based on unrealistic assumption.

(c) *It affects adversely on production and savings*: The progressive taxation, first, takes away the income from household and firm thereby reduces savings and capital formation which would eventually result into decline in production, income and savings in the economy.

(d) *It punishes prudent and virtue*: Prof. William Newmarch argued that progressive taxation is taxing a man being good to himself and being good to others; it allows extravagance and idleness. Similarly, J.S. Mill has called it 'graduated robbery'.

(e) *There is danger of tax evasion*: When higher rates of tax are levied on higher income slabs, the taxpayer tries to escape from paying tax to the government which leads to danger of tax evasion. For example, in India tax evasion was more during 1970s because the income tax rate was more than 50 per cent.

In conclusion, when we make a comparison between proportional and progressive tax the persons with higher income pay more in both proportional and progressive tax system. But the amount of the tax paid under the progressive tax is far more than the tax paid under the proportional tax for the same income. Moreover, the progressive taxation is based on 'principle of ability to pay'. People accumulate more income and wealth because of political, social and economic conditions developed by government activities. Thus, the progressive tax is more equitable compared to the proportional tax. A majority of the countries in the world at present have adopted progressive system of taxation. This is due to the fact that the sacrifice entailed in proportional taxation is less than it ought to be.

2.3.3 Regressive and Degressive Taxes

Another classification of taxes is 'regressive tax and degressive tax'. The principle of regressive and degressive taxes can be discussed as under:

(a) Regressive Tax: A tax is said to be regressive when the tax burden falls more heavily on the poor than the rich. It is the opposite of a progressive tax. It is explained in Table 2.3:

Table 2.3: Regressive Tax

Size of Income (₹)	Tax Rate (%)	Tax Amount (₹)
50,000	30	15000
1,00,000	20	20,000
2,50,000	10	25,000

Of course, the tax amount increased as there is increase in income-size but the tax is declined. Thus, under regressive taxation, the tax rate declines on increase in income level but here the burden of tax on each rupee will be more in case of low income people and less on high income group; that is why it is called 'regressive taxation'. It is explained as:

$$RGTB = \frac{TA}{TB} = \frac{15000}{50000} < \frac{20000}{100000} < \frac{25000}{250000}$$

$$\therefore RGTB = \frac{TA}{TB} = \frac{3}{10} > \frac{2}{10} > \frac{1}{10}$$

$$\therefore RGTB = 0.3 > 0.2 > 0.1$$

RGTB = Progressive Tax Burden

TA = Tax Amount

TB = Taxable Income or Tax Base

Since tax rate is not same on all income base, the burden of regressive tax is also not same, i.e. 0.3, 0.2 and 0.1, so it is differ from income group to income group on all persons. It can be illustrated in Fig. 2.4.

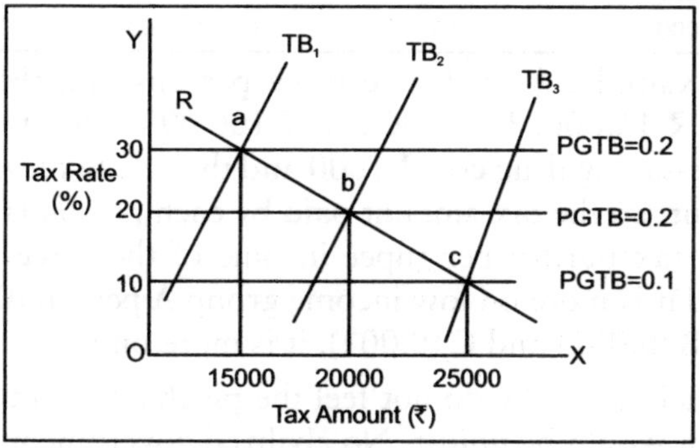

Figure 2.4: Regressive Tax

Tax rate is measured along 'OY' axis; the tax amount or proceedings is measured along 'OX' axis. RGTB line measures the burden of regressive tax on each tax base or taxable income. TB_1, TB_2 and TB_3 curves represent tax base or different level of taxable income. The regressive tax rate is not same on all levels of income, ₹ 50000 (TB_1), ₹ 100000 (TB_2) and ₹ 250000 (TB_3). It is 30 per cent on ₹ 50000, 20 per cent on ₹ 100000 and 10 per cent on ₹ 250000, thus, the burden of tax on each rupee is not same, i.e. 0.1, 0.2 and 0.3 (RGTB). It shows that the burden of regressive tax is more on low income and less and less on higher and higher income levels. Hence, R curve (we by joining a, b and c points) shows the progressive tax rate, it declines downwards from left to right as the level or slab of income increases.

Besides, there are several taxes on commodities whose burden falls mainly on the poor. The tax on all essential commodities may be considered as regressive taxation. For example, tax on salt, match box, etc. is regressive tax because the percentage of the tax paid by the poor will be more compared to the rich. The rich with more income pay less and the poor with less income pay more in percentage terms. The following example explained in Table 2.4 gives its explanation.

Table 2.4: Regressive Tax

Value of Life-Saving Drug (₹) 1	Tax Amount (₹) (Tax rate=10%) 2	Size of Income (₹) 3	Tax Burden on Each Rupee of income 2/3=4
1,000	100	A's -15,000	0.007
1,000	100	B's -50,000	0.002
1,000	100	C's -100,000	0.001

For example, A, B, C are three persons and their annual income is ₹ 15,000, ₹ 50,000 and ₹ 100,000 respectively. They need a life-saving drug cost ₹ 1000 and the sale tax levied on it is 10 per cent. So the tax amount paid by each person is ₹ 100 but when the tax burden per rupee income of the three persons is calculated it is more on low income group A person (0.007) and more on B (0.002) and C (0.001), it is more on poor.

The rich generally do not feel the pinch of such taxes. Such tax system would be unjust. No civilized government imposes a tax which is more burdensome on poor than rich people.

(b) Degressive Tax: Degressive taxation is an admixture of both progressive and proportional tax systems. Under degressive taxation, a tax may be progressive up to a certain limit or slab of income beyond which a uniform or same rate of tax continues. In this case, there will be a less tax burden on the higher income groups and more tax burden on the smaller income groups. It means the people with higher and higher income do not make a due sacrifice in the form of tax to the government. The burden of tax imposed on them is relatively less. This will happen when a tax is only mildly progressive, i.e. when the rate of progression in tax is not sufficiently steep. It is illustrated in Table 2.5.

Table 2.5: Degressive Tax

Size of Income (₹)	Tax Rate (%)	Tax Amount (₹)
50,000	10	5000
1,00,000	20	20,000
2,50,000	30	75,000
5,00,000	30	1,50,000

The annual income is divided into three slabs, ₹ 50,000, ₹ 1,00,000 and ₹ 2,50,000 in the above table and tax rate on them are 10 per cent, 20 per cent and 30 per cent, respectively. If income is above ₹ 2,50,000, the tax rate will be same, i.e. 30 per cent. However, the amount of tax is increased on every increase in income-size but the tax burden will be lesser and lesser as the higher level of income increases. The degressive tax is shown in Fig. 2.5.

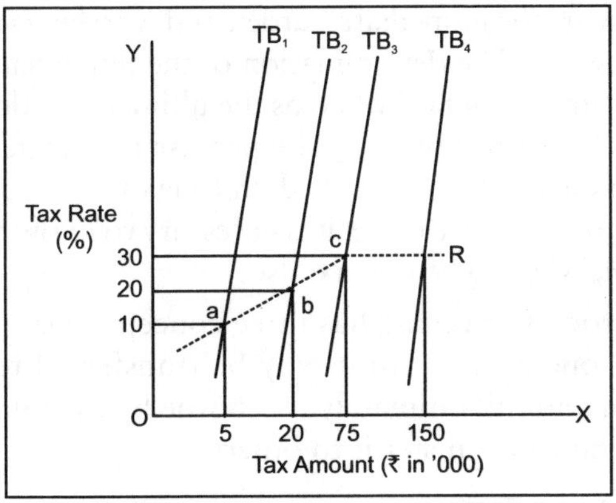

Figure 2.5: Degressive Tax

TB_1 (₹ 50,000), TB_2 (₹ 1,00,000), TB_3 (₹ 2,50,000), and TB_4 (₹ 5,00,000), curves show the taxable size of income or income slabs. Tax rates are measured along OY axis and tax amount along OX axis. The degressive tax is shown by 'R' curve which is drawn by joining the points a, b, c and d. It rises upwards till c-point which shows that the tax rate is progressive beyond that it becomes straight and horizontal which shows that the tax is same or proportional. Under this tax system, the annual income could be divided into slabs, say four or more. The Indian income-tax system at present is digressive because the annual income is divided into four slabs and on each slab tax rate is different. Low tax rate is levied on low income size; it further increases as income size increases but it remains constant beyond the last slab of income. It means richest of the rich in India pay proportional tax beyond last income-slab. Such tax system is said to be degressive.

2.4 BURDEN OF TAXATION

When a person pay tax to the government, he or she has to give up a certain part of his or her income to the government, it is called burden of tax on taxpayer. The burden of tax falls on person ultimately who bears it. For example, if a person pays ₹ 10 as tax to the government, the burden of tax will be ₹ 10. In some cases, the burden of tax is not on the person from whom the tax is collected but on the person who actually paid it. Therefore, it is necessary to know who bears the immediate burden and who bears the ultimate burden of the tax. The determination of the immediate burden of tax is called 'impact of tax' whereas the ultimate burden of the tax is known as 'incidence of tax'. The process to transferring of tax from one person to another is called 'shifting of tax'. To understand the meaning of incidence of tax it is necessary to know the meaning of *impact and shifting* of the tax also.

Thus, process of taxing has three concepts, viz. (i) the tax is imposed on one person, (ii) it may be transferred to second or other person and (iii) ultimately it is borne by the final consumer or person who can transfer it to others.

2.4.1 Impact of a Tax

Impact of a tax means the immediate money burden of the tax on person who pays it initially. In other words, it means the person who initially pays the tax to the government bears its burden. For example, if the tax is imposed on the shirt, the immediate burden of the tax would be on the manufacturers of the shirt, though they transfer it to the final customer. However, the immediate or initial money burden of tax falls on the manufacturers. It is initial burden but not ultimate burden of tax.

2.4.2 Shifting of a Tax

The tax-burden may or may not be on the same person who pays it initially. It can be transferred from person to another person but it depends upon the type of tax. When the tax on a commodity, say a shirt, is imposed by the government its immediate money burden would be on the producer. Initially, producer should pay the tax to the government but when he sells the shirt to a consumer the tax burden would be transferred to the consumer. Thus, ultimately the tax is paid by the consumer. Hence, the process by which the money burden of a tax is transferred from one person to another person is known as 'shifting of tax burden'.

The tax may be shifted both forward and backward. If the tax is shifted by the producer to the dealer; the dealer to the wholesaler; the wholesaler to the retailer and finally to the consumer; it is known as forward shifting. On the other hand, if the tax is shifted from the producer to the suppliers of raw materials it is known as backward shifting. If the cigarette producer shifts the tax on cigarette to the suppliers of the raw materials it is known as backward shifting. On the other hand, if any tax is imposed on the dealer, he may shift part of the tax to the producers, it is also called backward shifting. The direct taxes like income tax, tax on property cannot be shifted. The tax is paid, in this case, by those on whom it is imposed. Only the taxes on commodities, i.e. the indirect taxes, are shifted.

2.4.3 Incidence of a Tax

Incidence of tax refers to the money burden of a tax on the person who finally bears it. It is the "final resting place of the tax burden". In other words, incidence of tax is the money burden of a tax that finally settles or comes to rest on the ultimate taxpayer. The incidence of the tax is on that person who cannot shift the tax burden further to any other person. In the case of income tax, the ultimate burden clearly falls on the person who pays it on his income. But in certain cases income tax will also be shifted to other persons. For example, a tax on income is collected from the doctor instead he would shift it to his patients. Shifting generally takes by increasing the price of the commodity and service. The manufacturer increases the price of the product and shifts the tax burden forward to the consumer. In this case, it is the consumer who ultimately pays the tax; but the amount of tax is collected through the manufacturer. Here the incidence and impact of a tax are distinguished and they are on different persons. In this example, the impact of tax is on the manufacturer, but the incidence is on the consumer. In other words, the impact of a tax comes to rest with the final payee. A tax is compared to an unwanted baby. Hence, people on whom the impact of a tax falls always try to shift it.

Ursula K. Hicks in her book *Pubic Finance* classifies incidence of tax in to 'formal incidence' and 'effective incidence of taxation'. Formal incidence refers to the final resting place of the tax or the direct money burden as explained by Dalton. The concept of incidence of tax discussed above, according to Hicks, is the 'formal incidence'. Incidence in the modern context does not only mean the direct money burden of tax, it also includes the effective incidence of a tax. Effective incidence means the study of general effects of taxation. According to Ursula K. Hicks, if we make a comparison between an economy with a taxation policy in operation and another similar economic system without the tax policy the difference between the two is the effective incidence of the tax.

According to Dalton, the indirect money burden of a tax is the effect of a tax. The reduction in the consumption of a commodity as a result of a tax, according to Dalton, is called the indirect real burden of the tax. Thus, any tax policy which affects the market demand, production, investment activities, employment, etc., may be defined as effective incidence of tax.

2.4.4 Differences between Impact and Incidence

Though impact and incidence are the burden of tax, yet there are main differences between the two are shown in Table 2.6.

Table 2.6: Differences between Impact and Incidence

Impact	Incidence
(i) It is initial burden of tax	(i) It is final or ultimate burden of tax
(ii) It is felt by the person who pay it originally or initially	(ii) It is felt by the person who finally bears the burden of tax
(iii) It can be shifted to others	(iii) It cannot be shifted to others
(iv) It is direct action	(iv) It is indirect action

2.4.5 Determinants of Incidence of Tax

The incidence of tax plays a very important role in taxation policy of modern government. The economic welfare of the community depends upon the government budget policy wherein the tax policy has crucial role to play. The taxes are being imposed on the basis of the ability to pay of the taxpayer but the even or just distribution of tax burden depends upon certain conditions. The burden of tax might be shifted forward or backward and fully or partly; sometimes the shifted tax burden might be more than the actual tax rate. Hence, it is necessary to know the factors determining the incidence of tax as follows:

(i) Changes in Budget Policy: Modern economist Prof. Musgrave has defined 'incidence' as "a change in the distribution of income available for private use which arises as a result of change in budget policy". The change in budget policy generally refers to the change taxation and public expenditure policy. According to Prof. Musgrave, by keeping public expenditure constant, raising or reducing tax rate and substituting one tax for another tax would effect on distribution of income in the country. Thus, he said that the change in distribution of income due to change in tax is 'tax incidence'. Further, he contends that there are two types of tax-incidence, viz. (i) specific tax incidence and (ii) differential tax incidence. The *specific tax incidence* means the change in income distribution due to change or modification in tax rate such as income tax. According to Prof. Musgrave, the *differential tax incidence* means the difference in distribution of income due to the result of two tax policies or alternative tax that have equal yield.

(ii) Changes in Price: Price acts as a medium of shifting tax-burden. Tax is also considered as the component of total cost of production so imposition of tax or modification of existing tax may result into change in price of output or commodity but it depends upon demand and supply conditions and nature of commodity. For example, if a tax is imposed on car, the price of car increases thereby the incidence of tax will be on the customer, provided the demand for car is inelastic.

(iii) Elasticity of Demand and Supply: The elasticity of demand shows buyers strength and the elasticity of supply shows sellers strength. So the elasticity of demand and supply determine the shifting of tax or incidence. For example, if a tax is imposed on petrol, its burden will be shifted on consumer in form of raising petrol-price, provided the demand for petrol in inelastic. Or if a tax is imposed on onion, an agricultural produce, the tax cannot be shifted on consumer but it will be borne by producer because its supply is inelastic. Thus, the shifting of tax or tax-incidence depends upon the degree of elasticity of demand and supply of commodity or service. Greater the elasticity of demand for taxed-commodity, higher will be the incidence of tax on seller; greater the inelasticity of demand for taxed-commodity, higher will be the incidence of tax on buyer. Similarly, greater the elasticity of supply for taxed-commodity, higher will be the incidence of tax on buyer; greater the inelasticity of supply of taxed-commodity, higher will be the incidence of tax on seller or producer.

(iv) Nature of Commodity or Service Demanded: Incidence of tax depends upon the nature of commodity or service. The commodities are classified into three categories, viz. necessaries, comforts and luxuries. The demand for necessaries is inelastic, comforts moderately elastic and luxuries more elastic. If tax is levied on necessary commodity or service, the incidence of tax will be on consumer, for example, tax on life-saving drugs, income-tax on doctor, service tax on lodge, etc. are entirely shifted on consumers. The consumers bear the tax burden ultimately because they are necessary to them. In such cases, sometimes, the size of incidence of tax may be more than actual tax rate. If tax is levied on comforts, the incidence of tax will be partially on consumer and be partially on seller, for example, tax on chairs, radio, bicycle, fan, etc. comfort items are partly shifted on consumers. If tax is levied on luxury commodity or service, the incidence of tax will be low on consumer and more on seller or producer, for example, tax on car, tax on HD TVs, ACs, etc. are borne more by sellers or producers and less by consumers. In case of comforts and luxuries, the demand is elastic so the tax-burden on them should be shared by buyers and sellers both.

(v) Nature of Commodity Supplied: The incidence of tax also depends upon the nature of commodity supplied. Generally, the commodities are classified as (i) manufactured commodities or industrial goods and agricultural commodities and (ii) consumer commodities and capital goods.

The supply of industrial goods like TV, cloth, freeze, etc. is more elastic so after imposition of tax the supply of these can be re-adjusted to retain profit. In such cases, the incidence of tax would be shifted on buyers. On contrary, if tax is imposed on agricultural goods the burden of tax will be borne by the producer or sellers because the re-adjustment of supply of these goods is not possible.

The supplies of consumer goods are elastic whereas the supplies of capital goods are inelastic. If tax is imposed on consumer goods like TV, cloth, freeze, etc., the incidence of tax will be on buyers because there is provision for re-adjustment in supply to retain profit. On contrary, if tax is imposed on capital goods like machines, tools, equipment, etc., the incidence of tax will be retain by producers or sellers because the supply of capital goods is inelastic so there is no scope for re-adjustment in supply.

(vi) **Supply of Factors of Production:** The tax burden can be shifted either forward or backward. Forward shifting of tax is possible through raising the price of commodity. The backward shifting of tax is possible by reducing price of factors of production but it depends upon the supply conditions of the factors of production or inputs. For example, the supply of labour is inelastic the incidence of tax on commodity can be shifted on labour by reducing their wage. Hence, the incidence of tax depends on the condition of supply of inputs in the factor-market.

(vii) **Importance of Time Element:** The incidence of tax depends upon the time elements. The time element plays significant role in supply of commodity. The supply remains inelastic in short-run because the size of plant, scale of operation, etc. remain constant. Thus, in short-run, if the tax is levied its burden will be borne by seller or producer because there is no room for re-adjustment in supply. But in long-run, the supply is elastic because the size of plant, scale of operation, etc. are changeable. Thus, the incidence of tax will be on buyers in long-run.

(viii) **Geographical Area of Operation:** There are taxes applicable to various geographical areas, for example, local tax, state tax and central tax. Each tax has its area of operation, for example, municipality tax is applicable in that municipality-area only. The state and central taxes have wider area of operation. Hence, local taxes are not shiftable. The state and central taxes are shiftable, for example, state sales tax can be shifted easily over a wide area.

(ix) Economic Conditions: The shifting of tax burden generally depends upon the economic or business conditions prevalent in the economy. During inflation cost price, etc. are rising so under such economic situation the incidence of taxes is easily shiftable. But during deflation the incidence of tax cannot be shifted on buyers because demand, price, etc. are falling.

(x) Seasonal Changes: The shifting of tax burden is also depends on seasonal changes in demand and supply conditions. For example, in summer there is much demand for fans so the tax on fan burden can be shifted to buyers but in winter-season the tax burden will be borne by seller or producer.

(xi) Market Conditions: The shifting of tax burden depends upon the market conditions prevalent in the country. In monopoly and monopolistic markets, the tax on commodity burden can be shifted to buyers because buyers have no alternative. But in perfect competition market, the tax on commodity burden will be retained by the sellers or producers because the price elasticity of demand is perfect or very high.

2.5 EFFECTS OF TAXATION

In modern context, taxation is not only the measure of raising revenue for government but it is also used as instrument of redistribution of income and wealth to achieve socio-economic justice in the country. The taxes have their indirect money burden on the economy. The indirect money burden of tax on the economy is called 'effect of taxation'. The effects of taxation may be good as well as bad. According to Dalton, "the best system of taxation from the economic point of view is that which has the best or least bad economic effects". Dalton has discussed the effects of taxation mainly under three heads: (a) Effects on production, (b) Effects on distribution, and (c) Other effects.

2.5.1 Effects of Taxation on Production

According to Dalton, the effects of taxation on production can be discussed in the following three ways:

(a) Effects on the ability to work, save and invest.

(b) Effects on the desire to work, save and invest.

(c) Effects on the distribution of resources between different industries and places.

These effects are discussed as under:

(a) Effects on the ability to work save and invest: A tax on income of a person would reduce the efficiency of a person thereby his ability to work. Taxes should not be imposed on the poor people because taxes reduce their income, which is already low. The reduction in income through taxation reduces the level of consumption of the poor thereby it reduces their ability to work. The intensity of the effect is so serious that it reduces the ability to work not only of present generation but also of the future generations, which determines the production. Moreover, the efficiency of poor people also depends on necessaries of life so they should not be taxed. There is need to protect the poor from imposing heavy taxes.

If the additional income of the people is taken away in the form of taxes their ability to save also comes down. In other words, people who generally save are affected by a tax on income. Dalton is of the opinion that heavy taxes on the rich also reduce their ability to save. The decline in ability to save as an impact also reduces the ability to invest.

Generally, the reduction in ability to work, save and invest will have bad or adverse effects production, income, employment, etc. in the economy.

(b) Effects on the desire to work, save and invest: The effects of tax generally depend upon its nature. If a tax is temporary one, it will not have much effect on the desire to work and save. People do not think seriously about such taxes as they are expected to be short-lived. According to Dalton, the effects of taxation on the desire to work, save and invest depend upon (i) the *nature of taxes* and (ii) the *nature of individual's reaction to taxation.*

***(i) Nature of Taxes*:** The nature of tax is an important factor influencing the desire to work and save. The purpose of taxation is to encourage the desire to work, save and invest. But it depends on nature of tax. The effect of tax differs from tax to tax. Some taxes have only favourable effects on desire to work, save and invest but some other taxes have both bad and good effects on desire to work, save and invest. Some examples are:

(a) *Tax on Windfall-Gains*: It is unexpected short-run profit arises due to sudden rise in price. The taxes on such income have no bad effect on desire to work, save and invest.

(b) *Tax on Monopoly-Profit*: It has neutral effect on desire to work, save and invest because the monopoly compensates the tax-burden by increasing production.

(c) *Individual Taxes*: Income tax, wealth tax, expenditure tax and inheritance tax are the important individual taxes. They generally have bad effects on desire to work, save and invest.

(d) *Commodity Taxes*: Sales tax, costume duties, excise duties, etc. are commodity taxes which have bad effects on desire to work, save and invest.

In brief, a highly progressive income tax will have the adverse effect on the desire to work and save. Because of income tax takes away some part of the tax payer's income and it will have the adverse effect on the desire to work and save. Generally, progressive taxation will have greater adverse effect on the desire to work and save as compared to the proportional taxation. Progressive taxation takes away a greater part of the increased income and therefore acts as a disincentive for greater desire to work and save.

***(ii) Nature of Individual's Reaction to Taxation*:** It is the human psychology that every individual reacts against tax but the degree of it is different. Prof. A.C. Pigou called such the psychological reaction of tax-payer as 'announcement effect of taxation'. However, the reaction of any person to taxation depends upon several factors which are discussed as under:

(a) The elasticity of demand for income: It means the tax payers psychology to work more to maintain same level of income after imposition of tax on income. It is discussed as under:

(a) If the *demand for income is inelastic,* the effect of taxation on the desire to work, save and invest is favourable. The demand for income inelastic means the individual desires to maintain the same level of income after imposition of tax. In other words, when the income is reduced by taxation, the individual will work more to maintain the same level of income. In such cases, the effect of taxation on the desire to work, save and invest will be positive. Such tendencies among the individuals will make them to work hard.

(b) If the *demand for income is elastic*, taxation may result in lesser desire to work save and invest. Such individuals are not interested to work more. These individuals are not interested in maintaining the same level of income; nor did they worry about their reduced income. Naturally, such individuals prefer leisure to work. Greater elasticity of income will thus have an adverse effect on the desire to work and save. Therefore, Dalton has rightly suggested the government to measure the elasticity demand for income before the imposition of the taxes.

(c) If the elasticity of demand for income is unity, there is no effect on desire to work, save and invest.

(b) Economic Conditions: The economic conditions such as boom and depression influence on taxpayers' psychology whenever taxes are levied by the government. During boom-period the prices, profits, etc. are rising so imposition of taxes may not discourage the desire to work, save and invest. On contrary, taxes may discourage the desire to work, save and invest during depression-period because price, profit, etc. are falling.

(c) During War-Period: Generally, during war-period the prices are rising because of huge public expenditure and shortage of civilian-goods. So imposition of taxes during war may not discourage the desire to work, save and invest.

(d) Types of Industries: Imposition of tax on profits of already well-established industries may not discourage the desire to work, save and invest. But it discourages the newly established industries.

(c) Effects on the distribution of resources between different industries and localities: Taxation may be used as fiscal instrument for allocation of resources between industries and locations. Taxation can affect not only size and growth of production but also its composition and pattern. When a tax is levied on a commodity its price will rise but its demand will decline thereby its profit will be reduced so the producer will decline the production of that commodity thus some resources will be thrown out of employment. Such resources will move to another industry or location for employment. Hence, generally, the factors of production move from high taxed industries to low taxed industries. For instance, tax on harmful drugs, alcohol and tobacco may reduce the production of these commodities and the resources released from these industries will move to the production of necessary goods industries which are not taxed or taxed low. In the same way, heavy taxes on luxuries may divert both production and demand to the industries producing essential commodities for the common man.

Resources may also move from high taxed localities to low taxed localities. If taxation is heavy in one place compared to other places, the industries migrate from the high taxed localities to low taxed localities. For instance, some of the states in India such as Gujarat are providing tax concessions to attract industrial investments. They not only provide tax concessions but also provide other infrastructure facilities for the development of industries in their regions. As a result of it, the factors of production move from one place to another place. However, the movement of resources after taxation also depends on the elasticity of demand and supply conditions commodities taxed.

In brief, according to Dalton, whether the taxation has good effect or bad effect depends on the use of the tax-revenue by the government. Taxation may have adverse effect on production, if money collected by way of taxation is simply wasted. But money collected by the government in the form of tax is spent on production activities, the taxation is not waste.

2.5.2 Effects on Distribution

Reduction of inequalities of income and wealth is a major task in a majority of the welfare countries. The taxation policies would help the government to reduce income inequalities in the country. According to Wagner, a German economist, taxation is an important tool which can be used to reduce the inequality of income and wealth. But the effects of taxation on the distribution of income and wealth depend upon mainly two factors: (i) the nature of the taxation and tax rates and (ii) kinds of taxes.

(i) Nature of the Taxation and Tax Rates: There are various taxation systems and they have effects on income and wealth of the community. They can be studied as under:

***(a) Progressive Taxation*:** A steep progressive tax policy reduces the gap between the rich and the poor. In the progressive tax policy, the tax rate increases with increase in the level of income of the people. The rich under this system pay more and the poor either pay less or are exempted from paying the tax. Thus, the progressive taxation helps in reducing the gap between the rich and the poor. But there is fear that the progressive tax may adversely affect production and employment. Therefore, the governments should be cautious while imposing steep progressive taxes.

***(b) Proportional Taxation*:** Since the tax rate is same on all sizes of income under this system, the inequalities in income and wealth continues as before, if sizes of income remain same. The increase in income of rich would lead to widen the gap between rich and poor.

***(c) Regressive Taxation*:** Progressive taxes increase inequalities of income and wealth as their incidence is felt mainly on the poor. Tax on commodities, particularly on the necessaries, is regressive as it falls mainly on the poor. But if the taxes are imposed on luxuries, which are generally purchased by the rich, will help in the reduction of inequalities of income and wealth. Therefore, there is a need to make the commodity taxes progressive by imposing tax on the goods purchased by the rich.

***(d) Death Duty*:** It is a tax levied on inheritors or legal heir while transferring the income and property of deceased man. It is also progressive tax. It may lead to equal distribution of income and wealth thereby it may reduce income inequalities in the community.

(ii) Kinds of Tax: Broadly, taxes are classified into direct taxes and indirect taxes. Income tax, wealth tax, profit tax, death duty, etc. are the examples of direct tax; they are also called individual taxes. Sales tax, excise duties, custom duties, etc. are the examples of indirect taxes; they are also known as commodity taxes. Direct taxes having progressive in nature generally reduce the inequalities in income and wealth. The commodity taxes are regressive in nature so they widen the gap between rich and poor: richer becomes rich; poorer becomes poor, for instance Indian tax system.

However, the distribution of income and wealth in the community depends upon the just taxation system of the government.

2.5.3 Other Effects

Like production and distribution, there are other economic activities and situations that are being influenced by the taxation. They are also considered as the other effects of taxation. They are discussed as under:

(i) Effects on Employment: Taxation results in the reduction of the disposable income of the individuals. This reduces the ability to spend, save and invest of the people. A decrease in the aggregate expenditure of the community reduces the demand for output thereby the investment activities will be reduced and eventually the size of employment will be declined.

(ii) It Controls Inflation: Taxation is being used as a measure to control prices during inflation. Levying of new taxes and raising of existing tax rates would reduce the purchasing power of the people thereby the demand. So it would help to maintain price stability. Similarly, the tax exemptions would encourage savings and investments that would raise production and supply thereby prices would be stabilized.

(iii) It Fights Depression: Taxation is being used as an anti-depression measure. There is shortage of purchasing power in the hands of people during depression so price, demand, etc. economic activities are falling continuously so there is need for transfer of purchasing power to the hands of people. Removal of some taxes, reduction in tax rates, etc. tax policies allow more purchasing power with the people thereby the demand for goods and services will be increased, investment activities will be encouraged thus the economy will be recovered from depression or deflation.

In brief, tax policy has regulatory effects on economic activities such as production, consumption, distribution, savings, investment, income, employment, etc.

2.6 TAXABLE CAPACITY

Taxable capacity refers to the maximum capacity that the people of a country can contribute by the way of taxation to the government exchequer, both in ordinary and extra-ordinary situation. In other words, the tax-burden bearing limit of the people of a country, beyond which it suffers them in various respect.

2.6.1 Definitions of Taxable Capacity

The taxable capacity has been defined as under:

(i) **The Taxation Enquiry Commission of India (1953-54):** It has defined taxable capacity as "the capacity of different sections of the community may be said to refer the degree of taxation, broadly speaking, beyond which productive efforts and efficiency as a whole begin to suffer".

(ii) **Prof. Musgrave:** Prof. Musgrave defines the term taxable capacity as "the sacrifice the community is able to sustain". He defined taxable capacity in both national or interregional and international context. It implies the greater the per capita incomes, the greater the taxable or the ability to contribute.

(iii) **Sir J. Stamp:** He defined absolute taxable capacity as "the maximum amount, the citizens of a country could give towards public expenditure without having a real unhappy and down trodden existence and without dislocating the economic organization too much".

(iv) **Findlay Shirras:** Findlay Shirras defines taxable capacity as "the maximum amount which the citizens of a country can contribute towards the expense of the public authorities, without having to undergo an unbearable strain". In brief, taxable capacity is the limit of squeeze ability. In other words, taxable capacity stands for the maximum amount which the state can get from the community by way of taxes, without affecting the living standard and productive capacities of the people. It is the maximum amount of taxation that can be raised and spent to produce the maximum economic welfare of the community.

(v) Prof. Dalton: Dalton makes a distinction between the absolute taxable capacity and the relative taxable capacity. The *absolute taxable capacity* refers to the maximum amount that can be collected from a community without causing any unpleasant effects. The *relative taxable capacity,* on the other hand, means comparing the taxable capacity of two or more communities.

According to Prof. R.N. Bhargava, "absolute taxable capacity is just another name for optimum taxation". Optimum taxation according to him is reached when people are taxed according to the principle of maximum social advantage. It means the people are taxed up to the point where the marginal sacrifice from taxation is equal to the marginal benefit from public expenditure. On the other hand, relative taxable capacity means those who have greater capacity to pay may be made to pay more taxes and vice versa.

(vi) Prof. Coline Clark: According to Clark, the maximum taxable capacity of the most of the countries is 25 per cent of the national income. Moreover, the limit is not fixed but it may vary from time to time in the same country and country to country in same time-period.

However, Sir J. Stamp's definition is a more suitable and practicable definition of 'taxable capacity'. Therefore, the taxable capacity is the difference between real income and minimum consumption expenditure. It can be expressed as:

$TC = Y_t - E_{mc}$

TC = Taxable Capacity, Y_t = Real Income,

E_{mc} = Minimum Consumption Expenditure

2.6.2 Methods of Measuring Taxable Capacity

It is essential to measure the limit of taxable capacity. Generally, it accepted that the limit of taxable capacity is reached when the heaviness of taxation affects adversely on production and consumption. Prof. Amotoz Morag says that the taxation limit is reached when the 'marginal social cost' or of additional taxation exceeds the cost of borrowing from bank. The additional taxation means increase in income-sacrifice by taxpayers or higher disutility of taxation. If additional taxation is used to finance the public expenditure, it would curtail consumption and production both, the people would be put to worse-off. So Prof. Morag suggested to use 'deficit finance' in-lieu of additional taxation to finance public expenditure. Therefore, the equality between marginal social cost of additional taxation and government revenue is the limit of taxable capacity. It is illustrated in Fig. 2.6.

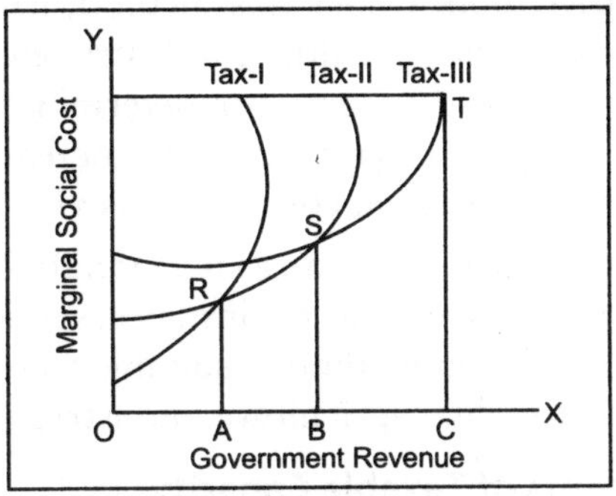

Figure 2.6: Limit of Taxable Capacity

Marginal social cost of tax is measured along OY axis, the government revenue along OX axis. Tax-I, II and III are different taxes levied to raise government revenue to finance public expenditure. The government revenue is OA at Tax-I, AB at Tax-II and BC at Tax-III so the total tax revenue is OA+AB+BC = OC. As more and more taxes are imposed the marginal social cost increased from RA to SB and TC. At Tax-III the marginal social cost (TC) is equal to government revenue (OC), i.e. TC = OC. At this stage if more government revenue is required to finance public expenditure, the government should use deficit finance method or borrowing from bank instead of levying additional taxes. Any additional taxation beyond OC will affect adversely on consumption and production or suffers community. Thus, the limit of taxable capacity is where marginal social cost of taxation is equal to government revenue.

Generally, taxable capacity depends upon the national income. Prof. Shirras has suggested the following two methods to estimate the taxable capacity:

(i) Income Method: It is also known as personal or aggregate income method. Under this method, the national income is estimated by adding-up the income of every individual on the basis of income tax returns. The taxable capacity would be calculated on the basis of national income: higher the national income, higher is the taxable capacity; lower the national income, lower is the taxable capacity.

(ii) Product Method: Under this method, net produce from various sources such as agriculture; industry, etc. are added-up to estimate the national income for determination of taxable capacity of the people. If net production increases, the taxable capacity will be increased; on contrary, it is vice versa.

Income method is suitable to estimate taxable capacity where income-data are easily available, for instance, service sector, trade, industry, etc. Production method is suitable to estimate taxable capacity from sectors like agriculture, industry, etc.

2.6.3 Determinants of Taxable Capacity

The taxable capacity depends on many factors. Any change in these factors change the limit of the taxable capacity of a country. The determinants of the taxable capacity are studied as under:

(i) Size of Population: Like national income, the size and growth rate of population determines the taxable capacity of a country. Given the national income, the increase in size and growth rate of population, generally reduce the individual income thereby the taxable capacity would decline; on contrary it would be vice versa. But where the population increases national income, the taxable capacity will be high.

(ii) Methods of Taxation: The governments can raise more revenue by judiciously combining variety of taxes, say direct and indirect taxes. If we do not bring all the citizens of the country under the tax-net, the taxable capacity will go down. In other words, the taxable capacity is low where single line taxation, direct or indirect taxation, is used; it will be high where multiple taxation, say both direct and indirect taxation, are sued together.

(iii) Purpose of Tax Revenue: If the taxes are collected by the government for spending on unproductive expenses, people may not come forward to pay more taxes, in such cases taxable capacity will be low. The government may also face resistance from its citizens in the payment of taxes. On the other hand, if the governments spend more tax-money on education, health and developmental activities, the people may not hesitate to contribute towards the state exchequer in such cases the taxable capacity will be higher.

(iv) Distribution of Income and Wealth: The taxable capacity depends on the type of distribution of national income and wealth among the people. If there is equal distribution of income and wealth among the people, it reduces the taxable capacity. On contrary, if there is unequal distribution of income and wealth among the people, it increases the taxable capacity in the country. Rich people having more income and wealth are capable to pay more taxes; the poor having less income and wealth are not capable to pay taxes or pay less tax. But the governments should act wisely and impose more taxes on the rich and collect more tax revenue. Progressive system of the tax is advisable in such cases.

(v) Psychology of Taxpayers: Psychology of the taxpayers is equally important in the determination of taxable capacity. If people are more patriotic in sentiment, they bear more taxes; if they are less patriotic in sentiment, they bear fewer taxes. The government should design different types of taxes for different income groups based on their psychology.

(vi) Stability of Income: The taxable capacity depends upon the stability of income of the people. The incomes of the farmers in India depend upon the monsoons. Monsoons are uncertain. This may adversely affect the taxable capacity. If incomes are more stable, like in industrial countries, the taxable capacity is more and there is scope for imposing fresh taxes on stable incomes.

(vii) Inflation and Deflation: During inflation the rise in the prices takes away some part of the income of the people in form of high price so it reduces the income of the people and their tax-paying ability. During deflation the income of the people is at low level so there are not able to pay the taxes. Thus, the taxable capacity is low in abnormal economic situations like inflation and deflation.

(viii) Level of Economic Development: Generally, the developed countries have a higher level of income so their taxable capacity is also higher. On the other hand, the taxable capacity in the developing countries like India is relatively less because of low level of income.

(ix) Political Stability: If the political conditions are not stable the investment activities in almost all the sectors of the economy come down. The uncertainty will result into fall in all economic activities. This adversely affects the taxable capacity. On the other hand, the stable political conditions help in raising the taxable capacity of the governments.

(x) Standard of Living: The standard of the people depends upon factors such as the per capita income and availability of goods and services. The national income influences these factors. The standard of living represents the pattern of consumption or consumption expenditure. The rich people have higher standard of living because they more income and wealth so they have more taxable capacity. If the general standard of living of the people is low, the taxable capacity of the people will be low.

(xi) Policies and Administration: The taxable capacity also depends upon the tax policy and tax department administration efficiency. The tax evasions are less where the tax policy is popular and the tax department is fair and efficient so taxable capacity will be higher because people pay tax without feeling it is burdensome.

2.6.4 Importance of Taxable Capacity Study

The study of the concept of 'taxable capacity' has greater significance in public finance because of the following aspects:

(i) Economic Development and Planning: Gathering of financial resource is essential for financing economic development programmes in the country. The taxable capacity helps the government to know how much revenue is possible from tax sources to finance for developmental activities.

(ii) Public Expenditures: Modern governments have various functions such as defence, civil administration, economic services, social services, general services, etc. So they need money to perform these activities. The taxable capacity help the government to design its expenditure plans: government cuts its coat according to its cloth. The unplanned public expenditure distorts the economy.

(iii) Comparison of Tax Burden: Taxable capacity helps the central of federal government to compare tax burden between states or regions of the country.

(iv) Avoidance of Un-necessary Taxes: Taxable capacity helps the government to avoid levying of un-necessary taxes that affect adversely on production and consumption.

(v) Re-allocation of Resources: It helps the government to formulate suitable tax policy for re-distribution of resources between sectors for economic development of the country as whole. For example, tax-revenue collected from industrial sector and rich people is used for the development of backward area, agriculture, rural area, uplift of poor, etc.

It is essential to the government to assess the exactness of taxable capacity before it decides to levy new taxes and raising of existing tax rates.

2.7 THEORIES ON TAX BURDEN DISTRIBUTION

Definitely, tax is a burden on the people, it is ultimately distributable among the people of the country. Whether direct tax or indirect tax, commodity tax or service tax, its burden ultimately fall on the entire community so tax system should be based on principle of equity means its burden must fall equally on all the people of the country, according to paying ability; if it is so, then it is called justice in taxation. There are various theories came into light to advocate the principle or theory on right distribution of tax burden. These are:

2.7.1 Physiocratic Theory

France's Physiocratic School of Economic Thought advocated this theory. According to this school, agricultural land alone yields net return and it adds to the wealth of the country so government should levy direct tax on the land and collect its revenue. But this theory suffers some shortcomings. They are:

(i) Land alone is not productive but there are other factors that yield net return for instance labour, capital, etc. Industry yield more income than agriculture.

(ii) Land—Tax-revenue is not enough to meet the increasing government expenditure.

(iii) It is uneven distribution of tax burden on landholder because there are people who have more income and wealth than landholders. If non-landholders pay no tax, it will be unjust or unfair.

(iv) It is difficult to calculate exactly the earning of land so it is not easy to impose tax on land.

So this theory is considered as unscientific thus discarded.

2.7.2 Financial Theory

This theory advocates the method of collecting tax revenue. It states "Pluck the goose with as little squealing as possible". It advocates collecting of maximum tax revenue from the public but under such tax system the burden of tax fall more on weak and poor people. It is generally opposed by all. This attempt was made in India in form of broadening the base of taxation it means bringing more and more people under the tax system.

2.7.3 Horizontal and Vertical Theory

This theory is also known as 'Principle of Equity'. Modern economists advocated this theory; they said that the burden of tax should be distributed on the principle of equity or equality, it means fairness or justice in distribution of tax burden among the people or taxpayers. There are two types of equity, namely (a) Horizontal Equity and (b) Vertical Equity. Horizontal equity means people of like circumstance having same economic status and vertical equity means people of unlike circumstances having differ in economic status. The theory advocates that people of same economic status, i.e. equality in income and wealth, should pay equal amount of tax and people of unlike economic status, i.e. inequality in income and wealth, should pay unequal amount of tax, equal tax on equal economic status people is called 'Horizontal Equity' and different amount of tax on different economic status people is called 'Vertical Equity'. This is shown in following tables:

Table 2.7: Horizontal Equity Theory

Taxpayer	Income (₹)	Tax Amount (₹)	Tax Burden/Per Rupee
A	10,000	1000	0.1
B	10,000	1000	0.1
C	10,000	1000	0.1

Table 2.7 shows that A, B and C are taxpayers who have like or similar circumstance, i.e. equal income or ability status; they pay equal amount of tax so the burden of tax per rupee income is ₹ 0.1, thus, the tax burden is same on these all tax payers. This table is also illustrated in Fig. 2.7.

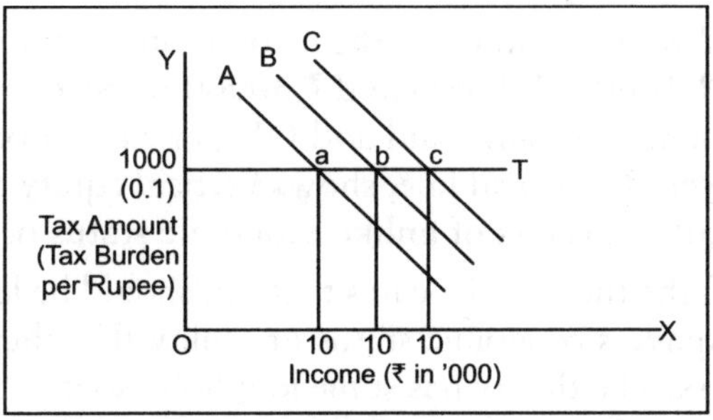

Figure 2.7: Horizontal Equity Theory

In Fig. 2.7, A, B and C are the income curve of taxpayer A, B and C, i.e. ₹ 10,000 each. OX axis measures income and OY the tax amount paid or per rupee tax burden on each taxpayer. T, horizontal line, shows horizontal equity or same tax burden on all taxpayers of like economic status or ability.

Table 2.8: Vertical Equity Theory

Taxpayer	Income (₹)	Tax Amount (₹)	Tax Burden/Per Rupee
A	10,000	1000	0.1
B	20,000	2000	0.1
C	30,000	3000	0.1

Table 2.8 shows that A, B and C are taxpayers who have unlike or dissimilar circumstance, i.e. unequal income or ability status; they pay different amount of tax but the burden of tax per rupee income is ₹ 0.1, thus, the tax burden is same on these all taxpayers. This table is also illustrated in Fig. 2.8.

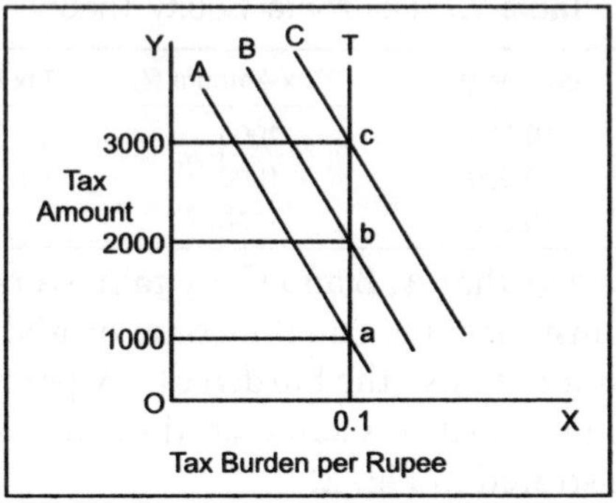

Figure 2.8: Vertical Equity Theory

In Fig. 2.8, A, B and C are the income curve of taxpayer A, B and C, i.e. ₹ 10000, ₹ 20000 and ₹ 30000 respectively. OY axis measures the tax amount paid and OX per rupee tax burden on each taxpayer. T, vertical line, shows vertical equity or same tax burden on all taxpayers of unlike economic status or ability.

In brief, the theory advocates that tax should be levied on the basis of taxpayers economic status or ability that they feel equal burden of tax. The theory has some loopholes so it is criticized as:

(i) It is difficult to define like and unlike circumstances, for instance, the taxpayers of equal income status may not have equal size of family so they cannot be treated alike.

(ii) The concept burden of tax is vague. There are various types of tax burden, for example, money burden and real burden of tax; direct and indirect burden of tax. The theory has not taken these aspects into account.

2.7.4 Cost of Service Theory

It is the oldest theory on distribution of tax burden. Government produces various services to its people so the government have to gather fund to meet the cost of production of these services. Hence, the theory advocates that the cost of these services must be the basis of taxation; and each taxpayer has to pay tax equal to the cost of service he/she received from the government. In other words, tax is price paid by the individuals who receive service worth its cost from the government. According to this theory, government is a producer of services to its people and in return collects price in form of tax just equal to its cost. But this theory is unacceptable and also criticized on the following grounds:

(i) It is difficult to estimate the cost of service to every individual, for instance police service, defence service, etc.

(ii) It is unsuitable to 'Welfare State'. Welfare state spends more money on social welfare schemes, employment scheme, relief services, etc. schemes so in such services taxation is unsuitable and unacceptable.

(iii) Tax is a compulsory payment by the people to the government and in return not benefit will be given to taxpayers.

2.7.5 Benefit Approach or Theory

This is the oldest theory on taxation or distribution of tax burden. The seventeenth century political theoreticians advocated this approach to taxation. This theory was supported by German writers like Grotius and Pufend, Aobbes, the Physiocrats and Locke; further held by eighteenth-century writer such as Hume and Rousseau. The theory advocates that the people should pay tax proportion to the benefits received from the government. People receive various benefits from government services such as defence, police service, public utilities, etc. For production of these services government spends its revenue that should be collected in form of tax. So everyone should pay tax as price in proportion to the benefit receives through these services by government.

In other words, the benefit principle conforms to a universal gut feeling that one should pay for what one gets. Government provides service or good, for example, police service, thus it collects revenue by levying tax in proportion to the cost of production of the service thus people should share these costs in proportion to their marginal benefits. In brief, the benefit principle of taxation taxes people in proportion to the marginal benefits they receive from a governmentally provided good or service.

Benefit Principle is different from Cost of Service Principle because the former considered the demand side and the latter considered the supply side; however, it is very much similar to Cost of Service Principle. This theory favours Proportional Tax System. The theory held that the need for service such as protection should be measured in proportion to income or wealth held by the taxpayer. It is nothing but user charge, for instance toll or charge for highway use. But the theory is not generally accepted by all, it is criticized as under:

(i) Rousseau said that the rich people need more protection to their income, wealth, assets, business, etc. than poor so the approach is more beneficial to rich.

(ii) Sismondi argued that the need for protection service increases more rapidly than income and wealth so it calls for progressive taxation, not proportional taxation.

(iii) J.S. Mill said that the protection is urgently needed by the poor so it calls for progressive taxation, not proportional taxation.

(iv) de Viti de Macro argued that each citizen uses public service in proportion to his or her income so it calls for progressive taxation. Since marginal utility of income of rich diminishes as income increases, there is need for progressive taxation, not proportional taxation.

(v) It is difficult to estimate the benefit receives by an individuals from government service or expenditure, for instance defence service, police service, etc.

(vi) The approach advocates benefit be the basis of taxation, it is private commercial rule; thus, it is not applicable to welfare state.

(vii) Under this principle, poor have to pay more tax because they receive more benefit from government services in countries like India; so it is not acceptable principle.

(viii) Benefit Principle advocates the proportional tax system, i.e. per capita tax burden on rich and poor should be same. Thus, it is regressive taxation so not acceptable.

(ix) This principle is unsuitable to welfare states because it fails to achieve socio-economic objectives of the state.

Despite the criticisms, the benefit approach has several advantages; they are discussed as under:

(i) Unlike 'Ability-to-Pay' approach, the benefit principle does not discourage efforts increasing income and wealth.

(ii) It is useful in price determination of government services like electricity, transport service, etc.

(iii) It is useful to local bodies or government to assess the properties that are benefited from public works such as roads, streetlight, etc.

However, since benefit approach advocates regressive tax system, it is not acceptable in the modern context.

2.7.6 Bowen and Lindahl Models

Modern governments, usually, collect funds from various sources to provide public services. Taxation is the most common source of revenue in mixed economies; but the burden of tax should be distributed among the beneficiaries of government service. Under the benefit theory, tax levels are automatically determined, because taxpayers pay proportionately for the government benefits they receive. In other words, the individuals who benefit the most from public services pay the most taxes. In analyzing the benefit approach, two models have been discussed: the Bowen Model and the Lindahl Model.

(a) Bowen Model: Prof. Bowen has explained that different taxpayers pay different prices for a social service or good on the basis of ability-to-pay and benefit received. Bowen's model has more operational significance because it demonstrates that when social goods are produced under conditions of increasing costs, the opportunity cost of private goods is foregone. For example, if there is one social good and two taxpayers, namely A and B, their demand for social goods is represented by 'a' and 'b' demand curves; therefore, the total demand for social good is DD. The total demand curve is the sum of a+b demand curves. The supply curve is shown by SS, indicating that the social good is produced under conditions of increasing cost. The production cost of social good is the value of foregone private goods; this means that DD is also the demand curve of private goods. It is illustrated in Fig. 2.9.

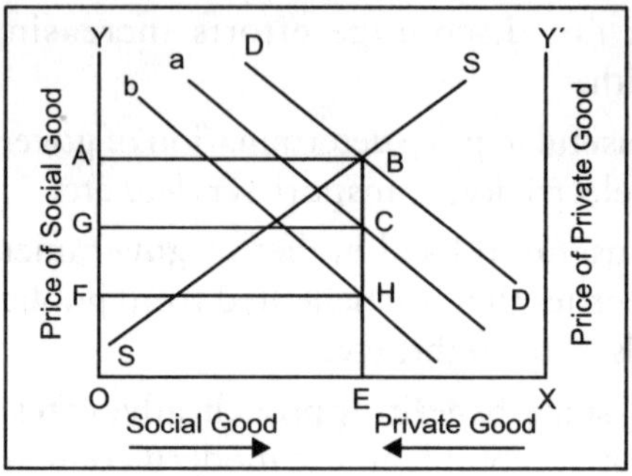

Figure 2.9: Bowen Model

Price of social good is measured along OY-axis; XY′ measures price of private good; social good is measured from O to X and private good is measured from X to O axis. The intersection of the cost or supply SS and demand curves DD at B determines how, according to taxpayers' desires, a given national income should be divided between social and private goods; hence, there should be OE social goods and EX private goods. Simultaneously, the tax shares of A and B are determined by their individual demand curves. The total tax requirement is the area ABEO; out of which A is willing to pay GCEO and B is willing to pay FHEO. Other than this equilibrium level of output and demand there is either cost or price is higher or lower than total tax revenue required by the government, for instance, at higher demand price of social good will be higher than the tax requirement.

(b) Lindahl Model: Erik Lindahl too argues that the tax burden should be distributed among different people according to their ability-to-pay and benefit received from the social good or service provided by government. Further, he says that in accordance with individual preference three sets of decisions have to be undertaken to solve three problems, namely (a) extent of state activity means total amount of public expenditure and tax, (b) allocation of the total expenditure among various goods and services to satisfy social wants, and (c) allocation of tax burden among various individuals. These decisions are mutually independent and must be rendered jointly. To explain his model Lindahl assumes one type of social good and community of two tax payers, A and B. Jointly A and B must contribute to total cost of production of social good, produced by government. The Lindahl model is illustrated in Fig. 2.10.

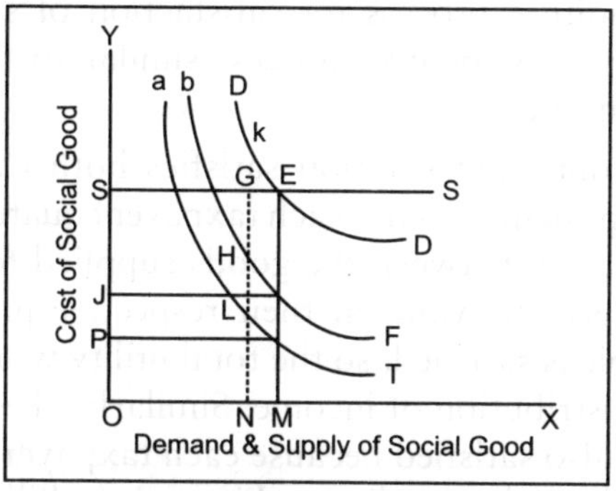

Figure 2.10: Lindahl Model

Demand and supply of social good is measured along OX axis and the cost of social good along OY axis. SS is the supply curve of social good produced by government to satisfy social wants; it is assumed that production of social goods is linear and homogenous. Curve 'a' is the demand curve of taxpayer A, and curve 'b' is the demand curve of taxpayer B. The vertical summation of the two demand curves results in the community's total demand schedule for the social good, shown by curve 'DD'. A and B pay different proportions of the cost of the social good. When OM is the amount of social good produced, at the intersection point 'E' where SS intersected with DD, A contributes TM and B contributes FM; the cost of supply is EM (=OS). Other than OM supply either increases the combined cost share of A and B more than willing to contribute or leads to short-fall of willing to accept. For instance, if government produces social good at 'N', i.e. ON size, A taxpayer will share NL and B taxpayer will share NH cost of social good but total unit cost will be NK which is more than NG that to be received from taxpayers by the government, the unit cost will be higher by GK. In other words, at ON level output the combined contribution by taxpayers to the government for social good, i.e. NK is greater than the required contribution, i.e. NG. On contrary, if supply is more than OM level, the combined contribution by taxpayers will be less than required contribution.

Lindahl concludes that the taxpayers contribute more till the equilibrium level of social good production is attained. Thus, the revenue expenditure process for satisfaction of social wants is determined by a competitive process similar to that applies in private good market.

Lindahl's optimum solution satisfies both the benefit and ability-to-pay principles. Since each taxpayer equates his marginal rate of substitution between the goods supplied for satisfaction of social and private wants at their respective price ratios, the benefit principle is satisfied; so the total utility will be maximum with a given distribution of income. Similarly, the ability-to-pay to principle is also satisfied because each taxpayer paid different price for social good according to his paying ability.

However, these models too fail to give correct interpretation of correct income distribution and taxation; differential pricing cannot take to just distribution of income. Lindahl is concerned only with allocation branch problem; he failed to explain ability to pay principle in true way, just distribution of income is taken for granted.

2.7.7 Ability-to-Pay Principle

The ability-to-pay principle of taxation is most generally accepted theory. It stands in sharp contrast to the benefits principle. Ability-to-pay principle rests on the idea that the tax burden should be geared directly to one's income and wealth. As the ability-to-pay principle has come to be applied in modern economies, it contends that individuals and businesses with larger incomes should pay more taxes—both absolutely and relatively—than those with more modest incomes. It does not make any connection between use and payment but simply states that the individuals who are most able to bear the burden of the tax should pay the tax. Taxes are based on taxpayers' ability to pay; there is no *quid pro quo*.

According to Prof. R.A. Musgrave, ability-to-pay is the "ideal ethical basis of taxation". The term 'ability' was previously known as 'faculty' which means property and income. During first half of sixteenth century, Guicciardini advocated progressive taxation based on 'faculty' but later by end of same century Bodin supported a proportional taxation based on 'faculty'. Since then it was restated and amended by the writers like Bodin, Rousseau, Sismondi, J.S. Mill, Wagner and Franklin Roosevelt.

J.S. Mill, in his classical version of ability doctrine, rejected the 'benefit approach' arguing that it is regressive taxation because poor need more protection service from government so it is against the true idea of justice. So, J.S. Mill states the ability-to-pay principle as "just distribution of taxes prevails when all contributes to the common goods so as to incur equal sacrifice". The principle of ability-to-pay is based on the dictum "all should be treated equally under law".

Grounds of Justification: The ability-to-pay principle is justified on the three grounds; these are:

(i) *Psychological effects of tax-payment upon taxpayer*: Psychologically, every taxpayer should feel that he or she has made equal sacrifice in the payment of a tax.

(ii) *Diminishing marginal utility of income*: The marginal utility of income diminishes as the income increases. Thus, the burden of tax should more on rich than poor that amounts to equality in sacrifice.

(iii) *The faculty interpretation*: Property, income and wealth of individual represent his or her the tax-paying ability. The part of income that bears the tax burden is called 'Economic Surplus' by Prof. Hobson; higher the economic surplus, higher will be the tax burden.

Measurement of Ability: 'How to measure ability-to-pay of person?' is the fundamental problem of the 'Ability-to-pay Principle'. To solve this problem two approaches come into existence, namely 'Subjective Approach' and 'Objective Approach'. The subjective approach has developed 'Sacrifice Theory or Principle' and objective approach has developed 'Faculty Theory or Principle' to measure ability-to-pay of the person. For implementation of both the principles, there is need for a quantitative measure for ability-to-pay. The welfare of the person depends on various factors such as consumption, holding of wealth, enjoyment of leisure, etc.; some of them are measurable, some others are not measurable. So a comprehensive measure is not possible, however, some observable measure are undertaken to measure the ability-to-pay of the persons; these are considered as 'Index of Ability-to-Pay' that are discussed as under:

(i) Property: Property and wealth is considered as the index to measure ability-to-pay tax; but it is not the primary test of ability because of the following reasons:

(a) All properties do not yield income for instance, rented buildings yield income whereas own-use buildings do not yield income.

(b) Income from property is not continuous, it depends upon use and demand conditions for instance, land-property unutilized for any purpose does not yield income.

(c) Income from property differ from place to place and use to use for instance a house-building yields more rent in city than in village.

(d) A tax is levied on value of property, it is unjust if the property does not yield income.

However, property is considered as supplementary test of ability because of the following reasons:

(a) The ownership of property gives the owner additional capacity to pay tax.

(b) Income from property gives more ability to pay tax than income from service for instance inherited property give more tax-paying ability.

(ii) Income: Income is the important test of tax-paying ability of a person, it is primary test of ability. Adam Smith and classical economists had argued that income should be the primary test of tax-paying ability of a person. Adam Smith advocated that the wages compose of real subsistence income should be exempted from taxation because it is burdensome on poor; the income above the subsistence level should be taxed. This advocates progressive taxation.

The development of industrial and money economy shifted the tax-base from property to income, income is in various forms such as rent, interest, wages, profit, dividend, remuneration, commission, etc. The gross income includes the cost elements so 'net income' should be considered as the primary index of ability. Adam Smith was the first to advocate income as the index of ability, now it is generally accepted by all.

***(iii) Family-Size*:** The size of the family of taxpayer is the other index of ability. With same amount of income, the large size family taxpayer feel more tax burden than small size family taxpayer. But it is not primary index of ability.

***(iv) Consumption*:** The taxation based on income and property may not be equitable and may lead to tax-evasion; for this reason, Prof. Fisher and Prof. Kaldor advocated taxation on expenditure. According to them, consumption expenditure should be the index of measuring tax-paying ability of an individual. Prof. Hobbes had argued that the tax should be levied on what he or she uses and not on fruits of labour. The consumption tax is more favourable to savings and investment thereby economic growth.

In spite of its merits, consumption taxation fails to get prominence as base of taxation, however, income is the most widely accepted index of ability-to-pay tax of person.

Approaches: There are two approaches evolved to solve the fundamental problem of measuring the ability-to-pay of the tax-payer; these approaches are:

***(a) Subjective Approach of Ability-to-Pay Principle*:** When an individual pay a tax to the government out of his income, he or she has to give up or sacrifice that part of his or her purchasing power or consumption or welfare; it effects on the psychological or mental attitude of the taxpayer. What the taxpayer feels about paying of tax is subjective factor and it differ from taxpayer to taxpayer. Hence, the subjective approach is based on the psychological or mental reactions of the taxpayers. Moreover, the subjective approach states that if tax burden is to be distributed equally among the people, each taxpayer should make equal sacrifice.

The subjective approach is based of J.S. Mill's 'Principle of Equal Sacrifice'. According to Mill, all should be treated equally under the law as well as in all affairs of government; equity in taxation means equality in sacrifice. Hence, J.S. Mill states the theory "Taxpayers are said to be treated equally if their tax payments involve an equal sacrifice or loss of welfare." He, further, argued that the people with same income or ability or marginal utility of income have to pay same amount of tax but the people with dissimilar income or ability or marginal utility of income have to pay different amount of tax so that the distribution of tax burden or sacrifice of welfare should be equal. In case of dissimilar situation or differ in tax amount to be paid there are 'three forms of equal sacrifice principle'. They are discussed as under:

***(a) Equal Absolute Sacrifice*:** Under this principle, the people with higher income should pay higher amount of tax and low income people should pay low amount of tax so the utility sacrifice due to tax should be equal to all or burden of should be same on all taxpayers. It is mathematically expressed as:

$$[U(Y) - U(Y-T)]_A = [U(Y) - U(Y-T)]_B$$

A and B are taxpayers, U = Total Utility of Money, Y = Income, T = Amount of tax paid to the government. The equation implies:

Total Utility Sacrifice by A = Total Utility Sacrifice by B

For example: A's income is ₹ 100 and B's income ₹ 200, assuming the value of U = 1 util for A and U = 0.5 util for B; A paid tax amount ₹ 10 B paid tax amount ₹ 20 to the government. By substituting these values in the equation:

$$[1(100) - 1(100-10)]_A = [0.5(200) - 0.5(200-20)]_B$$

$$100-90 = 100-90 = 10 \text{ util}$$

A's Utility sacrifice = B's Utility sacrifice = 10 util

This principle calls for arbitrary progressive tax system so it is regressive in nature. This principle is rejected by economists because the burden of tax will be more on low income group than high income group people.

It is very difficult to measure exactly the rate of decline in marginal utility of money as income increases; thus the rate of progression has to be fixed arbitrarily. Prof. A.C. Pigou, however, said that the high degree of progression should not affect the social status of the taxpayer.

***(b) Equal Proportional Sacrifice*:** Under this principle, an individual with higher income should pay more tax than those who have lower income but the ratio of sacrifice to the income should be same for all taxpayers. It can be expressed as:

$$\frac{\text{A's Utility Sacrifice due to Tax}}{\text{A's Income}} = \frac{\text{B's Utility Sacrifice due to Tax}}{\text{B's Income}}$$

According to this principle, the taxation is more progressive than 'equal absolute sacrifice principle'. The marginal utility of money declines with increase in income. The mathematical representation of 'equal proportional sacrifice principle' is given below:

$$\left[\frac{U(Y)-U(Y-T)}{(Y)}\right]A = \left[\frac{U(Y)-U(Y-T)}{(Y)}\right]B$$

A and B are taxpayers, U = Total Utility of Money, Y = Income, T = Amount of tax paid to the government. The equation implies:

A's Sacrifice to Income Ratio = B's Sacrifice to Income Ratio

For example, A's income is ₹ 100 and B's income ₹ 200, assuming the value of U = 1 util and U = 0.5 util for B; A paid tax amount ₹ 5 at tax rate 5 per cent and B paid tax amount ₹ 20 at the tax rate 10 per cent, to the government. By substituting these values in the equation:

$$\left[\frac{1(100)-1(100-5)}{100}\right]A = \left[\frac{.5(200)-.5(200-20)}{200}\right]B$$

$$\left[\frac{5}{100}\right]A = \left[\frac{10}{200}\right]B = \frac{1}{20} = 0.05$$

This principle calls for more progressive tax system than 'equal absolute sacrifice principle'. However, the required tax burden distribution depends on the level and slope of marginal utility of money schedule, initial distribution of income and amount of tax revenue to be collected by the government.

(c) Equal Marginal Sacrifice: Under this principle, the marginal sacrifice, i.e. the sacrifice of the last unit of money of taxpayer for all the different taxpayers should be the same so that the aggregate sacrifice of the community as whole should be least. It has considered marginal sacrifice, not the total sacrifice. The least aggregate sacrifice of the community means maximum welfare to all. In other words, the burden of tax should be so distributed that the marginal sacrifice income utility of all the tax payers must be the same and the community should enjoy maximum welfare or income utility after taxation. Hence, Prof. A.C. Pigou defines the marginal sacrifice principle as "Thus the distribution of taxation required to conform to the principle of least aggregate sacrifice is that which makes the marginal not the total sacrifice borne by all the members of the community equal." This principle is mathematically expressed as:

$$\left[\frac{dU(Y-T)}{d(Y-T)}\right]A = \left[\frac{dU(Y-T)}{d(Y-T)}\right]B$$

A and B are taxpayers, U = Total Utility of Money, Y = Income, T = Amount of tax paid to the government, *d* denotes change. The equation implies:

A's sacrifice on last unit = B's sacrifice on last unit of income of income

For example, A's income is ₹ 100 and B's income ₹ 150, assuming the value of U = 1 util; A paid tax amount ₹ 5 at tax rate 5 per cent and B paid tax amount ₹ 9 at the tax rate 6 per cent, to the government. Further, the income of A and B changed to ₹ 101 and ₹ 151 respectively. By substituting these values in the equation:

$$\left[\frac{dU(Y-T)}{d(Y-T)}\right]A = \frac{1(101-5.05)-1(100-5)}{(101-5.05)-(100-5)} = \frac{1.05}{1.05}$$

$$\left[\frac{dU(Y-T)}{d(Y-T)}\right]B = \frac{1(151-9.06)-1(150-6)}{(151-9.06)-(150-6)} = \frac{0.94}{0.94}$$

$$\left[\frac{1.05}{1.05}\right]A = \left[\frac{0.94}{0.94}\right]B = 1$$

This principle calls for more progressive tax system than 'equal proportional sacrifice and equal absolute sacrifice principles'. However, the required tax burden distribution depends on the level and slope of marginal utility of money schedule, initial distribution of income and amount of tax revenue to be collected by the government. Under this principle, the tax burden will fall more on rich and less on poor.

Figure Illustration: All the three principles, discussed above, are illustrated in Fig. 2.11

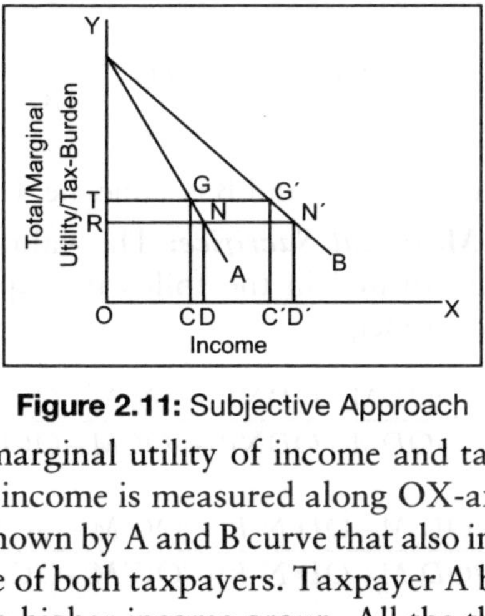

Figure 2.11: Subjective Approach

Total and marginal utility of income and tax are measured along OY-axis; income is measured along OX-axis. A and B are the taxpayers, shown by A and B curve that also indicate marginal utility of income of both taxpayers. Taxpayer A belongs to lower income and B to higher income group. All the three concepts of equal absolute, equal proportional and equal marginal sacrifice principles are illustrated in Fig. 2.11 as:

(i) ***Equal Absolute Sacrifice*:** Tax amount paid by A is OTGC and B is OTG′C′, B's tax amount is higher than A but the addition sum of both is equal to the tax amount government required to collect to pay for production of public services. The total utility of income of taxpayer A and B is respectively OCM and OC′M; after tax payment, the net total income utility is TGM for A and TG′M for B so the sacrifice of the both is same, it is shown as:

$$U(Y) - U(Y{-}T)_A = U(Y) - U(Y{-}T)_B$$

$$OCM - (OCM - OTGC)_A = OC'M - (OC'M - OTG'C')_A$$

$$OTCG_A = OTC'G'_B$$

So the tax burden on A and B is same, i.e. OT = CG = C′G′.

***(ii) Equal Proportional Sacrifice*:** The values illustrated in the above diagram are substituted in the following equation of equal proportional sacrifice principle:

$$\left[\frac{U(Y)-U(Y-T)}{(Y)}\right]A=\left[\frac{U(Y)-U(Y-T)}{(Y)}\right]B$$

$$\left[\frac{OCM-(OCM-OTGC)}{OCM}\right]A=\left[\frac{OC'M-(OC'M-OTG'C')}{OC'M}\right]B$$

$$\left[\frac{OTGC}{OCM}\right]A=\left[\frac{OTG'C'}{OC'M}\right]B$$

So the tax burden on A and B is same, i.e. OT = CG = C′G′.

***(iii) Equal Marginal Sacrifice*:** The values illustrated in Fig. 2.11 are substituted in the following equation of equal marginal sacrifice principle:

$$\left[\frac{dU(Y-T)}{d(Y-T)}\right]A=\frac{(ODM-ODNR)-(OCM-OCGT)}{(ODM-ODNR)-(OCM-OCGT)}=\frac{RTGN}{RTGN}$$

$$\left[\frac{dU(Y-T)}{d(Y-T)}\right]B=\frac{(OD'M-OD'N'R)-(OC'M-OC'G'T)}{(OD'M-OD'N'R)-(OC'M-OC'G'T)}=\frac{RTG'N'}{RTG'N'}$$

$$\left[\frac{RTGN}{RTGN}\right]A=\left[\frac{RTG'N'}{RTG'N'}\right]B=1$$

The marginal sacrifice of total income utility of each taxpayer is equal or same, i.e. RTGN = RTG′N′.

In brief, tax burden will be more on low income group than high income group under equal absolute principle but tax system will be less progressive in nature; under equal proportional and equal marginal principle the taxation will be more and highly progressive respectively, burden of tax on higher income group will be higher and highest respectively and it will be lower and lowest respectively on low income group.

Limitations of Subjective Approach: This approach has some limitations that are discussed as under:

(i) It is difficult to equalize the marginal sacrifice of all the taxpayers because even with equal income the size of family, taste, psychology, etc. differ from person to person.

(ii) Sacrifice is a subjective phenomenon so it cannot be measured; it can be realized by the person who makes sacrifice. In such case, it is difficult to equalize the sacrifice of all taxpayers.

(iii) The utility of hard-earned money income is more than easy-earned money income, for instance, salary is hard-earned and income from property is easy-earned money income. In such case, it is difficult to measure the sacrifice of all taxpayers.

(iv) The subjective approach is based on law of diminishing marginal utility but whether this law applies to income is doubtful case. It is difficult to say that marginal utility of income declines as income increases, it is based on situation and attitude of the person.

(v) The progressive tax structure is fixed on arbitrary basis so it is difficult to equalize between marginal sacrifice of taxpayers.

(vi) The scope of application of this approach is limited, no finance minister formulate progressive tax policy on the basis of this principle. It is difficult to measure both ability and sacrifice.

***(b) Objective Approach*:** Since subjective approach has practical difficulties, some economists, particularly American, have presented objective approach to measure the ability-to-pay tax. Prof. Seligman has used the term 'Faculty' to measure ability in objective term so the theory is called 'faculty theory of ability-to-pay'. This approach is contrary to 'subjective approach'. The theory takes into account the money value of taxable capacity of taxpayer instead of his or feeling of sacrifice. Subjective approach is individualistic approach because it considers sacrifice of income or utility at individual level but we have to consider at society or macro level. The ability-to-pay capacity of an individual and the benefit enjoys by him or her depend on economic structure of the society so the objective approach takes into account the economic structure wherein the person earns income and wealth that constitutes the ability-to-pay tax. In other words, objective approach gives social flavor as against the subjective approach that gives feeling of individual sacrifice.

To measure ability faculty theory has taken into account three indices, namely income, property and consumption expenditure. According to this approach, tax can be levied on the basis of tax-paying ability of individual so it calls for progressive tax system.

Defects and Limitations: The objective approach has some defects and limitations; these are:

(i) Prof. Seligman found out some defects with measurement of ability of the theory (a) it is difficult to reach every personal property, (b) lack of uniformity in assessment of property and income, for instance property in villages and cities and (c) it calls for general property tax which is regressive in nature.

(ii) The faculty theory suffers the following limitations:

(a) The theory has taken into account income and wealth as the index of measuring ability-to-pay but it fails to consider other factors such as individual status, economic situation, etc. that also influence of ability, and (b) The theory fails to consider the factors like family-size, source of income, nature of income, etc. that determines ability.

However, the faculty approach is supplement to the subjective approach.

In practice, in spite of limitations and criticisms, the ability-to-pay theory is most widely accepted theory of tax burden distribution.

2.8 MODEL QUESTIONS

(a) Questions each needs answer in 2-3 sentences (2 Marks each)

1. What is public revenue?
2. What do you mean by tax revenue?

3. Give the meaning of non-tax revenue.
4. Name any two sources of tax revenue.
5. Name any two sources of non-tax revenue.
6. State any two characteristics of tax.
7. Mention any two administrative revenues.
8. What is escheat?
9. Give difference between tax and price.
10. Give difference direct tax and indirect tax.
11. Mention the difference between proportional tax and progressive tax.
12. Mention the difference between regressive tax and degressive tax.
13. What do you mean by burden of tax?
14. What is impact of tax?
15. What is incidence of tax?
16. Write any two determinants of incidence.
17. Give difference between impact and incidence of tax.
18. Give difference between incidence of tax and effect of tax.
19. How does tax reduce the ability to work?
20. How does tax reduce the income and employment in the economy?
21. Define taxable capacity.
22. Give the difference between absolute taxable capacity and relative taxable capacity.
23. Mention any two determinants of taxable capacity.
24. Highlight any two importance of taxable capacity.
25. What is justice in taxation?
26. Give the statement of physiocratic theory of taxation.
27. What does financial theory state?
28. What is horizontal equity? What do you mean by vertical equity?

29. Give any two reasons for unacceptability of cost of service theory.
30. Mention the central idea of benefit approach.
31. What does Bowen model state?
32. Give the meaning of ability-to-pay.
33. Name the approaches to ability to pay theory.
34. What do you mean by equal marginal sacrifice?

(b) Questions each needs short-note type answer (5 Marks each)

1. Give a brief account of tax revenue.
2. Write a note on sources of non-tax revenue.
3. Discuss in brief merits and demerits of direct tax.
4. Write a short-note on merits and demerits of indirect tax.
5. Write a note on proportional tax and progressive tax.
6. Explain in brief the regressive tax and degressive tax.
7. Write a note on determinants of incidence of tax.
8. Discuss in brief the determinant of taxable capacity.
9. Write a note on measurement of taxable capacity.
10. Write a short-note on physiocratic theory and financial theory of taxation.
11. Give a brief account of horizontal and vertical equity theory.
12. Discuss briefly benefit approach.
13. Narrate briefly Lindahl model.
14. Write a note on index of ability-to-pay.
15. Explain briefly the objective approach of ability-to-pay theory.

(c) Questions each needs essay type/long answer (10/15 Marks each)

1. Define public revenue, explain its sources.
2. Define tax, explain its characteristics and burden.
3. Explain the merits and demerits of direct tax.

4. What is indirect tax? Explain its merits and demerits.
5. What is tax? Explain its various types.
6. What is incidence of tax? Explain its determinants.
7. Define tax, explain its effects.
8. What is taxable capacity? Explain its various determinants.
9. Define taxable capacity. Explain its measurement and importance.
10. Explain Bowen and Lindahl models of tax burden distribution.
11. Discuss the ability-to-pay theory on distribution of tax burden.

3

Public Expenditure

3.1 PUBLIC EXPENDITURE

It is another aspect of operation of public funds of public finance. It helps to know the real purpose of functioning of the government. It decides success and failure of the government.

3.1.1 Meaning and Scope

Public expenditure is the expenditure incurred by public authorities like central, State and local governments for the purpose of the satisfaction of the collective needs of the society or citizens. Public expenditure is used as an effective tool for promoting the economic and social welfare of the citizens. The scope of public expenditure is changing as the functions and responsibilities of the government are expanding in the recent years.

Classical Economists' View: The classical economists including Adam Smith supported for the passive role of government. According to them the role of the government was just like an observer in the process of development and suggested for least interference in all economic activities. According to these economists the important functions of the government were as follows.

(i) Expenditure on defense to protect the country from foreign aggression.

(ii) Expenditure on maintenance of internal law and order which is essential to promote economic activities.

(iii) Expenditure on administration of the country which helps in bringing co-ordination among economic activities to achieve economic and social welfare.

(iv) Along with this the governments should also spend certain amount of money for building infrastructure which promotes economic activities.

Modern Economists' View: Classical views were with the 'police States' but modern states are 'welfare-States' so the basic objectives and scope of public expenditures underwent changes. In the recent years, increase in urbanization and industrialization has led to an increase in the role of government. There is a manifold increase in the activities of the modern governments. According to Wagner, a German economist, increase in the government activities both economic and non-economic causes for an increase in the government expenditure. He further advocated that the modern governments have to perform both old and new functions with more efficiently and completely. There will be additions to the existing economic activities and hence the governments are expected to spend more than the previous years. The governments are adopting both developmental as well as welfare activities causing for an increase in their expenditure. Some economists have termed this process as "deepening and widening" of governments' activities so as to achieve certain pre-determined socio-economic objectives.

Twentieth century economist Prof. R.A. Musgrave has advocated that the modern governments are forced to do the activities like (i) reallocation of resources, (ii) re-distribution activities, (iii) stabilizing activities, and (iv) commercial activities.

J.M. Keynes strongly advocated for an increase in public expenditure to attain speedy progress of the economies. He advocated the principle of 'functional finance approach' for to come out of the situations of great depression and the same principle can be successfully introduced for the development of the underdeveloped countries. The pump-priming, multiplier and acceleration principles propounded by Keynes have been successfully adopted by modern governments for the process of economic development. The application of these approaches has not only brought success but also boosted their confidence in increasing public expenditure on a large scale. Further, these principles have increased the active role of government in a "welfare state" and have resulted in an enormous increase in public expenditure and its scope.

3.1.2 Comparison between Private and Public Expenditure

Private expenditure means the spending by private individuals, companies, organizations, etc. for the purpose of their own benefits. Public is not allowed to enjoy these benefits, for examples, private parking places, gardens, halls, buildings, etc. Public expenditure means the spending by government for the purpose of common good or benefits of all citizens of the country. There are similarities and dissimilarities between private and public expenditures. They are enlisted in Table 3.1.

Table 3.1: Comparison between Private and Public Expenditure

Private Expenditure	Public Expenditure
I Similarities	
(i) Maximum returns with minimum cost	(i) Maximum returns with minimum cost
(ii) Flexible in nature: increase or decrease according to need	(ii) Flexible in nature: increase or decrease according to need
(iii) Increases productivity	(iii) Increases productivity
II Dissimilarities	
(i) Income determines the expenditure.	(i) Expenditure determines the income.
(ii) It has private motive or profit.	(ii) It has social motive or benefit.
(iii) It is voluntary.	(iii) It is compulsory.
(iv) It is short-view plan with foreseeable future.	(iv) It is long-view plan for long-run benefit of the society.
(v) It is for personal advantage, for example, education.	(v) State has no personal advantage, for example, education.
(vi) It has narrow scope.	(vi) It has wider scope.

3.2 TYPES OF PUBLIC EXPENDITURE

Public expenditure has been classified into various types or categories on the basis of certain factors such as benefits given, revenue received in return of services rendered, government functions, etc. The different classifications of public expenditure by the economists are studied as under:

(i) Benefit-based Classification: German economist Cohen and American economist Plehn have classified public expenditure as:

(a) Public expenditure *benefitting the entire community* such as defence, general administration, education, etc. The entire people irrespective of rich and poor get benefits from public expenditure.

(b) Public expenditure *benefitting the certain people* such as poor-relief, etc. Not the entire community but the selective people are benefitted from public expenditure.

(c) Public expenditure *benefitting the certain people and the entire community both* such as administration of justice, public health, etc. Rich and poor both are benefitted from public expenditure.

(d) Public expenditure *benefitting particular groups* such as subsidies granted to particular industry, farmers, etc.

This Cohen-Plehn classification is overlapping so it is not satisfactory.

(ii) Revenue-Received-Based Classification: This classification was done by F.S. Nicholson on the basis of revenue received by the government in return to its service rendered. It is as follows:

(a) Public expenditure *without direct return of revenue*: Government expenditures on poor-relief activities, war, etc., yield no direct income in return to the government.

(b) Public expenditure *without direct return of revenue but indirect return of revenue*: Government expenditures on education, public health, etc., yield no direct income in return to the government but indirectly yield return to the government by way of making the people the better taxpayers.

(c) Public expenditure *with partial direct return of revenue*: The public expenditures on goods and services partly borne by the people, for example, subsidized railway service, bus service, fertilizer, education, etc.

(d) Public expenditure *with full return or profit*: The public expenditures on production of goods and services by the government undertakings yield full return or profits, for example, post office service, central bank services, government industries, etc.

This classification is also not clear cut and it is also overlapping, for example, the expenditure on education appears in group (b) and (c) both.

(iii) Dalton's Classification: Prof. Dalton has classified public expenditures into two types on the basis of return to government in form of goods or service. They are as follows:

(a) *Purchase Prices*: Dalton defines purchase price as "payments by the public authority to any of its employees by way of salaries and wages, or to the contractors, whom it employees, are purchase prices". Government pays salaries and wages to its employees and in return gets service from them.

(b) *Grants*: Dalton defines grants as "payments of old age social insurance (by Govt) are grants". Government spends money but does not expect any commodity or service in return is called grant, for example, social security schemes.

This classification is also not clear in some cases like payment of interest on public debt: it is purchase price from present point of view but it is grant from past point of view when it was received and used.

(iv) Adam Smith's Classification: On the basis of the functions of the government, Adam Smith classified the public expenditures into three groups. They are studied as follows:

(a) *Protective Functions*: It is the primary duty of the government to protect its people from internally and externally. For maintenance of internal law and order police force, civil administration, courts, etc. are required so government spends on these functions. They are generally called 'administration-expenditures'. To protect the nation from external aggressions the government has to maintain defence forces such as army, air and naval forces. They are generally called 'defence-expenditures'.

(b) *Commercial Functions*: The government has to support commercial activities in the country for its economic development. The grants, subsidies, tax reliefs, organizing of industrial exhibitions, etc. functions have to be carried out by the government so it has spent on these activities.

(c) *Development Functions*: To increase national income and to improve social welfare are also equally important functions of the government. Government expenditures on development of infrastructure such as roads, railways, waterways, airways, power, etc. increase the national income. Similarly government spending on education, health, public recreation, collection of social statistics, etc. improves the social welfare of the people. They are generally called 'development expenditures'.

Smith's classification is also considered as overlapping because some items of expenditure come under more than one group for instance, defence expenditure: it is for protection and progress both.

(v) J.S. Mill's Classification: J.S. Mill classified public expenditure into two categories on the basis of the nature of government functions:

(a) *Optional Expenditures*: It refers to government expenditure on its non-necessary or non-obligatory functions, for example, education, health, etc.

(b) *Obligatory Expenditures*: It refers to government expenditure on its necessary or obligatory functions, for example, law and order, administration, defence, etc.

This classification is also overlapping because the expenditures like public education, public health, etc. come under both categories. Such expenditures cannot be avoided.

(vi) Roscher's Classification: Roscher classified public expenditures into three categories on the basis of merits and demerits of the particular expenditure. They are as follows:

(a) *Necessary Expenditures*: These are the expenditures which have to be borne by the government and they cannot be postponed, for example, administration, defence, etc.

(b) *Useful Expenditures*: It refers to government expenditure which is desirable but can be postponed, for example, poor relief, education, social security schemes, etc.

(c) *Superfluous Expenditures*: The expenditure which may or may not incur by the government is called superfluous expenditure, for example, allowances, reliefs, etc.

It is also not a scientific classification because no state or government would spend on un-necessary activities. Useful and superfluous expenditures may become necessary due to changing conditions, for example, poor relief, flood relief, public health, etc.

(vii) G.F. Shirras's Classification: Prof. Shirras has classified public expenditures on the basis of government's primary and secondary functions. They are discussed as follows:

(a) *Primary Expenditures*: Defence, law and order, repayment of public debt, etc. are the primary functions of government so the government expenditures on these heads are called 'Primary Expenditures'.

(b) *Secondary Expenditures*: Public health, education, public under takings, etc. are the secondary functions of the government so the public expenditures on these heads are called 'Secondary Expenditures'.

This classification is also not acceptable the primary and secondary are the relative terms so it is difficult to say which more important and which is less. Public health, education, public undertakings, etc. are also more important from development point of view.

(viii) A.C. Pigou's Classification: Prof. Pigou classified public expenditures into two groups namely:

(a) *Non-Transfer Expenditures*: The expenditure that purchases current services or productive resources for the use of government authorities is called 'exhaustive' or 'real' or 'non-transfer expenditure', for example, expenditure on army, navy, air force, civil, education, judiciary, etc. services. It gives rise to creation of some output or money income. Government purchases these services by paying them salary otherwise these services would be used for alternative purposes. For instance, government pays salary to public school teacher to purchase his or her service.

(b) *Transfer Expenditure*: The expenditure on existing property rights to private persons is called 'transfer expenditure', for example, payment of interest on government debts, pensions, sickness benefits, etc. and subsidies on production of social goods like sugar, milk, house, etc. It does not create any income or output. It transfers money from government to recipients.

Prof. Pigou's classification is satisfactory because people are directly benefitted from non-transfer expenditures and indirectly from transfer expenditures.

(ix) J.K. Mehta's Classification: Prof. J.K. Mehta considers that public expenditure is a cost to the government so he used cost concepts such as 'prime cost' and 'supplementary cost' as basis of his classification of public expenditures. He classified public expenditures in to two groups as:

(a) *Constant Expenditures*: Mehta defines constant expenditure as "constant expenditure is that the amount of which does not depend upon the extent of the by the people, in whose interest it is incurred, make of services that are financed by it". It incurs irrespective of the size of people using it, for instance, defence or police expenditures incur irrespective how many people use it.

(b) *Variable Expenditures*: Mehta defines variable expenditure as "variable expenditure, likewise, is that which increases with every increase in the use of public services by the people for whose benefit it is incurred". It depends upon the number of people using it, for instance, expenditure on postal service depends on the number of people using it.

Mehta's classification is different from others because he used cost as basis and others used benefit as basis. Mehta too admitted that the classification of public expenditures is difficult task because some costs may be placed in both groups, for example, the police expenditure may increase due to increase in population.

(x) Economic and Other Classifications: Despite above discussed classifications, economists have done still more classifications for convenience of study and interpretation of the concepts. They are discussed as under:

(a) *Economic Classification*: Public expenditures are classified as (i) Revenue Expenditures and (ii) Capital Expenditures for the sake of economic interpretation of the government expenditures.

The public expenditure which does not result into asset creation is called Revenue Expenditure, for instance, current expenditures on civil administration, defence, commercial undertaking, grants, public utility services like railway, post telegraph, etc.

The public expenditure which does result into asset creation is called Capital Expenditure, for instance, capital expenditures on capital transactions of defence, commercial undertakings, etc.

If government spends on salary of army, it is revenue expenditure but if it on purchase of land, construction of building, purchase of arms, tanker, etc., it is capital expenditure.

(b) *Plan and Non-Plan Expenditure*: The public expenditures are also classified as (i) Plan Expenditures and (ii) Non-Plan Expenditures for the sake of economic interpretation of the concepts.

The current expenditures on investment and developmental activities are called Plan Expenditures, for instance, development of industry, agriculture, infrastructures, etc., for the sake of development of the country. It is also known as Development Expenditures.

The obligatory expenditures on part of government are called Non-Plan Expenditures, for instance, interest payments, pensions, statutory transfers, defence, civil administration, education, health, etc. In other words, the expenditures by the government for its commitments or obligatory works are known as non-plan expenditures. It includes both development and non-development expenditures of the government.

This types of classification is being practiced in countries like India. It is most useful for formulation, review and implementation of policy objectives.

3.3 PRINCIPLES/CANONS OF PUBLIC EXPENDITURE

Like canons of taxation, there are some canons or principles to govern the public expenditure. These principles are discussed as follows:

(i) Principle of Maximum Social Advantage: It is necessary that all public expenditures should satisfy one fundamental test, i.e., the test of 'Maximum Social Advantage'. The government should always try to maintain an optimum level of public expenditure by balancing social benefits and social costs. It means each rupee spent by a government should promote maximum welfare of the society as a whole. The public funds should not be allocated and used for the benefit of a particular group or a section of society. The prime objective of the government should be general welfare. Government exists for the benefit of the governed and hence there is necessity of justification of the government expenditure. This can be successfully done if the governments spend the money for the benefit of the community as a whole.

(ii) Canon of Economy: The canon of economy means that the state should be economical in spending money. The main objective of the government is to maximize social benefit. But at the same time, there is need for utmost economy in public expenditure. The state should not spend more than the necessary amount. The main objective of this canon is to avoid extravagance and corruption. Economy does not mean niggardliness. It only means that extravagance and waste of all types should be avoided. The objective of the social benefit can be maximized when there is no waste. Public expenditure has great potentiality for public good but it may also prove injurious and wasteful. For example, if three street lights are installed in the place where two street lights are necessary. Thus, if revenue collected from the taxpayer is diverted for wasteful expenditure, it would be obviously uneconomical. To satisfy the canon of economy, it will be necessary to avoid all duplication of expenditure and overlapping of authorities. Further, public expenditure should not adversely affect saving. In case government activity damaged the individual's will or power to save, it would be repugnant to the canon of economy.

(iii) Canon of Sanction: According to Shirras 'the canon of sanction is that no public expenditure should be incurred without the sanction of proper authority'. It means that before the actual expenditure is incurred, it should be sanctioned by a competent authority. Unauthorized expenditure will lead to extravagance, over spending and misuse. The object of this canon is to avoid the possibilities of unwise and reckless spending. It also means that the amount must be spent on the purpose for which it was sanctioned. The canon of sanction also includes that the expenditure of the government should made for which it has been sanctioned. Further, the state should see that the sanctioned amount is properly utilized. It means there is need for auditing of the public expenditure. That is, all the public accounts at the end of the year should be properly audited to see that the amounts have not been wrongly spent or misappropriated.

(iv) Canon of Elasticity: The canon of elasticity requires that the expenditure policy of the state should be able to change itself with the change in requirements of the country. In other words, the public expenditure should be flexible in nature. It means the public authorities should have the opportunity to vary the expenditure according to the needs or circumstances. A rigid level of expenditure may prove a source of trouble and embarrassment in bad times. Increasing the public expenditure at a higher level is not difficult. The modern governments find it relatively easy to increase the scale of expenditure. But elasticity is needed most in the downward direction. There will be serious social discontent when the governments reduce the expenditure. It is very necessary, therefore, that when the public expenditure has to be increased, it should be increased gradually. A short spell of prosperity in the economy should not lead to long-term commitments in expenditure. To avoid embarrassment at a time of fall in revenue of the government there is need for a fair degree of elasticity in public expenditure.

(v) Canon of Surplus: The classical school of thought believes the theory of surplus in the budget. They advocate the principle of avoidance of deficit in public expenditure. It means the public expenditure should be kept well within the revenue of the State so that a surplus is left at the end of the year. The state should live within her means like a private individual. But the modern economists, especially Keynes, do not regard surplus budgeting as a virtue, rather deficit budgeting is more useful in raising the levels of income and employment in the underdeveloped countries. Deficit budget is also important during depression because it increases the purchasing power of people and this would increase the aggregate effective demand which may help in raising the level of income and employment. But the governments should be careful as deficits running over a number of years are considered bad for the financial stability of the country.

(vi) Canon of Equitable Distribution: This canon advocates that the expenditure should be carried out in such a way that the inequalities in the distribution of income are reduced. This objective can be achieved by providing more benefits to the poorer section of the community by allocating more funds for health, education, and housing and on those programmes which generate employment opportunities for the poorer section of the community. Along with this there is need for allocation of more money for the poverty alleviation programmes which help the weaker sections of the community. This will help in increasing the productivity and the standard of living of the poorer sections of the community.

(vii) Promotion of Economic Growth and Stability: The main objective of the modern governments is to promote economic growth and stability. Public expenditure is effectively used by many governments to these twin objectives. The expenditure of the government should be designed in such a way that it not only promotes economic growth but also helps to achieve economic stability.

Thus, for obtaining maximum benefit from each rupee spent by the state there is need to obey the principles of public expenditure, discussed above. The success of all governments depends upon the effective implementation of the functional finance. It means the public expenditure should be directed to the achievement of economic and social objectives set by the planners.

3.4 WAGNER'S LAW

Adam Smith, in his book *Wealth of Nations* advocates that the government expenditures should be restricted only to their activities such as defence against foreign aggression, maintenance of internal peace and order and public development works. Other than these functions were considered beyond the scope of the state and such expenditures were treated as unjust and wasteful.

But there had been a spectacular expansion in the functions of state that have resulted in phenomenal increase in public expenditure. For this we shall take a look at contributions by Adolph Wagner and Peacock-Wiseman.

Adolph Wagner, the German economist made an in depth study relating to rise in government expenditure in the late 19th century. Based on his study, he propounded a law called "The Law of Increasing State Activity".

Wagner's law states that "as the economy develops over time, the activities and functions of the government increase". Further, he continues "Comprehensive comparisons of different countries and different times show that among progressive peoples (societies), with which alone we are concerned; an increase regularly takes place in the activity of both the Central Government and Local Governments constantly undertake new functions, while they perform both old and new functions more efficiently and more completely. In this way, economic needs of the people to an increasing extent and in a more satisfactory fashion, are satisfied by the Central and Local Governments." Wagner's statement indicates the following points:

(i) In the progressive societies, the activities of the Central and Local Government increase on a regular basis.

(ii) The increase in government activities is both extensive and intensive.

(iii) The governments undertake new functions in the interest of the society.

(iv) The old and the new functions are performed more efficiently and completely than before.

(v) The purpose of the government activities is to meet the economic needs of the people.

(vi) The expansion and intensification of government functions and activities lead to increase in public expenditure.

(vii) Though Wagner studied the economic growth of Germany, it applies to other countries too both developed and developing.

According to Wagner, as the country experiences the economic growth and development it also experiences increase in functions and activities of government so there is increase in ratio between the public expenditures on these functions and activities and gross national product (GNP) as the GNP increases. For its justification, he divided public expenditure into two categories, namely, (a) expenditure for internal and external security, and (b) expenditure for cultural and welfare activities such as public education, health, infrastructure facilities, banking, etc. Further, he argued that the government or public sector produces goods and services far better than private sector in terms of quality and quantity and it controls market crisis created by private sector.

In other words, Wagner contends that the income elasticity of public expenditure (E_{ype}) is greater than unity($E_{ype}>1$), if GNP increases by 10 per cent the public expenditure will increase by 15 per cent. It means public expenditure increases much more than increase in income of the people.

Peacock-Wiseman Views: Peacock and Wiseman conducted a new study based on Wagner's Law. They studied the public expenditure from 1891 to 1955 in U.K. They found out that Wagner's Law is still valid. The findings of Peacock and Wiseman are:

(a) "The rise in public expenditure greatly depends on revenue collection. Over the years, economic development results in substantial revenue to the governments, this enabled to increase public expenditure".

(b) There exists a big gap between the expectations of the people about public expenditure and the tolerance level of taxation. Therefore, governments cannot ignore the demands made by people regarding various services, especially, when the revenue collection is increasing at constant rate of taxation.

(c) They further stated that during the times of war, the government further increases the tax rates, and enlarges the tax structure to generate more funds to meet the increase in defence expenditure. After the war, the new tax rates and tax structures may remain the same, as people get used to them.

Therefore, the increase in revenue results in rise in government expenditure. Wagner's law and Peacock-Wiseman views emphasize on the fact that public expenditure has tendency to increase overtime.

3.5 CAUSES OF INCREASE IN PUBLIC EXPENDITURE

In recent years, there has been an enormous increase in public expenditure because the functions and activities of the state have been increasing manifold. In the past, the state was regarded as a 'Police State' that was concerned with defending the country from foreign aggressions and maintenance of law and order within the State. But in modern time states are regarded as a 'Welfare States' because their main objective is to promote the welfare of its citizens. Hence, it has to provide not only social security but also to look to economic stability with growth. The economic growth calls forever increasing investment expenditure. The increase in activities and functions of modern states has led to increase in public expenditure. They are discussed as under:

(i) Increase in Area and Population: The enormous increase in population of the countries like India has led to cultivation of the barren and uncultivated land. To cater to the needs of the growing population the modern governments are not only brought the 'no-man's' land under their supervision but also have introduced intensive methods of cultivation. Growing population has forced the governments to acquire more lands for the purpose of construction of cities and towns. It made the governments to spend more on these activities. Thus, increase in population in many countries of the world at present has led to increase in public expenditure.

(ii) Increase in the Functions of the Modern Governments: The modern governments are no longer police states; they are 'welfare states'. Increase in developmental and welfare activities of the state have resulted in a tremendous increase in their functions. Wagner's law too advocated that as economic developmental activities take place it also give room for increase in public expenditures.

The modern governments are performing the both (a) old functions such as administrative, maintenance of internal law and order and the functions related to the protection against foreign aggression more intensively and (b) new functions such as better utilization of natural resources, economic growth and reduction of economic inequalities. Besides, governments particularly in the underdeveloped countries are adopting popular schemes in the name of welfare programmes to please the people. Such state activities have become causal factors for an increase in the public expenditure. These issues are already studied in Wagner's law.

(iii) Inflationary Situation and Rising Cost of Public Services: In the recent years the cost of living has been increasing at a faster rate due to inflation. The government has to give subsidies and to arrange fair price shops for poor and common people so it is additional burden on the government exchequer. Likewise, the government has to undertake both developmental and welfare schemes to satisfy the plan objectives so naturally the governments have to buy goods and services at the prevailing prices in the market. This requires larger funds at the disposal of the government. In addition to this the salary and pensions benefits given to the government employees have enormously increased in the recent years.

(iv) Increase in Cost of Development Process: Most of the countries have development plans. These countries are spending huge amount of money for the development of agriculture, industry and service sector. As a result of this there a continuous improvement in all these sectors on the one hand and on the other there is increase in the production and national income in these countries. Further, there is steady increase in the per capita income and improvement in the standard of living of the people. Because of these developmental activities there is a corresponding improvement in public revenues and public expenditures.

(v) Defence and War Activities: The modern governments are spending a lot of money on accumulation of war equipment and building armed forces. The countries have to spend not only for fighting wars but also for the prevention of the wars. For instance, India at present is allocating more than 30 per cent of its budget for defense because of maintenance of balanced power in the region and fear of war. There is continuous increase in this expenditure year after year. India is also fighting against proxy wars waged by the terrorists. This is causing huge burden on the government exchequer. Thus, war and the money spent on the prevention of the wars is becoming a major source of expenditure of the modern governments.

(vi) Provisions of Public Utility Services: The modern governments are termed as welfare governments. They are making provision for various public utility services such as supply of water, electricity, transport services, etc. As these are essential services many governments have taken the responsibility of providing these services to their citizens. Recently though there is privatization of some of these services, to protect interest of their citizens many governments are making provisions in the budget for these services. As there is a continuous increase in the population and urbanization the expenditure on all these services is also increasing. Naturally, the public expenditure is also increasing.

(vii) Expansion in Social Services: In modern times, there has been a remarkable expansion in social services like education, public health measures and medical aid. Expansion in educational facilities has led to the establishment of schools, colleges and technical institutions in a very large number. The number of hospitals and medical colleges has been increasing continuously to meet the growing requirements of the public. Public health and sanitary measures are taken on a vast scale. The governments have also undertaken slum areas improvement programmes. The manpower requirements in providing these services are also increasing. As a result of this the governments are expected to spend more money on these services. This is also considered as productive investment, since it leads to increase in income and employment. The development of human resources is another major task of the modern governments. Making provision for providing these services naturally builds human capital particularly in the developing countries. Thus, allocation of more resources for these activities is another important reason for the increase in the public expenditure.

(viii) Economic Development: All developed or under-developed countries have given top priority to economic development activities to raise the standard of living of the people. The programmes of economic development need allocation of large amount of state resources. The governments are spending a large amount of money on creation of economic and social overheads. Several measures have been taken for the development of agriculture, industry and infrastructure. The state is expected to create all necessary infrastructures according to the requirements of the industry such as construction of roads, airports, railways, generation of electricity, making provisions for water supply, etc. The net result of such development activities is the huge increase in the government expenditure.

(ix) Technological Changes: The competitive nature of the present market is call for technological innovations. The modern governments have encouraged research and development (R&D) activities to encourage the development of science and technology that results in a large increase in government expenditure.

(x) Extravagance: Duplication and multiplication of governmental works in the recent years is common. The number of government departments and ministries has been increasing, particularly in democratic countries like India. The salaries, dearness allowance, travelling allowance, pension, etc. expenditures of public representatives like MP, MLA, MLC, etc. have been increasing continuously. Besides, the wrong allocation of resources, wastage of valuable resources of the state on populous schemes is also responsible for increase in government expenditure.

(xi) Political Factors: To enlist the support of the people the political parties in a democratic set up are providing concessions and benefits to the people like fare concessions, self-employment schemes, etc. Such benefits and concessions are given at the expense of the public fund only. The demand for such benefits multiplies over a period of time. Thus, the regional and sectional demands for creation of amenities will result in intensive as well as extensive increase in state functions. As a result of this the old functions are being performed more thoroughly and many new functions are being undertaken, causing for an increase in the state expenditure.

(xii) Welfare Activities and Growth of Transfer Expenditure: The modern States are making liberal provision for social security schemes such as free medical aid, free education, old-age pensions, provident fund schemes, etc. These are known as transfer expenditure. There is a phenomenal rise in the transfer expenses of the state in the recent years. Such schemes have substantially pushed up the State budgets.

(xiii) Creation of Employment Opportunities: Creation of more and more employment opportunities is a major objective of the modern governments. To generate more and more employment opportunities, the states are launching ambitious schemes of public works. Naturally, the public expenditure of the state is increasing.

3.6 EFFECTS OF PUBLIC EXPENDITURE

The governments spend significant amount of resources for defense, administrative, developmental and other welfare activities. There is need to know the impact of public expenditure on the level of employment, production and income as well as on the distribution of income in the country. The following are the main effects of public expenditure:

(i) Effects on Production: According to Dalton, Public expenditure has direct and indirect effects on production in the economy. Dalton in his book *Public Finance* states that a correct view of the effects of public expenditure on production can only be evaluated by examining its effect upon the following factors:

(a) Effects upon ability to work, save and invest,

(b) Effects on willingness to work, save and invest,

(c) Effects on diversion of economic resources as between different uses and localities.

The nature of effects of public expenditure on all these factors is discussed as under:

(a) Ability to Work, Save and Invest: Public expenditure helps to increase the ability of the people to work, save and invest. The expenditure made by the government on means of communication and transport, education, public health, scientific research and industrial research, controlling of human, animal and plant disease and expenditure on social insurance like health insurance, unemployment insurance and old-age pensions, etc., will increase the efficiency of the people to work. For instance, the productivity of labour has been increasing in India because of the infrastructural development, education, health, training, etc. programmes by the governments.

Further the government expenditure on social security schemes like unemployment allowances, old-age pensions, widow allowances, free education, etc. could increase the purchasing power of the people, particularly low income groups. It entails into the promotion of efficiency of these people. The net effect of such expenditure will be on the increase in the efficiency of the people and their ability to work and save. In other words, the public expenditures on these programmes initially increase the work efficiency of the people and thereby income, savings and investment abilities could be improved during the course of time.

Money spent by the government on increasing the salary and wages and providing essential commodities at cheaper rates would increase the purchasing power of the people thereby it raises the ability to work, save and invest.

The expenditure made by the government on maintenance law and order would help to increase in the level of investment. Increase in the level investments leads to increase in production and income of the people. As a result of this their ability to work, save and invest will also increase. For instance, the maintenance of law and order reduces the number of strikes and lockouts thereby it reduces man-days losses.

On the other, if a large amount of money is spent on production of intoxicants and harmful drugs the health and efficiency of the people will be affected adversely. This will have an adverse effect on the ability to work, save and invest. At the same time, the invaluable resources of the economy should be used mainly for diverting them towards creation of productive assets. Increased expenditure on transport and communication, educational institutions, hospitals irrigation projects, etc., will increase the ability of the society to work, save and invest. Thus, public expenditure should be incurred on the projects which bring maximum benefit to the entire community in terms of ability to work, save and invest.

***(b) Willingness to Work, Save and Invest*:** Peoples' willingness to work, save and invest generally depends on the character of public expenditure and its policy. If the people find that their future is insecure, they will not work, save and invest. If they find the future is secure, they will work, save and invest. For example, old-age pension, provident fund benefit, insurance against risks and sickness and government employment, etc., provide security and safety to the people and hence, it increases their willingness to work, save and invest.

There is, also, scope for discouraging willing to work, save and invest by social security schemes, for instance, the social security schemes like widow pension, old-age pension, fair price shops, etc. in India have reduced the willingness of work of the family members. Therefore, there is need to regulate public expenditure in such a way that it should not adversely affect the desire of the people to work, save and invest.

***(c) Diversion of Economic Resources*:** Public expenditure diverts resources from private sector to public sector. But there are differences of opinions on such diversion of resources. The expenditures of the government on defence, police, and civil administration are generally considered as a waste. However, in reality these are not unproductive expenditures because these expenditures are essential to maintain internal and external security of the nation. Expenditure on all these items helps to promote of economic activities smoothly. Internal and external security and a stable and good administration could assure effective and optimum use of the resources in the country.

Diversion of resources from the private use to the public use for the construction of infrastructure facilities like roads, railways, irrigation projects helps in promoting economic growth. This type of public expenditure also provides incentives to private investment by enlarging the size of the market.

Through the system of bounties and subsidies a government may succeed in diverting resources to hitherto neglected channels and thus create new industries. This helps in increasing production in the existing industries also.

In addition to this, by spending money on development of backward areas, the government may add to the total production of the country. A wisely conducted policy of public borrowing stimulates saving and the habit of investment in the community, which are certainly beneficial to producers. If the borrowed money is invested by the government in the development of infrastructure facilities, aforestation, education, training, research, public health schemes, etc., it will increase efficiency and production of the country.

Diversion of resources through public expenditure between different localities helps in increasing productive power and may thus help in reducing regional and territorial inequalities. Development of backward areas may be undertaken by making provisions for loans, subsidies and other facilities to the industries of those areas.

It may be, thus, concluded that the wise public expenditure has a significant influence on production. In other words, it assists production indirectly by adding the power to work and save as well as by a profitable diversion of resources. Besides, it also encourages production through state enterprises.

Till recent time, the discussion of the effects of public expenditure was mostly confined to the indirect effects on production as discussed above. However, with the Keynesian revolution, it has come to be realized that public expenditure can exercise directly an important influence on the level of economic activity, accelerate economic growth and help to maintain economic stability. According to Keynes, public expenditure has a direct influence on the level of effective demand. For instance, the increase in public expenditure during a depression helped to create more demand and thereby increased the level of output and employment of depression hit economies during 1930s.

(ii) Effects on Distribution: Public expenditure is also used as a powerful weapon, in the hands of the government, to achieve an equitable distribution of wealth among the people of the country. To bring about just and equitable distribution of wealth and income among the people of the country the government would use not only its taxation policy but public expenditure policy also. The expenditure policy of the government should be framed in such a way that it benefits the poor the most. The rich are in a position to make provisions for their better living so they protect themselves. But the poor are helpless so there is need to provide them the facilities like health, education and employment opportunities. Such policy measures could reduce the gap between the rich and the poor. These policy measures are inevitable in both developed countries like USA and developing or underdeveloped countries like India.

There are certain public expenditures to benefit the poor, e.g., poor relief, old-age pensions and unemployment and sickness benefits. Of course, some US economists like Milton Friedman strongly oppose such public expenditures but the benefits derived from such social services by the poor may be regarded as a net addition to their incomes. Further the revenue collected by taxing the rich will also help in reducing the inequalities of wealth distribution provided this money is spent for the benefit of the poor.

If public expenditure is really to make the distribution of wealth more even and fair, it must be progressive. It means more money should be spent by the government to generating employment opportunities for the poor. This naturally helps to reduce the gap between the rich and the poor.

"Public expenditure must be so arranged as to confer a maximum benefit on the community as a whole" must be the guiding principle. Granting of old-age pensions, supply of social goods at the subsidized rates will have positive effect on distribution that would reduce the inequalities of income and wealth in the country.

Moreover, if most of the public expenditure is to be incurred for the welfare of the common people in general and the poor people in particular, it would result into bring about a more equitable distribution of incomes and wealth in the community.

(iii) Effects on Economic Development and Growth: Already a discussion is done above on the effects of public expenditure on production and distribution. It is also noticed that the sphere of state activity has very much widened in modern times. As a result public expenditure on several new items is increased manifold. Generally, public expenditure affects the level of income and employment in the country. Keynes had shown that the government could remove widespread unemployment during period of great depression through liberal public expenditure on public work. Thence the public expenditure is being used as fiscal policy measure to raise the level of income and employment in the country.

Keynes further argues that when government increases its investment expenditure on public works, it increases the level of income and employment much more than its said investment expenditure, it depends upon the value of 'Income Multiplier', in the country.

This happens because when government increases its investment expenditure, the employment opportunities in all the sectors in which the government has spent money will increase. Meanwhile the increase in income of the people in these sectors generates demand for consumer goods. When these people spend their additional income on the purchase of consumers' goods, the demand for consumer goods will increase that leads to increase in production of consumer goods initially thereby the demand for capital goods will be increased. As its consequence more employment opportunities will be generated. This process of increased demand and increased production expenditure continues to create employment opportunities and income of the people. Thus, effect of public expenditure on generating new employment opportunities is not only confined to the sectors where the government has spent its money its effect is felt on private sectors also.

The developing economies have adopted Keynes' deficit financing policy successfully to increase income and employment opportunities in their countries. The directed public expenditure policy in developing economies in the areas like building social and economic infrastructure such as sound educational base, adequate public health measures and medical aid, etc. would improve human capital in the form of physically strong and healthy skilled labour that would I go a long way in raising the income and employment in the country. The government would also launch public enterprises and build-up heavy and core industries of strategic importance by public outlays. It could also promote agricultural development by making adequate provision for the supply of critical inputs in the form of irrigation facilities, fertilizer improved seeds and pesticides. In such ways, public expenditure can be used as an instrument of raising the level of income and employment in the country. Through public expenditure government would raise the rate of capital formation as well as promote economic development in the country. Thus, it would provide employment and build up productive capacity of the economy.

The Indian government has been spending billions of rupees on schemes of capital formation such as irrigation projects, power generation, construction of roads, railways, building huge steel plants, machine-making industry, heavy engineering and heavy electrical industry, fertilizer industry, etc. under the five-year plans. This has substantially added to the volume of employment and productive capacity in the country. These are important steps towards removing unemployment and poverty in the countries like India, USA and others.

Thus, the government through its public expenditure policy could create additional employment opportunities and added to people's incomes.

Thus, the governments of both developed and under-developed countries would achieve economic development and growth by increasing their expenditure on and capital formation. Public expenditure in both developed and underdeveloped or developing countries, therefore, plays a very vital role in raising the level of income and employment in the country.

(iv) Effects on Economic Stability: Economic stability is most desired economic situation by all countries. It refers to continuation of prevailing normal economic conditions in the country. In other word, there should not be any ups and downs or oscillations in economic activities such as depression, recession, inflation, deflation, etc. There are much cyclical fluctuations of economic activities in free market or capitalist economy like USA. Keynes has suggested fiscal policy measures to control such business cycles so as to maintain economic stability or price stability. As a part of fiscal policy, public expenditure plays both direct and indirect role in achievement of economic stability by controlling economic ups and downs in the economy. It is discussed as under:

(a) Public Expenditure Policy during Depression: Depression is that economic situation when the economic activities like demand, price, employment, output, investment, etc. are at lowest or bottom level in the economy. There is mass discontentment in the country. To lift the economy from this lowest level the government must create employment opportunities through its autonomous investment in public works activities like road construction, public utility activities, public sector industries, and social security schemes, etc. so as to increase purchasing power of the public for raising of effective demand. Thus, the increase in public expenditure helps the country to recover from depression.

(b) Public Expenditure Policy during Inflation: Inflation is that economic situation when the economic activities like demand, price, unemployment, investment, etc. are at highest or peak level in the economy. It also creates mass discontentment in the country. This situation warrants the decline in excess supply of money and credit and increase in production. To recover from inflation the government must reduce its expenditure on non-productive activities like wages and dearness and other allowances of civil servants, extravagancy on ministers, defence expenditures, etc. but the expenditures on production activities must be raised and continued to enable the economy to raise supply of goods and services.

To recover the economy from depression and inflation the government should follow built-in stabilizer public expenditure policy so as to maintain economic stability.

3.7 MODEL QUESTIONS

(a) Questions each needs answer in 2-3 sentences (2 Marks each)

1. What is public expenditure?
2. What do you mean by the scope of public expenditure?
3. What would be the role of government according to classical?
4. Name any two functions of government advocated by classical.
5. Name any two modern government activities advocated by R.A. Musgrave.
6. Who advocated principle of 'functional finance approach'?
7. Name the principles that have increased the active role of government in a "welfare state".
8. Give difference between private and public expenditures.
9. Mention any two similarities between private and public expenditures.
10. Mention any two dissimilarities between private and public expenditures.
11. Name the types of public expenditures mentioned by Dalton.
12. What do you mean by 'Plan Expenditure'?
13. What do you mean by 'Non-Plan Expenditure'?
14. Name any two canons of public expenditure.
15. Give the statement of Wagner's Law.
16. Give the statement of Peacock and Wiseman.
17. State any two causes of increasing public expenditure.
18. How does inflation increase the public expenditure?
19. What is 'effect of public expenditure'?
20. Mention any two effects of public expenditure on production.
21. Mention any two effects of public expenditure on distribution.

22. How does public expenditure support economic growth?
23. How does public expenditure support economic stability?

(b) Questions each needs short-note type answer (5 Marks each)

1. Give a brief account of Classical and Keynesian views on public expenditure.
2. Write a note on similarities and dissimilarities between private and public expenditure.
3. Discuss in brief Dalton and Adam Smith's classifications of public expenditure.
4. Write a short-note on canons of public expenditure.
5. Write a note on Wagner's Law.
6. Explain in brief the causes of increase in public expenditure.
7. Write a note on the effects of public expenditure on production.
8. Discuss in brief the effects of public expenditure on distribution.
9. Write a note on effects of public expenditure on economic, development, growth and stability.

(c) Questions each needs essay type/long answer (10/15 Marks each)

1. Define public expenditure, explain its various types.
2. Define public expenditure, explain its various canons.
3. Explain the meaning of private and public expenditure, give their similarities and dissimilarities.
4. Explain Wagner's Law.
5. What is public expenditure? Explain the various causes for its increase.
6. What is public expenditure? Explain its various effects on economy.

4

Public Debts

4.1 PUBLIC DEBT

Like private individual or firm, government also borrows loans and advances from various sources like individuals, banks and financial institutions, etc. of domestic and foreign countries. But public borrowing or debt is different from private debt. Government raises loans of various types such as funded and unfunded, internal and external, redeemable and irredeemable, productive and unproductive, etc. Government borrows loans when it feels that its revenue is less than its expenditure. Moreover, there are various reasons for raising of public debts like to overcome deficit in budget, to recover from depression, to achieve economic development, to meet war expenses, etc. purposes. Many economists have considered public borrowing is the suitable method of financing budget deficit as it controls inflation and achieves economic development. For example, India practiced this method after second five-year plan to achieve economic growth with stability.

Public debt has both positive and negative effects on the economy. Thus, the country, developed or developing needs a sound public debt to take the economy on right track of economic development. The growing public debt should not put the country in 'debt trap' so suitable methods are being used to repay the public debts.

4.1.1 Meaning and Definitions

Generally, public debt refers to loans borrowed by a government within the country or outside the country. In other words, public debt includes money that is owed to individuals, mutual funds, hedge funds, pension funds, foreign governments, etc. Like individuals, every government has to borrow when its expenditure exceeds its revenue. But it is not a source of revenue like taxes. However, in wider sense, the term public revenue covers all types of income, hence; public revenue includes the money borrowed by a government. Like other forms of revenue, the amount borrowed by the government during any given year constitutes income of that year. We may, therefore, call public debt the 'revenue' of the government. But the basic difference between the public debt and other sources of revenue is that the public debt has to be repaid by the government to the lenders whereas the other types of income like tax are need not be re-paid by the government to the payers. The government collects taxes from the public without any commitment or promise. But public loans or debts are collected by the treasury or government from banks, institutions and individuals on the conditions given in writing that these would be repaid and interest would be paid thereon regularly, either yearly or half-yearly as per the terms of the loan.

Moreover, the concept of public debt has been defined by many economists and some of them are discussed as under:

(i) Prof. J.K. Mehta has rightly defined public debt as, "Public revenue, therefore, consists of the money that the government is not obliged to return to the very individual from whom it is obtained. Public debt on the other hand, carries with it the obligation on the part of the government to pay money back to the individuals from whom it has been obtained".

(ii) According to Prof. Findlay Shirras "National debt is a debt which a state owes to its subject or to the nationals of the other countries".

(iii) Prof. P.E. Taylor defines, "The debt is the form of promises by the Treasury to pay to the holders of these promises a principal sum and in most instances interest on that principal. Borrowings is restored to in order to provide funds for financing a current deficit".

(iv) According to Carl. S. Shoup, Public debt as "the receipt from the sale of financial instrument by the government to individuals or firms in the private sector, to induce the private sector to release manpower and real resources and to finance the purchase of these resources or to make welfare payments or subsidies".

The definitions implies that public debt includes money that is owed to individuals, mutual funds, hedge funds, pension funds, foreign governments, etc.

In other words, public debt or national debt or public borrowing means the government borrowing either by selling its bonds, treasury bills, etc. or directly from provident funds, social security funds, mutual funds, finance corporations, banks, etc. for a specific period with promise under some terms and conditions like payment of interest, etc.

4.1.2 Sources of Public Debt

The term 'public' refers to the government that includes local, state and central or federal governments. The government borrows loans and advances from various sources. They can be broadly classified into two types, viz., (i) internal sources and (ii) external sources. They are discussed as under:

(i) Internal Sources: Internal sources refers to sources within the country. Government borrows loans and advances from the domestic people, commercial banks, financial institutions, money market and central bank within the country. For example, Government of India's borrowing from Indians, Indian Commercial Banks, Reserve Bank of India, Provident Fund Organization, Life Insurance Corporation of India, etc. It borrows in two types of modes, viz., (a) by selling its bonds, treasury bills, debt-receipts, etc. and (b) by borrowing directly.

(ii) External Sources: External sources refers to foreign people, commercial banks, central banks, international financial institutions, etc. or sources outside the country. The government borrows loans from the foreign people, foreign banks, international and foreign financial institutions, etc. For example, Government of India's borrowing from foreigners such as Americans, British people, foreign commercial banks, foreign central banks, foreign financial institutions and international financial institutions such as World Bank, International Monetary Fund, etc.

4.1.3 Purposes or Objectives and Causes of Public Debt

During pre-modern days the government functions were minimal and they were expected to follow an ideal system of balanced budget. The classical economists like Adam Smith strongly advocated the balanced budget and economy in public expenditure. But modern governments have increased their activities both intensively and extensively as they moved from 'police state' to 'welfare state'. This has necessitated the need to find additional sources of finance. Hence, modern governments have come to rely upon public borrowings to meet their financial requirements. The growing importance of public debt, the objectives or purposes and causes of public debt and its increase are discussed as follows:

(i) Government borrows to finance budget-deficits: The deficit incurs in budget when public expenditure exceeds public revenue. It happens naturally during occurrence of unexpected events such as floods, famines, etc. During such situation government may have to raise income by levying taxes so it takes the help of public debts. Beside, during post-1930s great depression period most of the countries including both developed and underdeveloped countries followed Keynes' 'Principle of Deficit Financing' to achieve economic development as well as recovering from economic depression. So governments deliberately creates deficit in budget by increasing expenditures on developmental and economic recovery activities and so created deficit could be met through public debts. During such circumstances the government borrows from internal and external sources.

(ii) It is used as a policy-measure to fight depression: Depression is an economic condition of falling prices, increasing unemployment, lack of investment, declining output and no hope for the future-profits. This situation may be removed through raising of demand for goods and services in the economy, in the words of Keynes raising of effective demand. This can be done by increasing the public expenditure on public works like construction of infrastructure and social security schemes such as unemployment allowance, old-age pension, etc. in the country. To meet such public expenditure raising of public revenue is necessary. Taxation is not the right choice of raising revenue during depression so the best method of raising revenue is public debt. Tax-imposition during depression could further reduce the effective demand through its adverse effects on incentive to work and invest. Hence, government should resort to borrowings especially from banks to meet public expenditures to increase employment and income during depression. Thus, it helps to stop further fall in prices and other economic activities and recover the economy from depression and take the economy to prosperity.

(iii) It is used as a policy-measure to curb inflation: Inflation is an economic condition of continuous rising prices in the country. It is worse than depression. There is mass discontentment, increasing unemployment, decline in investment and thereby decline in output during inflation. To control inflation there is need for reduction of purchasing power of the community, hence, the government by raising debt from the public can withdraw a large volume of purchasing power from them. But some modern economists advocates taxation as the better mode of curbing inflationary trend as compared to public debt. It is because money received through public borrowing increases the liabilities of the government for its repayment if the amount taken has not been properly utilized in productive channel. However, the surplus revenue amount raised by public debt may easily be left idle in the treasury to curb inflationary pressures.

(iv) It is best method of financing economic development: Public debt is a boon to underdevelop or developing countries for financing their developmental programmes. They always suffer from the shortage of funds. The government also cannot resort to heavy taxation, because of low taxable capacity. Thus, these countries use public debt as method of financing for poverty-eradication and developmental programmes such as infrastructural development, agricultural development, etc. Hence, the governments of underdeveloped countries resort to public borrowing from the people or from governments and individuals of foreign countries or both to finance huge developmental expenditure of their countries so as to make necessary pre-conditions for economic take-off.

(v) It is necessary to meet unprecedented expenses: It becomes inevitable to government to raises loans to meet the expenditures on relief activities during the unprecedented events like famine, floods, earthquakes and epidemics, etc. So public debts are necessary under such typical conditions.

(vi) It is required to finance war: To defend the country from external aggression is the primary function of every state or country, whether democratic, socialist or communist. The government should have adequate fund for its defence purpose. It is essential to purchase weapons from foreign countries. Hence, the government borrow for defence purposes.

Since modern age is an atomic age, there is increasing international tension so the country needs large funds to maintain its defence services and up to date equipment to protect itself from foreign aggression. Moreover, the modern wars are difficult to be financed by taxation alone as heavy taxation adversely affect production. Hence, government borrows from within the country as well as outside the country to finance war.

(vii) It is essential for development of infrastructure: Creation of infrastructure refers to the development of essential services or basic facilities like railway, roads, airways, waterways, communication, power, finance, public health, education, etc. Private investment will never come forward to carry out such schemes because they need huge long-term investment and yield less returns. In the interest of the nation, it is the duty of the government to create such social and economic overhead capital in the economy. It borrows loans for these purposes. Public debt is justified in such cases.

(viii) It is essential to finance public enterprises: Public sector is the sector established by government for specific purposes under laws, for example, postal department, central bank, defence industries, power plants, railway-services, core and basic industries, etc. Public sector enterprises have an important role to play in economic development of underdeveloped or developing countries. Since the profit of margin is low and requires long-term huge capital the private sector deliberately avoid to establish these industries though they have national interest. So these are inevitable to public sector, therefore, government borrows to finance the investment in these industries or sectors. These are generally productive enterprises in key areas of production like steel, cement, etc. Modern governments have resorted to public debt to run these public sector enterprises.

(ix) It is used for creation of productive assets: There are several items of public expenditure which result in the creation of permanent income yielding assets. Irrigation dams, railways are examples of this type. In such cases these assets can be created out of borrowed funds. The income from such assets or fees charged on beneficiaries can be used to repay the loan. The best example of this in recent years in India is the implementation of the Konkan railway line on the west coast by public borrowing in the three states which will benefit from this project. If public debts are raised for creation of income-yielding assets, they have positive effects on the economy.

(x) It is necessary for better allocation of resources: The resources like money or finance and physical resources are being distributed among various sectors or industries but it depends upon the prevailing practice in the country. If the country has free-market economy then resources are being distributed on the basis of price, for example, more investment fund flow to high return yielding industries like manufacturing of high priced cars, luxurious or private goods. But low priced public goods industries suffer lack of capital and have adverse effect of entire economy. This amounts to misallocation of resources. To avoid the misallocation of resources, the government may act to put the existing level of resources at an optimum level. Public debt helps to reallocate resources from surplus area to deficit areas. Public debt could be used for investment in public goods and services industries as well as industries in backward areas.

Moreover, the misallocation of resources is generally created by monopolistic competition. The government has to take over these monopolistic firms or encourage the entry of other firms so that the misallocation of resources may be checked. For this the government has to provide long-term finance and the government itself has to borrow to meet the needs of such firms.

4.1.4 Private Debt and Public Debt

There are similarities and dissimilarities between private debt and public debt. C.F. Bastable wrote about the analogy between private debt and public debt as "in all essential points the analogy between public and private debt does hold good and should never be lost sight of it". It means both debts are regulated by same lending principle, i.e. to repay debt as per terms and conditions. But J.B. Say said that "There is this grand distinction between an individual borrower and borrowing government that in general, the later borrows capital for the purpose of barren consumption and expenditure". However, the similarities and dissimilarities between private debt and public debt are discussed as under:

(a) **Similarities:** Classical economists advocated that there is analogy or comparison between private and public debts. The similarities between the both are as follows:

(i) Diversion of fund from one use to another use: Both private and public debts divert the resources from one use to another use. When a private borrower borrows fund for investment purpose from another individual who has fund for consumption purpose it is diversion of fund from one use to another use. Similarly, the diversion of fund from one to another use takes place when government borrows funds for investment from individuals who have fund for some other purposes.

(ii) To meet immediate or temporary needs: Whether government or private individual both borrow fund to meet their immediate or temporary needs. For example, at the time of emergency like natural calamities both private and government borrow loans to meet the relief expenditures.

(iii) Capacity to repay: The borrowing capacity of both private and government depends upon their loan-repay capacity. It is normal constraint to borrowing capacity.

(iv) Disposal income of lender diminishes: The borrowing act generally reduces the disposal income of the lender, it is true in case of both kinds of debts.

(v) Fear of bankruptcy: The debt-trap takes place when the burden of debt service exceeds the loan-repay capacity of the borrower, whether private or government. It leads to the state of bankruptcy.

(vi) Same lending principle: The lending principle of private and public debts is same. The borrower has to pay interest on loan and repay the principal amount after specific period or as per terms and conditions agreed by both borrower and lender.

The above comparisons or similarities support the classical economists' argument that there is analogy between private and public debts. Hence, they considered that the consequences of debt applicable to private borrowing are also applicable to government borrowing.

(b) Dissimilarities: Modern economists disagree with classical economists' arguments. According to modern economist there are dissimilarities between private and public debts so there is no analogy between the both. Prof. A.H. Hansen put it in his words as "An internal loan resembles ordinary (private) borrowing in purely formal way and it is obvious that every analogy to private borrowing must be completely false". It means there is no analogy or comparison between private and public debts, hence the dissimilarities between them are as follows:

(i) State of spending power of the borrower: The impact of borrowing on spending power of borrower is differ from government to private individual or company. The private debt definitely increase the purchasing power of borrower but it is not true in case of government borrowing. Because of the other fiscal devices to raise resources like taxation, etc. with the government and the resources of the country are more or less fixed at the particular point of time, the public debt could not increase the purchasing power of the government.

(ii) Debt services: Repayment of principal amount of the loan and payment of interest on the loan are called 'Debt Services'. The debt services cannot reduce the spending power or

expenditures of the government but it reduces the spending power or expenditure of private individuals or firms. If a private individual pays debt services out of his disposable income, it will reduce his spending power on consumption expenditure. It is not so in case of government because it has many other sources of payment of debt services, for instance, taxation, issue of new currency, etc.

***(iii) State of insolvency*:** The excess borrowing or heavy borrowing excess over repay capacity generally leads to bankruptcy or insolvency. It is applicable to private borrower because of limited income and assets but it is not applicable to government because government has many ways to repay its debts for instance levying additional taxes on people for repayment of its debts. Similarly, raising of fresh loans, issuing of new currency, raising price of products of public sector industries, imposing capital levy, diverting of fund from subsidies, etc. are the other methods of repayment of public debts being used by government. So there is no question insolvency in case of government.

***(iv) Matter of public policy*:** Public debt is a matter of public policy of government. Government uses public debt as a measure to control economic situations like inflation, deflation, etc. and as a method of financing development programmes in the interest of the nation; it borrows even when fund is not necessary. But in case of private debt, private individual or firms borrow fund when they need it and it is for the benefit of their own. Thus, private debt is not a matter of public policy.

***(v) Method of repayment*:** Private individuals or firms repay loans by using their income and wealth but government has various sources or methods to repay its loans. For example, government use tax revenue to repay its debts but private individuals have no such source.

***(vi) Purpose of use*:** Private persons borrow funds for personal consumption and investment purposes but government borrows funds for welfare of the community and development with stability of the economy.

***(vii) Rate of interest policy*:** Government always thinks of borrowing funds at low rate of interest. It influences of rate of interest through its monetary and fiscal policies. But private persons have no such policy-measures to influence on interest rate so they borrow at high rate of interest.

Hence, the above discussed dissimilarities made it clear that there is no analogy between private and public debts. To sum-up, the modern economists' arguments are based on more realities than classical views.

4.2 EFFECTS OF PUBLIC DEBT

Effects of public debt refers to the changes or impacts happen in the economy after raising, spending and repayment of public debt. These changes may be beneficial or non-beneficial or costly to the people of the country at both micro and macro levels. If the effects are beneficial to the society as well as individual, it is 'positive effects' of public debt, for instance, public debt used for construction of dams improve economic position of both farmer and the nation. Unlike it, if the effects are non-beneficial or yields no returns, it is 'negative effects' of public debt, for instance, public debt used for extravagance of ministers or government officials yields no return.

However, the effects of public debt depend upon several factors. As Dalton points out several changes take place in the floatation of a government loan. When public debt is raised, money is transferred from the purchasers of government securities to the government and finally to those on whom the government spends money. When interest is paid through taxation there is a transfer of purchasing power from taxpayers to the holders of the government bonds. When the public debt is repaid, there is further transfer of purchasing power. All such transfers over a period of time affect the different segment of the economy in different ways. In brief, the effects of public debt mainly depends upon several factors.

(a) Determinants of Effects of Public Debt: The factors determining the effects of public debts can be discussed as follows:

***(i) Source of loan fund*:** Government mainly borrows from two sources namely (a) internal sources such as households or individuals, commercial banks, central bank and financial institutions of domestic country and (b) external sources such as foreigner investors, foreign banks, foreign governments, foreign central banks and international financial institutions like, World Bank, International Monetary Fund, Asian Development Bank, etc. In case of government borrowing from domestic sources, it is simply transfer of funds from private use to government use thus it makes no difference in quantum of loanable funds so there is no overall effects of public debts but if it is activation past idle savings of the private then public debts have effects on the economy.

In case if the government borrows funds from foreign sources, it increases the quantum of fund, thus it has effects on the domestic economy.

***(ii) Purpose of borrowing*:** The effects of public debts depend upon the purpose for which they are borrowed. If public debt is borrowed for purposes like wasteful expenditures on extravagances of ministers have no effect of creation of social and economic assets in the country. Such public debts have adverse effects on the economy such as inflation, decline in investment activities, etc. If public debt is borrowed for investment activities, creation of employment opportunities, creation of social and economic assets, it will have good effects on the economy like economic prosperity.

***(iii) Terms and conditions of debt*:** The terms and conditions refer to rate of interest, duration of repayment of loans. The rate of interest policy of government would effect on the investment activities of private firms or companies. If government pays high rate of interest on its debts, the fund will transfer from private sector to government sector so it reduces investments, production, income, etc. in private sector and it also lowers their tax paying capacity. Similarly, if government raises the tax rates to collect revenue for payment of interest on such loans and repayment of short-term loans, it has inflationary effect on the economy. The long-term public debts have positive effects on the economy.

If the terms and conditions are soft like low rate of interest, long-term, etc. public debts will have good effects on the economy.

***(iv) Size of public debt*:** The effects of public debts also depend upon the size of loans floated in the money market in form of savings certificates, treasury bills, bonds, etc. Larger the amount of public borrowing, higher will be its adverse effects on the economy, for instance, India has been facing difficult inflationary situation because of its heavy borrowing, and it pays every year more than 25 per cent of its government revenue for debt services.

***(v) General economic conditions*:** The general economic conditions prevalent in the economy too decides about the effects of public borrowing in the country. Heavy public borrowing during inflation reduces the purchasing power of the community thereby reduces the excess effective demand and increase in price level, thus, takes the economy to prosperity. Public borrowing during end of depression or the beginning of recession, increases purchasing power of the community through government investment activities and thus it takes the economy to recovery. Prof. A.G. Buchler points it as "Heavy government borrowing during boom periods may accentuate the rise of prosperity by its inflationary effects, while borrowing at the end of a depression or at the beginning of recovery may help to promote recovery".

(b) Ways of Effects of Public Debt: Generally public debt affects the economy in two ways namely (i) revenue effects and (ii) expenditure effects.

***(i) Revenue effect*:** When government borrows from public, either by floating treasury bills, bonds, savings-certificates, etc. or by direct borrow, it effects on the revenue side of the lenders (public) hence they change their budget that effects on their consumption-expenditure, savings and investment activities. Thus, this way of public debt effect is called 'Revenue Effect'. Usually people do not contribute to public debt by reducing their consumption as in case of taxation. Public borrowing is also met out of past savings. However, it may also change their consumption, saving and investment pattern. In brief, the adjustments they have to make in their budgets is the revenue effect.

***(ii) Expenditure effect*:** Government spends 'public-debt-fund' on public utilities, investment in production activities, administration, defence, etc. activities that yield various benefits the people thus such effect is called 'Expenditure Effect'.

Thus, by these two ways public debt effects on economy, in micro as well as macro levels. These several effects of public debt on economy are discussed as under:

4.2.1 Effects on Consumption

The effects of public debt on consumption depends upon how it financed by individuals. If they lend to the government out of their idle savings, consumption is not affected. If they buy out of past savings, it has only limited impact on present expenditure. But if they lend by cutting present savings, it may make them feel less secure and so they may reduce consumption. But if the people feel that they have invested in government securities which are considered safe investment, they may actually increase their consumption. However, the public debt reduces present consumption but it raises future consumption through supplementing the income of the lenders.

4.2.2 Effects on Investment and Production

If people buy government bonds and securities by withdrawing money from their industrial concerns or by selling debentures and shares of industrial concerns or financial institutions and even commercial banks subscribe to government loans out of funds meant for investment or for accumulation of stocks, then the investment is adversely affected, leading to adverse effects on production. If government utilizes this money in connected public enterprises, the total investment available for production may not be adversely affected on investment and production. On the contrary, if government utilizes it on non-productive works, the total investment may be adversely affected that resulting in adverse effects on production also. Thus, if the loans raised by the government are utilized for productive purposes directly, they increase the income of the community, leading to an increase in consumption, thereby increases the production.

4.2.3 Effects on Distribution

Public debt is bound to have effects on distribution of income because it involves transfer of purchasing power from one section to another. Generally, rich section of the society purchases government securities, but the burden of tax falls upon the common people, i.e. poor people. Public borrowing increases the inequalities of income and public debt adversely affects the distribution of income. If the bond purchasers and the taxpayers are the same persons, the redistribution of income will not occur, thus, increasing the gap of inequalities of income. Its effect can also be assessed by the way in which the public debt is used. If the public debt is used for public welfare programmes especially the poor, inequalities of income decrease. But on the contrary if the public borrowings and spending creates inflation, its favourable effects on distribution of income can be neutralized due to rise in prices.

4.2.4 Effect on Liquidity

Public debt is generally represented by bonds which are highly negotiable. Therefore, those people who hold bonds possess highly liquid form of assets, these assets or bonds can easily be converted into cash whenever the holding individual needs money. So, public debt increases the volume of liquid assets in the economy. Secondly the large quantity of such liquid government bonds can result into the failure of monetary policy. For example, when central bank tries to control inflation through monetary policy tools like bank rate, the commercial banks can increase their cash reserve by selling government bonds.

4.2.5 Effect on Resources Allocation

The public debt unlike tax finance has little effect on resources allocation. To a greater extent, public borrowing curtails business investment activities while decline of investment varies from one industry to another. In this way allocation of resources are not much affected by the manner of financing these units.

4.2.6 Effects of Public Debts on Cost Conditions

Public debt influences cost of production conditions in the country in two ways. On the one side, if public debts fund is being used for development infrastructural facilities like transport, power, irrigation, markets, etc. it reduces cost of production of both private and public sector industries. For example, if government starts professional courses like medical, engineering by investing public debt funds, the cost of education will be low to common people. On the other side, if spending of public debts raises the demand for labour and raw materials in the market, the prices of these factors will go up thereby the cost of production will be increased in the country.

4.2.7 Effects of Public Debts on Money Market

Government borrows fund from money market by floating its treasury bills, bonds and securities thus, it competes with the private borrowers. Generally government fixes higher rate of interest to borrow more fund from money market so it influences on all the transactions of the market. If it borrows from central bank at same rate of interest when the supply of fund is inadequate in the market, central bank issue new currencies to lend loan to government that results into increase in supply of money in the economy. For instance, Indian government has been practicing borrowing from Reserve Bank of India to finance the budgetary deficit since Third Five Year Plan as it is found a measure to control inflation with economic growth but the supply of currency expanded in the country.

4.2.8 Effects of External Debts on Economy

External borrowing is considered as a factor of economic development. External borrowing brings foreign currencies and enables the country to import capital goods, technology, technical know-how, basic and short-in-supply raw material, etc. to meet the requirement of developmental activities. In such cases, public debt has positive effects on the national economy. For example, the developing countries like India attained their present status of economic development with the help of foreign capital and the same story is true in case of so-called developed countries like UK and USA.

4.2.9 Effects of Public Debts on Private Sector

Generally public debt has positive effects on private sectors. Public debts spending on social security schemes, employment generating activities, etc. enhances the purchasing power of the people so it leads to increase in demand for goods and services produced by the private sector thereby their prices that yield them more profits, further it takes them to higher and higher developmental activities. Similarly, public spending on 'Research and Development' (R&D) and 'Science and Technology', public education, public health, etc. helps the private sector to reduce their cost on these activities. However, the private sector feel it burdensome when they feel the benefits they are being enjoyed from the public debt spending are than the burden of taxes they are paying to the government.

4.3 TYPES OF PUBLIC DEBT

Public debts have been classified in many ways. Government loans differ from one another. The differences are due to differences in the market in which debts are floated, the rate of interest offered, conditions for repayment and the purpose of utilization. Followings are the main classification of public debt:

4.3.1 Internal Debt and External Debt

On the basis of nature of sources public debts can be classified as internal debts and external debts. Internal debt refers to public loans within the country, while external debt refers to the loans taken by the government from foreign individuals, institutions and governments or outside the country. For example, the Government of India used to take types of loans; (i) Rupee loans which were taken by the government from the citizens of the country, and (ii) Sterling, Dollar, etc. foreign currency loans from foreign countries like UK, USA, etc. An external loan is invariably contracted in foreign exchange resources of the borrowing country. But the borrowing country has to pay heavy sum of money by way of interest and it can also pose a danger to economic and political independence of the country. For example, India's external debt position is very critical, it pays $65 out of borrowed $100 for external debt services. External debt is also known as foreign debt.

In case of internal debt the interest payment remains inside the country. It does not increase the total availability of resources within the country. It simply involves transfer of resources from the bond holders to the govt. In case of external debt, on the contrary, leads to total availability of resources for the debtor country because it represents transfer of wealth from the creditor nation to the debtor nation. However, when external debt is repaid, there is a transfer of resources from the debtor nation to the creditor nation.

4.3.2 Productive Debt and Unproductive Debt

On the basis of return public debts can be classified as productive debt and unproductive debt. Productive debts are those which are used for those projects which yield an income to the government. For example, the public debt used for the construction of railways, irrigation and power projects, public sector industries, etc. that yield income or return to the government. The income derived from these projects may be enough to pay the yearly interest on the loans incurred on these projects. Moreover, the principal and the interest both can be paid out of the income derived from these projects. Thus, productive loan should not be considered as a burden upon the government and the tax payers. On the other hand, unproductive debts are those which create neither any asset nor yield any income to the government. It is dead weight or useless burden on the community. For example, public debt raised for financing war, meeting famines droughts, earthquake, budgetary deficits, etc.

4.3.3 Funded Debt and Unfunded Debt

On the basis of duration of repayment the public debts can be classified as funded and unfunded debts. The funded debt is a long-term debt. This type of debt is repaid by establishing a separate fund. Every year the government credits a certain amount of money to this fund. Generally funded debt is borrowed for famine relief, factory building, ports and harbour construction, Railways, etc.

Unfunded debt on the contrary refers to a short-term debt. It is that type of debt for the payment of which the government sets up no separate fund. These loans are generally paid off within a year.

Treasury bonds are unfunded debt because they are to be repaid after three to six months when they mature and their maturity period never be a longer period more than a year. The interest on this type of debt is paid by the government out of its ordinary income. The principal amount is repaid by the government by contracting additional loans from the market. The unfunded debt is generally undertaken to meet the immediate financial requirements of the government, filling temporary gaps in the budgets.

4.3.4 Redeemable Debt and Irredeemable Debt

On the basis of nature of repayment the public debts are classified as redeemable and irredeemable debts. The redeemable public debts are those which the government promises to repay at some future date. Here the government has to make arrangements for repayment of the principal as well as the regular payment of interest. For example, National Savings Certificates, Vikas Bonds, etc. in India. New taxes may have to be levied to make these payments. Redeemable debts may be short term (3-9 months) or medium term (more than 9 months but less than 5 years) or long term (more than 5 years); there is low interest rate on short-term debts and high interest-rate on long-term debts, the medium is in between these two.

Irredeemable debt is one where there is no promise to repay the principal amount. The government pays only the interest regularly. It may be difficult to raise irredeemable loans in democratic countries where people may not contribute if there is no promise to repay the principal at some future date. Hence, redeemable debt seems to be reasonable and preferable to irredeemable debts on the ground of sound finance and convenient method of payment.

4.3.5 Voluntary Debt and Compulsory Debt

Voluntary debt is one where people are requested or invited to contribute to governments loan programme. The public borrowing by democratic governments results in voluntary public debt. No force or compulsion is used. For example, in India most of the loan floated by the government is oversubscribed on voluntary basis. Though, the rate of interest is lower that on other securities, the financial institutions and banks find them to be good liquid assets.

Compulsory debt implies force, i.e., government uses pressure or force for getting loans from the individuals and institutions.

Such compulsory debt is raised during an emergency such as inflation, war, etc. for example, Indian government introduced 'Compulsory Deposit Scheme' to its employees to fight inflation. People refuse to contribute to the government loans if they lose faith in the stability of the government. In such a case the government has to raise loans compulsory to meet its requirements. Compulsory loans are not common in modern days.

4.4 MERITS AND DEMERITS OF PUBLIC DEBT

There are differences of opinions among the economists and academicians regarding public debt. Classical economists have no belief in public debt that may do better for community. But mercantilists and modern economists have belief in public debt that it may enable the government. However, public debt has both merits and demerits, it is both boon and curse to the community.

4.4.1 Merits

Despite of classical economists' unacceptance of public debt, Malthus, J.S. Mill, Sidgwick and Cairnes have argued that it is not great evil. Modern economists like A.P. Lerner, A.H. Hansen, J.M. Keynes and others have argued that it enables the government to control the economy to achieve well defined goals. Hence, the conveniences or advantages or merits of public debt are discussed as follows:

(i) It helps economic development activities: Government needs huge amount for developmental programmes like infrastructure, public sector core industries, etc. Taxation is not a suitable method to finance developmental activities because taxes raise prices and put the economy into inflation crisis. So, public debt is the right method of raising fund to finance developmental activities as well as controlling effective demand to control rise in prices.

(ii) It enables the government to solve unemployment problem: Public debts empowers the government to undertake autonomous investment activities that directly leads to creation of employment opportunities in the country. Advanced countries use public debt as a method to recover economy from depression by creating employment opportunities, for example, USA; developing countries use it to solve unemployment problems, for example, India.

(iii) It helps to control inflation: Both developed and developing countries use public debt as a method to reduce excess supply of money in circulation for controlling inflationary situation. Public borrowing take away peoples' excess purchasing power thereby it controls demand for goods and services to control rise in prices.

(iv) It inculcates savings habits among people: Government gives interest on public loans so it encourages the people to save more from their income to avail this opportunity. Besides, productive public debts raises the productivity and income of the country that increases income as well as propensity to save of the people.

(v) It helps monetary policy: Monetary policy and fiscal policy are the complementary measures of government to regulate economic activities for attaining economic stability. Public debt is a part of fiscal policy operation so it helps the government to implement monetary policy successfully. For example, to control inflation, one the one hand, bank-rate will be raised under monetary policy to discourage borrowing and more public loans will be floated under fiscal policy on the other.

(vi) It helps for defence of the country: External debts brings foreign currencies and enables the government to import modern arms and ammunitions, defence technology to strengthen the defence, to have defence industries and maintain regional defence-balance.

In brief, public debt help the modern welfare states to carry out all its developmental activities in almost all fields of the nation such as economic, social, defence, etc.

4.4.2 Demerits

Classical economists have no belief in public borrowing because it creates threat to nation's sovereignty. David Hume says "Nations once they began borrow, would be unable to desist until they reached the point of bankruptcy". Adam Smith said about public debt as "In short, the ability to engage in loan finance makes for irresponsibility in sovereign". In brief, classical have the opinion that the public borrowing unnecessarily increases the power of government to borrow for wasteful and unproductive public expenditures. The dangers or demerits of public debt are discussed as follows:

(i) It increases governments' extravagance: When fund is made easily available by borrowing governments spend more on unnecessary activities like allowances to ministers and officials, unnecessary expansion of departments and ministries, etc. unproductive activities. So these are real burden on taxpayers when tax proceeds are used for repayment of such debts.

(ii) It enhances financial burden on the economy: Government have to pay interest regularly on debts and it have to repay loans so for this purpose either it imposes taxes or expand supply of money which lead to inflation thereby the debt burden on government increases further. Besides, some part of national income has to be used to pay external debt services so it increases the financial burden on government. So public debt is also as danger as private debt.

(iii) It creates international problems: External debts makes home currency weaker and weaker against foreign currency because the demand for foreign currency increases for purpose of external debt services. It results into decline in foreign exchange reserve stock and depreciation of home currency. It put nation into debt-trap that spoils the refutation of the country at world-level.

(iv) It disturbs money market: To raise more loan at low rate of interest government follows cheap money policy that expands credit supply unnecessarily. It floats more bills, bonds and securities to borrow more money but it creates instability in money market.

To resume, public debt is boon so long it creates national income yielding assets and takes the economy to prosperity but it becomes curse when it turns into unproductive, burden on taxpayers and crisis initiator.

4.5 BURDEN OF PUBLIC DEBT

There is a controversy on the question of public debt burden in economic literature. Before analyzing the burden of public debt, it is essential to know the meaning of burden of public debt. The burden of public debt refers to the sacrifice and negative effects on the community through a rise in taxation at the time of repayment of the principal and the regular interest payment, i.e. debt services.

The public debt burden is classified in to two types namely (i) primary burden and (ii) real burden.

(i) Primary Burden of Public Debt: When the government increases the taxes to repay the interest on public debt thus, income of the people are transferred to the government are losses loss of income to the people can be called 'financial or money or primary burden of public debt'. David M.C. Wright says, "The financial burden of the national debt is to be measured by the effects of interest charged and taxes levied to meet them. The relation which the taxes of interest bear to national money income is the question of primary importance".

(ii) Real Burden of Public Debt: The real burden or secondary burden implies that higher level of taxation due to rise in public debt has adverse effect on capacity and willingness to work, save and invest.

These burdens of public debt are direct or indirect so these two concepts can be explained on the basis of source of borrow as (a) Burden of Internal Public Debt and (b) Burden of External Public Debt.

***(a) Burden of Internal Public Debt*:** It is a matter of generally accepted fact that the internal debt should not leave any burden because there is only a transfer of purchasing power from one section to another within the economy. However, some important aspects of burden are to be considered to analyze the fact.

(i) Direct Money Burden: Direct money burden refers to the amount of goods and services sacrificed by the people due to rise in taxes to repay the debt. If the taxpayers and bond holders are the same, there is no direct money burden. Even if the taxpayers and bond holders are different, there is only a change in the distribution of income from the taxpayers to the bond holders. Thus on the whole as far as internal debt is concerned there is only a transfer of purchasing power from one section to another.

Money does not go out of the economy. Hence, there is no direct money burden of an internal debt on the economy.

(ii) Indirect Money Burden: This refers to the indirect effect of public debt on the money incomes. When the government spends its loans on development projects, it increases the government demand for goods which results in a rise in prices. This causes a reduction in purchasing power or the people. Sometimes, taxes are increased to meet the repayments so such an increase in taxation affects people's desire and ability to work, save and invest thereby the levels of production.

(iii) Direct Real Burden: The government repays the principal amount along with the interest by imposing new taxes on the people and floating of securities. But generally most of the tax payers are poor and common people and government securities purchasers are relatively rich people who earns income from them. In such a case, it results in the transfer of purchasing power from the poorer section to the richer sections of the community. With this change in the distribution of income, more burden will be fall on the poorer sections of the society. For example, in India more than 84 per cent tax revenue is being collected from commodity taxes that falls heavily on poor and common people.

(iv) Indirect Real Burden: Indirect real burden refers to the indirect effect on the desire to work and save. When government imposes additional taxes to repay public debt, if it levies indirect taxes on goods, it affects the poor people more. It adversely affects their willingness to work and save besides increasing the disparities in income.

(b) Burden of External Public Debt: External debt mean the money borrowed from individuals, associates, etc. belong to foreign countries External debt also consist of the loan taken from foreign governments. In the words of Prof. Dalton, "A loan is external if subscribed by persons or institutions outside this area". The burden of external debt like that of internal debt is being discussed as follow:

(i) Direct Money Burden: In the case of an external debt, the debtor country has to remit to the creditor country huge amounts of money every year by way of interest. After the expiry of the

debt, the principal amount has also to be remitted in terms of foreign currency. Thus, the direct money burden of an external debt is represented by the aggregate money payment in the form of interest as well as principal repayable to the creditor country.

(ii) Indirect Money Burden: Sometimes the amount of interest on external debt is paid in kind, i.e. in terms of goods and service. In other words, the debtor country exports to the creditor country goods and service on a large scale by way of interest payments. This inevitably results in a rise in the prices of these goods and services within the country, as a consequences, there is a decline in the economic welfare of the community. This represents the indirect money burden of external debt.

(iii) Direct Real Burden: According to Prof. Dalton, "Direct real burden is measured by the loss of economic welfare which these payments involve to members of the debtor community". The debtor government imposes new taxes on the people to pay off the external debt. It is obvious that the burden of these taxes will fall more on the poorer sections of the society. Hence, it is the direct real burden of external public debt. Not only that in an effort to pay the external debt, debtor community is deprived of certain benefits, in a real sense, it represents the direct real burden.

(iv) Indirect Real Burden: Indirect real burden depends upon whether the people's ability and willingness to work and save is affected by taxation imposed to repay the external debt. If it adversely affects the willingness and ability to work, save and invest, it has unfavourable effects on production. Due to heavy debt repayment government has to curtail its essential public expenditure reducing welfare. This represents the indirect real burden of external debt.

In brief, however, the money and real burden of public debt is least related with the purposes of borrowing but more related with the effects of its methods of payment of debt services on individuals and community as a whole.

4.5.1 Theories on Burden of Public Debt

Since mercantilists to post-Keynesians era various thoughts on burden of public debt came to existence. The effort is made to discuss the important theories as under:

(i) **Mercantilist Theory:** Mercantilists believed in 'State Role Policy'. They argued that all trade and commercial activities could be regulated by the government so they favoured public debts. According to them, State raise loans for beneficial investments.

(ii) **Classical Theory:** Classical economists had no single opinion on public debt, during nineteenth century and early part of twentieth century. So there are two different views or theories on burden of public debt by classical. They can be discussed as:

***(a) Early Classical Theory*:** Earlier classical economists condemned state intervention in economic activities and public debt. J.B. Say, Adam Smith, David Hume, David Ricardo, Gladstone and others opposed the government borrowing. They believed that public debt creates irresponsibility in government and it leads to wasteful and unproductive expenditures by government. They strongly believed in principle of 'Balanced Budget' and government's activities limits to maintenance of internal law and order and protection of nation from external aggressions so government collect tax revenue just equal to meet these expenditures. In other words, they advocated 'Policy of minimum taxation for minimum public expenditure'. They strongly advocated 'Laissez Faire Policy' (Free Trade Policy) and free competitive market economy that take care of the welfare of the entire community.

***(b) Latter Classical Theory*:** Latter classical economists like J.S. Mill, Malthus, Sidgwick, Cairnes, C.F. Bastable and others had liberal views regarding public debt. They had considered both the advantages of public debts to government and the lenders to government. Thus, the classical theory of public debt was formulated at the end of nineteenth century, Bastable represented it. The main contentions of the theory are; (i) the burden of public debt will be carried forward to future-time, (ii) there is no significant difference between internal public debt and external public debt and there is also analogy between private debt and public debt, and (iii) there is difference between public debt and tax.

Bastable has accepted the view that the burden of public debt could be shifted on future generation, i.e. the debts raised today will be repaid with interest by levying taxes on people tomorrow.

He also argued that there is analogy between private and public debts because both are regulated by same lending principle. Further he differentiated between debt and tax: a debt is voluntary, it depends upon lenders' willingness, but tax is compulsory, it levies on both willing and unwilling to pay.

(iii) Modern Theory: The modern theory of public debt is also known as 'The New Orthodox of Public Debt' or 'no burden theses'. J.M. Buchanan, in his book *Public Principles of Public Debt* says about the theory as "The currently dominant theory of public debt is called here the 'new orthodoxy' I have adopted this term because of the virtual unanimity which is to be found among scholars. The word 'new' modifies 'orthodoxy', and it should not be taken to suggest that the ideas themselves are 'new' or modern. Long before the 'new economics' came into existence, articulate statements of the currently ruling theory of public debt are to be found. And, even today, there is far from a one-to-one correspondence between the proponents of the 'new economics' and those who accept the new orthodoxy of debt theory. This may be quite simply illustrated by stating that Professor Pigou himself belongs to the latter group."

It is formulated during 'Great Depression of 1930's' so it is circumstance child of 'Keynesian Economics'. The modern theory has been formulated on the belief that "huge public debt is a national asset rather than a liability and continuous deficit spending is essential to the economic prosperity of the nation". The theory refuted classical theory assumptions like full employment, perfect competition, public debt is wasteful and unproductive, etc. The modern theory advocates that 'it is not wasteful but productive and an essential means to increase employment and to achieve economic development with stability. Prof. A.H. Hansen states the theory as "public debt is an essential means of increasing employment and has become an instrument of economic policy today". The theorists further argued that the public debt does not matter so long the national income rises.

J.M. Buchanan, in his book *Public Principles of Public Debt*, summarized the modern theory in his words as "the real sacrifice of private goods and services, that is real income, allegedly occurs during this initial period, and this sacrifice stems, not from the debt *per se,* but rather from the decision of the government to undertake the public expenditure in question. In this particular respect the financing of a public expenditure by borrowing is little different from financing it by taxation. In either case, the real burden is borne currently. Any shift of the primary real burden of public expenditure over time by changing the method of financing is impossible." Further, he advocates the statement of the theory that "public debt incurred now leaves not only an obligation to the future generation but also a claim". It means public debt simply leads to transfer of funds between future members of the community, i.e. taxpayer children inherit tax liability and bond-holder children acquire an equal asset means loss of taxpayers is offset by gainers of bond holders thus the whole net burden will be nil. Similarly, Keynes advocated the theory, in brief, as there is no burden of internal public debt as it has income-generating potentiality. Further modern economists contends that there is difference between internal public debt and external public debt because external debt imposes burden but internal debt does not impose burden. External public debt burden involves repayment of foreign loans with interest leads to transfer of goods and services to foreign countries.

The new orthodoxy of the public debt is based upon three basic propositions. These are:

(a) *The creation of public debt does not involve any transfer of the primary real burden to future generations*: It means the real burden of public debt falls on the initial generation and it cannot be transferred to future-generation.

(b) *The analogy between individual or private debt and public debt is fallacious in all essential respects*: It means a public debt internally held is different in nature from private debt. The impact of public debt on production, employment, income distribution, taxation, is different from impact of private debt.

(c) *There is a sharp and important distinction between an internal and an external public debt*: It means the burden of internal debt cannot be transferred to future-generation but the burden of external public debt can be transferred to future-generation. The domestic goods and services will be transferred to foreign countries when the payments are made for external debt services that reduces the real income of future generations.

These three propositions are clearly not independent of one another, but this means of classification does provide a useful model for exposition and initial discussion.

Criticism against Modern Theory: Some modern economists have disagree with the modern theory on 'no burden theses'. They refuted all the propositions of theory by their empirical studies. So the theory has been criticized as follows:

(a) The primary real burden of public debt can be transferred on future-generations. Many modern economists have the opinion that the primary real burden of public debt could be transferred to future-generation. It is true fact that the public debt raised to-day reduces future productivity by reducing present production potentiality of the economy as well as individual. The reduction in present consumption lowers future production of goods and services by curtailing present investments.

(b) There is analogy between private debt and public debt. The same credit policy regulates both public and private debts in money market. Likewise, the lending principle will be same. In case of both, the growth of debt matters, for instance the debt trap disrupt the economic situation.

(c) External and internal public debts are alike in impact is concern. The shifting of tax burden, raised to pay debt-services, to future generation reduces future consumption, savings and investment. In India the payment of both previous external and internal debt services are being paid out of budget of the current year that has impact on all economic values like production, distribution, consumption, savings, etc.

To sum up that the public debt whether external or internal does matter. It can be put in A.P. Lerner's words as "A statement that public debt does not matter must be understood in the same sense as when a man who finds that rumour has converted a twisted ankle into a broken neck tells his friends that he is perfectly alright".

4.5.2 Limits and Sustainability of Public Debt

'Is there any limit on public borrowing?' Is the basic question to be answered by the economists, academicians and the policy-makers? In practice, it is very difficult fix the ceiling on government borrowing, however, it depends upon type of its effects on the economy, for instance if the further public borrowing is detrimental to the national economy then that would be the maximum limit. It differs from economy to economy. If it is a developed economy, the limit of government borrowing depends on adequate taxation policy used to pay public debt services without creating or worsening inflationary situation and ensuring fair distribution of income and wealth in the country. Prof. A.H. Hansen said "Much of the discussion about the limits of the public debt is wholly unrealistic. There are no rigid and fixed limits. The problem is manageable one, and can best be taken care of by ensuring that taxation is adequate (1) to prevent inflation and (2) to provide a reasonably equitable and workable distribution of wealth and income."

In case of developing or underdeveloped economy, the limit on government borrowing is determined by the rate of growth of national income. So, the limit of public debt depends on the relative factors such as public sector policy and development, government investment policy, growth of national income, etc.

Sandra Švaljek, Institute of Economics Zagreb, wrote regard public debt limit and the sustainability of public as "History has shown that different economies cope with the debt burden in different ways. Sometimes crises appear even at low levels of share in the debt of the gross domestic product (GDP), whereas some economies function very well even when their public debt significantly exceeds the value of the total one year production in the country. Consequently, we cannot talk about the existence of absolute and universal boundaries of public debt. However, it can be said that these boundaries are reached when fiscal policy objectives are jeopardized." In other words, it means that the optimum of public debt is not reached until additional public expenditures like public investments that are financed by debt are capable to (a) increase the use of production capacities,

(b) increase or improve production capacity of the economy, and (c) enable the approaching to the desired distribution.

Sandra Švaljek, further argued that "Similarly, sometimes it is simply considered that new borrowing is a 'wise' move if it is consistent with other macroeconomic goals (current account balance, growth of private investments, inflation control, maintaining external credibility). If one assumes that all investments in economy should equal the total savings of residents and foreigners, and if new public sector borrowing, i.e. public sector deficit, is considered as the difference between public investments and public savings, then this deficit is balanced by savings of other sectors of domestic economy and/or external deficit (deficit on balance of payments current account). Consequently, the wisdom of new borrowing depends on the level of private savings, on the desired levels of private investments, and the desired deficit on the balance of payments current account." According to Sandra Švaljek if the above mentioned criteria of desirability of borrowing are hard to quantify, some simpler ratios are often applied as indicators of borrowing and the possibility of further borrowing depends upon the following ratios:

(i) The ratio of interest paid on public debt and collected taxes. This ratio shows to what extent the burden of interest is covered with tax revenues.

(ii) The ratio of interest and public expenditures. This indicator shows which share of public expenditures is "tied" due to public debt repayment obligation.

(iii) The interest/GDP ratio. Interest is put into a ratio with GDP because the tax revenues from which the debt obligation needs to be met depend on GDP.

(iv) The new borrowing/public expenditures ratio.

(vi) The share of new borrowing (i.e. deficit) in GDP.

(vi) The share of total debt in GDP.

According to Sandra Švaljek the last two are the most frequent and most important ones, and they also serve to define the criteria for admission to the European Monetary Union. Sandra Švaljek, further said that these indicators do not show whether the public debt limit has been reached; however, if they are monitored over a longer period of time, they can used for monitoring the dynamics of borrowing. Besides, these indicators are used in international debt comparisons.

In many countries, when possibilities of internal borrowing in the country are exhausted, the government turns to borrowing abroad. Since foreign debt can be serviced only through exports, the 'external public debt/exports ratio' is used as an indicator of the external foreign debt level sustainability.

Besides the above simple indicators of indebtedness, Sandra Švaljek said that a whole array of methods has been developed for assessing the long-term sustainability of the existing borrowing policy and these methods can be divided into three basic categories:

(i) Methods of assessment by using the solvency approach: Methods of assessment of sustainability of the public debt policy by using the solvency approach take a country's "budget constraint" as the starting point. The government budget identity was "discovered" in the 1960's and 1970's and was a result of the critique of the Keynesian model (Haliassos and Tobin, 1990). Unlike the Keynesian approach to deficit and debt, the methods of analysis of the financial policy of a country, which use the budget identity of that country as a starting point, stress the importance of the form of financing of the budget deficit, i.e. debt. Budget identity is actually the balance of government receipts and expenditures. Although the budget identity is often called budget constraint, it does not represent a constraint in itself, but the constraint consists of the limits explicitly or implicitly set for a country's possibility to issue a new debt, of the minimum level of the foreign exchange reserves set by the government itself, and also of the limitations of real resources that the government (under given political and economic circumstances) may collect by issuing money (Buiter, 1985). In the most general form, budget identity in a given period of time contains the following elements:

Money issue + new debt issue + sale of state property = government expenditures + interest on existing public debt - taxes - revenues from government property

The right side of this identity actually represents the financial deficit of the public sector, while the left side shows in what ways this deficit can be financed (Buiter, 1985).

(ii) Methods of monitoring the trend of debt as a share of GDP: In order for the borrowing policy to be sustainable, it is sometimes considered that the deficit does not necessarily have to be zero; instead, the aim is to stabilize the ratio of the nominal debt and the nominal GDP. The simplest approach to such conception of debt sustainability says that the growth rate of debt share in nominal output should be equal to the sum of the price growth rate and the real output growth rate (Gordon, 1993).

(iii) Time series analysis methods (Heinemann, 1992): In the last decade, debt sustainability has been tested by the time series analysis method. This method starts from the idea that long-term debt trend is of key importance for the sustainability issue. A debt is sustainable if it can be shown that during a longer period of time with unchanged debt policy, primary deficit and surplus values are balanced. A review of possible sustainability tests by using the time series analysis method was first provided by Hamilton and Flavin (Heinemann, 1992). They suggest testing of a hypothesis that the expected present value of future debt equals zero, which means that the current debt is equal to the present value of future surpluses.

There is no unique and generally acceptable definition of the sustainability of borrowing policy. At the same time, there is a higher degree of agreement about unsustainability. Any borrowing policy that is not unsustainable is frequently considered sustainable. In simple terms, a government debt policy is unsustainable if private subjects, both domestic and foreign, consider it as such. This means, for instance, that creditors, doubting a country's credibility, i.e. its ability to repay loans, will suspend further granting of loans and demand risk premiums. Domestic creditors may, for instance, expect a tax increase and emission of money in the future as well as related inflation, and even devaluation, which can all lead to reduced domestic currency savings, taking capital abroad, and finally to a financial crisis or balance of payments crisis.

Sandra Švaljek further argues that this scenario is common for countries with undeveloped financial markets but in countries with developed financial markets an unsustainable borrowing policy may cause a rise in the supply of government bonds, which leads to a drop in their prices and a rise in interest rates. State creditors will demand an even higher increase in interest rates if bonds are not indexed, and will also seek protection from possible loss by demanding risk premiums (Masson, 1985). In the Sargent and Wallace (1981) scenario, under the same conditions, an unsustainable debt policy will lead to a drop in the demand for government bonds and an increase in bond interest rates, which will prevent the state from possibility to control the money supply growth rate and the inflation rate.

To conclude on the limit of public debt and its sustainability, in the words of Sandra Švaljek, "it can be said that these boundaries are reached when fiscal policy objectives are jeopardized".

4.5.3 Public Debt vs. Tax

Taxes and public debts are the choices before government to meet its expenditures. Heavy taxation and reckless borrowing are not acceptable because both ruins the financial structure and economy as whole put the nation into problems such as inflation, mass-discontentment, bankruptcy, etc. So there must be a sound guiding principle of financing public expenditure without damaging the economy in any form. Prof. A.C. Pigou, in book *The Political Economy of War*, wrote "The general principle followed in financing public expenditure is that, the normal or ordinary and recurrent expenditure should be financed out of taxes, while non-recurrent and productive expenditures should be met out of loans".

However, taxation is advisable to meet public expenditures so long it has no adverse effects on economy including commerce, industry, etc. and public debt is advisable when tax system is unsatisfactory.

Difference between Public Debt and Tax: There are differences between tax and public debt as discussed under:

(i) The burden of tax falls on current income only but the burden of public debt falls on both current and future income. Public debt reduces both present and future purchasing power of people.

(ii) Tax reduces present consumption, savings and investments but public debt reduces both present futures consumption, savings and investments provided it is not used for productive purposes.

(iii) Public debts reduce the availability of public savings to private investments. Tax has no such adverse effect on private investment.

(iv) Tax is a compulsory payment but public debt is voluntary, people may or may not purchase government securities.

(v) Burden of tax is not equitable or cannot be diffused equally among all people but the burden off public debt can be diffused over long a period.

(vi) Taxes may control extravagant expenditures of individuals but public debt may encourage such expenditures with expectation of future incomes from public-debt investments.

This discussion does not imply that we have to give up one of the methods of financing public expenditures. A good tax system possesses taxes raise income up to a certain limit beyond that public borrowing can be used to raise the income for purpose of public expenditures.

4.6 PRINCIPLES OF PUBLIC DEBT MANAGEMENT

The management of public debt is very significant because there can be important economic effects of the changes in the size of the public debt on the functioning of the economy. These changes may co-operate or disturb the implementation of monetary and fiscal policy of the country. The main objective of public debt management is that the borrowing and repayment of public debt should not have adverse effects on the economic situation of the country. So, a set of principles are required to manage public debt. These are:

(i) Principle of Economy: The cost of public debt operation should be minimum. Government have to pay interest on public debts so this interest cost must be minimum. Similarly, the repayment of principal loans should not be burdensome on the people. Government impose taxes on people to collect money for debt services so these taxes should not impose heavy tax-burden on the people. The government interest rate policy influences on money market. The heavy taxation policy and high interest rate policies may jeopardize the functioning of the economy.

(ii) Principle of Satisfaction: The management of public debt should satisfy the needs of the investors. Prof. S.P. Naik, in his book *Essays in Public Finance and Planning* argued "public debt should be managed in such a way that the needs of the investors with regard to the types of government securities and terms of issues are satisfied". Government should offer attractive terms on short-term and long-term securities. It should assure high rate of interest while converting short-term securities into long-term securities. If such assurances are not given, it disturbs the security market.

(iii) Principle of Funding: The funding refers to converting of short-term debts into long-term debts. The public debt management must help to fund short-term debt into long-term debt without disturbing the economic stability. If interest-rate is raised by the government for conversion of short-term debts into long-term debts, the short run debt availability will be reduced thereby private investments will be affected adversely on the one hand and future debt service burden will be increased on the other, thus, it will lead economy to recession. The lowering of short-term interest-rate for funding purpose will encourage 'Hot Money Movement' that is short-term fund flow out of country which has adverse effect on the economy. Hence, the funding should be done in such a way that it satisfies the investors.

(iv) Principle of Co-ordination: The public debt policy must be co-ordinated with fiscal and monetary policies of the country. This co-ordination is essential to maintain economic growth with stability. If government forces the central bank of the country to lower interest rate for reducing public debt burden, that leads to credit expansion thereby the inflationary situation will be created in the economy. Therefore, there must be co-ordination among public debt, fiscal and monetary policies.

(v) Principle of Degree of Liquidity: The public debt should have a moderate degree of liquidity. If they have high degree of liquidity, it will lead to inflation for instance if a large proportion of total public debt is short-term debt and its more portion is held by the banks, it will lead to high degree of liquidity.

To sum-up, the policy of low interest leads to inflation and the funding of short-term debts leads to economic recession so the public debt must be managed in such a way that it should have least disadvantages.

4.7 METHODS OF REDEMPTION OF PUBLIC DEBT

Redemption of public debt means repayment of public debt. Public debt is to be repaid by the government on attainment of its maturity just as the private individual or organization has to repay the loan. It is better for the government to clear the debt as soon as possible because mounting public debt has a demoralizing effect on the people apart from the fact that public debt is subject to higher rates of taxation. Therefore the government in any case, should pay the interest on loan although in some cases the principal amount is not repaid. If the government fails to honour its promise, i.e., not paying the interest, its creditworthiness will be lost and it would not be in a position to raise new loans when circumstances warranted.

There are several advantages of public debt redemption. These are: (i) prompt repayment helps to cheek any tendency undertake extravagant expenditure on the part of the government, (ii) it helps to reduce the cost of debt management, (iii) every repayment reduces the burden of public debt on future generation, (iv) it helps flow back of funds to the public and this will help greater private investment, (v) it maintains confidence of the lenders, and (vi) it is very good measure to fight deflationary tendencies.

For repayment of public debts, government uses the following important methods.

4.7.1 Use of Budget Surplus

Government creates surplus in budget either raising more tax revenue excess over public expenditures or reducing public expenditures at given tax revenue. Whenever the government secures a surplus in its budget, it utilizes this surplus to pay off its debts raised from the people. Normally the government utilizes the budget surplus to purchase back its own bonds and securities held by the people in the money market. This results in an automatic liquidation of its debt liability.

This method is unsuitable during depression because it discourages the demand factor.

4.7.2 Sinking Fund

It is a very popular method of repayment of public debt. Under this method the government creates a separate fund known as the 'Sinking Fund' for the repayment of outstanding public debt. The government goes on crediting every year fixed sum of money out of its income to this fund. By the time the debt matures, the fund accumulated enough amounts to pay off the principal as well as interest charges. Generally the government credits amounts to this fund by transferring fixed payment of its annual income and by raising a new loan and credit the proceeds to it. According to Dalton, a sinking fund should be accumulated out of current revenues of the government like taxation, not out of new loans. For example, suppose the government floats a loan of ₹ 50 crores redeemable in ten years for the construction of a bridge, it can introduce an additional levy or tax (such as a levy on users of bridge or an additional taxation on petrol or vehicles) and divert this amount into sinking fund. If it is carefully planned, sufficient amount can be accumulated to repay the interest as well as the principal at the time of maturity of the loan. The fund created out of new loans is not 'true sinking fund'.

The sinking fund method is a systematic method of debt redemption. The budget of debt is spread over a number of years. It increases the credit worthiness of the government. However, it is a slow process of debt repayment.

4.7.3 Terminal Annuities or Annual Repayment

Government issues terminal annuities, a part of which matures every year according to serial number given so the debt can be cleared every year. This method of debt redemption is similar to 'Sinking Fund'. Under this method the government pays off its debt every year in equal annual installments which include both interest and principal. The main benefit of this method is that it leads to a fall in the burden of public debt every year.

4.7.4 Refunding

Refunding is a process by which old matured bonds or debts are replaced by new bonds or debts. It means the issue of new bonds and securities by the government to replace the old maturing debts or bonds. This method is used when the government finds it difficult to repay a debt on the date of maturity. It floats a new debt to replace the old debt usually short-term debts are replaced by the new long-term debts. Similarly, the government may pay the old debt with higher interest by borrowing new loans at a lower interest.

This method is adopted only when the government is not able to raise funds from any other source to repay debt. In reality the government only postpones its obligation to pay a debt to a future date. Thus, the total burden of the debt continues to increase in future.

4.7.5 Debt Conversion

Conversion of public debt means exchange of new debts for the old ones. Under this method, the loan is actually not repaid, but the form of debt is changed. The process of conversion consists generally in converting a public debt from higher to a lower rate of interest. The government that have borrowed loans at a time when the rate of interest was high, now converts it into new loans at a lower rate of interests in order to minimize the burden of the debt on the state. Moreover lower interest rates on public loans would mean a less unequal distribution of income.

Conversion is not strictly speaking a method of debt redemption because the volume of debt is not reduced. Further, government should enjoy the faith of the people to make them to agree to convert the old loan into a new loan. Therefore, conversion is a voluntary process requiring the consent of the bond holders. The government cannot force them.

There is only a subtle difference between refunding and conversion. In refunding the old debt is actually paid off by floating a new loan. In conversion, there is a variation in the original terms of loans such as rate of interest or other details.

4.7.6 Repudiation of Debt

This is the most drastic method of debt redemption. Repudiation of debt means simply that the government refuses to pay the interest as well as the principal amount. Thus, the debt is not repaid but it is destroyed.

Internally the government may repudiate a debt when it experiences financial ruin, bankruptcy or change in political setup. Repudiation of internal debt makes the people lose confidence in the government. Secondly, the government may find it difficult to raise new loans. Finally, there may be internal rebellion.

Similarly in the case of external debt the government may restore to repudiation when it faces a grave foreign exchange crisis, yet there may be severe consequences like social revolution, economic blockade and even military action.

Debt repudiation should not be adopted by the government because it is dishonest measures where the government fails to keep up its promise to repay. This practice was adopted in USA during the civil war period (1861-65) and USSR after the revolution (1917). Now no modern governments have adopted it.

4.7.7 Capital Levy

Capital levy means a heavy tax on property and wealth. According to some economist, the war time debt should be paid off the government by imposing a capital levy on the people. Such an idea was mooted by certain modern leading economists in Great Britain after the First World War. Dr. Dalton recommended capital levy as a method of debt repayment. It is a one time tax on capital assets. The richer sections reap huge amount of profit during war time through the rise in prices and as such they should be subjected to heavy taxation in the post war period for the repayment of war time debt, it is justified. The capital levy also satisfies the canon of equity.

4.7.8 Repayment of External Debts

The foreign debts are repaid by government through foreign exchange earnings. Government earn foreign exchanges by export surplus, invisible trade surplus and borrowing foreign-loans. If there is no export surplus, the country has to reduce its home-consumption. For example, India followed 'export or peril' policy during its fourth five year plan aiming to boost its export trade surplus.

4.8 MODEL QUESTIONS

(a) Questions each needs answer in 2-3 sentences (2 Marks each)

1. What is public debt?
2. What do you mean by the source of public debt?
3. What are the sources of public debt?
4. What is private debt?
5. Name any two similarities between private and public debts.
6. Name any two dissimilarities between private and public debts.
7. What do you mean by effects of public debt?
8. Name any two factors influencing effects of public debt.
9. What is revenue effect of public debt?
10. What is expenditure effect of public debt?
11. Name any two effects of public debt on economy.
12. Name any two types of public debt.
13. What do you mean by 'Funded Debt'?
14. Name any two merits of public debt.
15. Name any two demerits of public debt.
16. Give the meaning of public debt burden.
17. Distinguish between primary and real burden of public debt.
18. What is internal public debt burden?
19. What is external public debt burden?
20. Mention any two theories on public debt burden.
21. Give the statement of mercantilist theory on public debt.
22. Give the statement of classical theory on public debt.
23. Give the statement of modern theory on public debt.

24. What do you mean by limits of public debt?
25. Mention any two factors determining the limit of public debt.
26. Name any two methods of assessing sustainability of public debt.
27. Give any two difference between public debt and tax.
28. Name any two principles of public debt management.
29. Name any two methods of public debt redemption.
30. What is funding?
31. State any two advantages of public debt redemption.

(b) Questions each needs short-note type answer (5 Marks each)

1. Give a brief account of sources of public debts.
2. Write a note on similarities and dissimilarities between private and public debts.
3. Discuss in brief the effects of public debt on economy.
4. Write a short-note on types of public debts.
5. Explain in brief the causes of public debt.
6. Write a note on modern theory on public debt burden.
7. Write a note on the determinants of effects of public debt.
8. Discuss in brief the merits and demerits of public debt.
9. Write a note on direct and indirect burden of public debt.
10. Write note on principles of public debt management.
11. Discuss in brief the methods of public debt redemption.

(c) Questions each needs essay type/long answer (10/15 Marks each)

1. Define public debt, explain its various types.
2. Define public debt, explain its various sources.
3. Define public debt, explain the causes of public debt.
4. Define public debt, explain the similarities and dissimilarities between private and public debts.

5. Explain the various effects of public debts on the economy.
6. What is public debt? Explain its various types.
7. What is public debt? Explain its merits and demerits.
8. Explain the modern theory of public debt burden.
9. Discuss the limit and sustainability of public debt.
10. Analyze the principles of public debt management.
11. Narrate the various methods of public debt redemption.

5

Budgeting and Fiscal Policy

5.1 BUDGET

In layman's jargon 'Budget' means the fund sanctioned or authorized to use for specific purpose; it is common term used in college, school, business organizations, governments, etc. Its origin tells that the word 'Budget' has been derived from the French word 'Bougette' which means a small leather bag. Today, bag itself is not important, but people are anxious to see what the bag contains. Therefore, the bag contains economic bill presented by the Finance Minister before the Parliament every year. Every democratic government makes vigorous efforts for this end, maximizing the welfare of the community in the modern times. In order to achieve, the government takes in hand various socio-economic activities. This requires proper operation of the budgetary policy of the government. A budget therefore is not only a financial statement of actual and anticipated revenues and outlays of the government but is also a document of detailed programmes and policies of action which they desire to pursue in the coming years for raising the level of economic activity. So, budget is an instrument of fiscal policy.

5.1.1 Meaning and Definition of Budget

According to Gladstone, the budgets are not merely arithmetic but in thousand ways go to roots of prosperity of individuals relations of classes and strength of kingdom. Therefore, the taxation and expenditure policy help to narrow down the class distinctions. The expenditure and production policy aimed at removing poverty, unemployment and maldistribution of wealth and accelerating the rate of economic growth. The public borrowing policy aimed at accelerating the rate of saving and mobilizing of resources for the rapid development of the economy. In short, budget is a powerful instrument of economic activities or economic policy.

A budget is a statement of financial plan of the government. It includes the revenue and expenditure of the last completed financial year, the probable revenue and expenditure estimates for the current year, i.e. not completed year and the estimates for the anticipated revenue and proposed expenditure for the next financial year. In general, a budget shows the financial accounts of the previous year, the revised estimates of the current year, and the budget estimates of revenue and expenditure of the coming year. Further the estimates of the coming year are split up in to two parts, those based upon the assumption that the current year's taxes and their rates as per expenditure policy would continue, and those based upon the proposed changes therein. In this way, a budget becomes both a description of the policies of the government and the financial plans corresponding to them. In short, the budget is the annual financial statement of accounts for the preceding and current year, and the estimates of the revenue and expenditure of the coming year. Many economists have defined budget in different ways:

(a) Prof. P.F. Taylor: Taylor has defined budget as "Budget is the master financial plan of the government. It brings together estimates of anticipated revenue and proposed expenditure for the budget years".

(b) Rene Stourm: Stourm defined budget as "The budget is the document containing a preliminary approved plan of public revenue and expenditure".

(c) Prof. C.F. Bastable: Bastable defined budget as "The budget has come to mean the financial arrangement of a given period, with the usual implication that they have been submitted to the legislature for approval".

(d) Prof. Dimock: Dimock defined budget as "A budget is a balanced estimate of expenditure and receipts for a given period of time. In the hands of the administration, the budget is the record of past performance, a method of current control and a projection of future plans".

(e) Prof. Gildenhuys: Gildenhuys defined budget as "The budget is a political document through which money is appropriated according to value judgments and the budget process is a political process that takes place within a political arena".

After looking into definitions discussed above Prof. Thornhill and others have summarized the most important features of a public budget as follows:

(i) The budget, after its approval by the legislative authority, is enforceable. In other words, it has a sanction of public authority.

(ii) The results of most of the objectives to be realized by the budget are not quantifiable.

(iii) The budget brings together a variety of considerations.

(iv) As the objectives of action taken by public institution differ widely from those of private organizations, the processes for determining the content of a public budget are therefore unique.

(v) Authorities do not always adapt their expenditure to fit their available revenue.

(vi) It is the statement of expected revenue and proposed expenditure of the public authorities concerned.

(vii) It possesses periodicity which is generally in one current year.

(viii) Budget proposals should be clear.

(ix) It sets procedure in which the collection of revenue and administration of expenditure is to be executed.

(x) The anticipation of revenue and expenditure should make positive contribution to economic goal.

5.1.2 Types of Budget

Generally, budget has been classified into different types. These are:

(i) Balanced Budget: A budget is said to be balanced when the proposed expenditure and anticipated revenue both are equal.

According to Prof. Dalton, "A balanced budget is that when over a period of time revenue does not fall short of expenditure". In balanced budget, there is neither any deficit nor any surplus. However, the balanced budget is an accounting concept only. It is simply a balance sheet approach. At the initial stage we may have a balanced budget but later on as per the prevailing circumstances and in course of time it is bound to be either a deficit budget or a surplus budget. Thus, a balanced budget is a theoretical concept only. It can be expressed in terms of equation as:

$$B = R - E = 0$$

B= Budget, R = Anticipated revenue or income or receipts, E = Proposed expenditures.

When $R - E = 0$, $R = E$ so the budget is balanced

The concept of 'Balanced Budget' is advocated by classical economists.

(ii) Unbalanced Budget: When a budget shows that the government proposed expenditure and anticipated revenue are not equal, it is said to be an unbalanced budget. According to Prof. Dalton, "If over a period of time expenditure exceeds revenue, the budget is said to be unbalanced". In other words, over a period of time if there is no equality between proposed expenditure and anticipated income of the government then there is unbalance budget. It can be expressed in terms of equation as:

$$B = R - E \neq 0$$

B = Budget, R = Anticipated revenue or income or receipts, E = Proposed expenditures.

When $R - E \neq 0$, $R \neq E$ so the budget is unbalanced.

The concept of 'Unbalanced Budget' is advocated by modern economists.

The unbalanced budget may be 'Surplus budget' or 'Deficit budget'.

(iii) Revenue Budget: Revenue budget consists of revenue receipts and payments of the government such as tax revenues and non-revenues and expenditure is met from these revenues. Tax revenue comprise proceeds of taxes and other duties levied by the Union Government. Non-tax receipts of government mainly consist of interest and dividends on investments by the government, fees and other receipts for services rendered by government. The revenue expenditures consists of the expenditures of the government such as civil administration, defence, socio-economic services, etc. The revenue budget can be expressed as:

RB = RR–RE

RB = Revenue budget, RR=Revenue receipts or income, RE = Revenue expenditures.

If RB = RR–RE = 0, it is 'Balanced Revenue Budget';

If RB = RR–RE ≠ 0, it is 'Unbalanced Revenue Budget', it may be 'Surplus' or 'Deficit'.

If RB = RR–RE > 0, means RR is greater than RE value, it is called 'Surplus Revenue Budget' (Revenue Surplus) or If RB = RR–RE < 0, means RR is less than RE value, it is called 'Deficit Revenue Budget' (Revenue Deficit).

(iv) Capital Budget: Capital budget consists of capital receipts and payments. The main aim of capital receipts is raise fund for budgetary purposes. The capital receipts are (a) loans raised by the government from public which are called market loans, (b) borrowing of the government from Central Bank of the country and other parties, (c) loans received from foreign government, and (d) bodies and recoveries of loans generated by Central Government to State Governments and other parties. Capital expenditure is met out of capital receipts for acquisitions of assets like land, building, machinery, equipment, etc. and also investments in shares, bonds, etc. Besides, loans and advances granted by Central or Federal Government to State Governments, governments' companies, corporations and other parties are included in capital expenditure. Most of the expenditure on capital account or capital expenditure is developmental in nature. The capital budget can be expressed as:

CB = CR–CE

CB = Capital budget, CR=Capital receipts or income, CE = Capital expenditures.

If CB = CR–CE = 0, it is 'Balanced Capital Budget';

If $CB = CR - CE \neq 0$, it is 'Unbalanced Capital Budget', it may be 'Surplus' or 'Deficit'.

If $CB = CR - CE > 0$, means CR is greater than CE value, it is called 'Surplus Capital Budget' (Capital Surplus) or If $CB = CR - CE < 0$, means CR is less than CE value, it is called 'Deficit Capital Budget' (Capital Deficit).

(v) **Surplus Budget:** When the public revenue exceeds the public expenditure it is called 'surplus budget' or 'budgetary surplus'. In olden days, surplus budget was a common feature of the country's economy. However, nowadays surplus budgets are hardly visible.

(vi) **Deficit Budget:** Where the public revenue falls short of public outlay then it is said to be a 'deficit budget' or 'budgetary deficit'. Deficit budget becomes a common policy of underdeveloped or developing countries like India as a measure to finance developmental activities. Keynes advocated this policy as a measure to recover economy from depression.

(vii) **Interim Budget:** Interim is one which is prepared for an interim period, i.e. less than a full year. In case when there is a delay in preparing regular budget for full year then interim budget is prepared so as to meet the expenditure during the period.

(viii) **Ordinary and Emergency Budget:** The ordinary budget deals with the functions which are relatively permanent, while the emergency budget is concerned with the abnormal or exceptional circumstances like war, depression, etc. This kind of budget was introduced in America in 1933. The emergency budget could not gain much popularity and it was criticized on account of an instrument to hide the extent of wasteful spending.

(ix) **Supplementary Budget:** During the course of regular budget, if the expenditure exceeds the revenue or the government is required to incur expenditure on some specific project for which no provision was made in the regular budget, supplementary budget is prepared so as to meet this extra expenditure.

5.1.3 Functions and Objectives of Budget

Government have a specific policy on its budget, known as 'Budget policy' to perform a well-defined functions to achieve pre-determined goals. The nature of budget policy is too heterogeneous to permit a unitary explanation. Various functions must be distinguished and dealt with separately, even though they are part of an interdependent system. Prof. Gildenhuys and other modern economists have recognized the functions of a pubic budget as follows:

(i) **Satisfaction of Public Wants:** Richard A. Musgrave said that 'satisfaction of public wants' is one of the three major functions of public budget. Its function is to decide just what public wants should be satisfied, how much of such want satisfaction should be provided for, and who should bear the cost. The problem, then, is to provide for the satisfaction of public wants free of direct charge, and paid for out of general tax revenue. R.A. Musgrave called this function 'Service Branch'.

The budget is a policy statement declaring the goals and specific objectives anauthority wishes to achieve by means of the expenditure concerned. It is public policy expressed in amounts of money and is the actual embodiment of policy and of implied policy objective. In policy-making, realization of the most important objectives and aims should receive priority. As a policy-making document, the budget generally contains a definition of both the quantity and the quality of the envisaged service delivery. However, no normative guidelines exist by which priorities may be scientifically determined, thus, that is the result of political expedience.

(ii) **Redistribution of Income and Wealth:** The redistribution of wealth is one of the most important functions of a public budget. It requires that total integration should exist between the two sides of the budget—revenue policy and expenditure policy—in order to comply with a fiscal policy for the redistribution of wealth.

R.A. Musgrave argued that "To the extent that society wishes to undertake distributional adjustments, the tax transfer mechanism of the public budget furnishes an efficient tool by which to accomplish them and one that provides least interference with the market. This, however, leaves open the difficult question of how to determine just what adjustments are to be made." Musgrave has called it 'Distribution Branch'.

(iii) Work Programme: The budget is a work programme for the administrative authority, on which each department can base its own operational work programme. This function of the budget demands that the structure of objectives, the activity schedule, the resource schedule and the financial schedule is clearly expounded in the budget documents.

(iv) Source of Information: The budget serves as a source of information for everyone concerned; the information contained in the draft budget document is necessary for its consideration and, after approval, serves as the most important source of information to the administrative authority for executing its functions.

(v) Coordinating Instrument: The budget also serves as a coordinating instrument by which government activities can be integrated, because it is supposed to contain all the information on the policies, objectives and activities of the government in one document.

(vi) Control Instrument: The budget is also a control instrument to be used by the legislative authority over the executive authority and by the executive authority over the administrative authority and even for internal control within a single component of the administrative authority. Two types of administration control are important in this regard, namely, *a priori* control and *ex post* control.

(vii) Contribution to Stabilization: According to R.A. Musgrave, the contribution to stabilization is another important function of public budget. Budget policy, in coordination with monetary and debt policy, maintains an appropriate level of aggregate demand to achieve stability in the economy means control of inflation or deflation. Further, he said that the 'stabilization-function' works along with 'service-function' and 'distribution-function' to achieve budgetary-goals. Musgrave has called it 'Stabilization Branch'.

(viii) Employment Generating Instrument: Modern governments are using budget as an instrument to generate employment opportunities in the economy. It helps both developed and developing or underdeveloped countries to solve their unemployment problems, but the techniques of budgeting are different.

5.1.4 Rules and Norms for Public Budgeting

The recent experiences enabled the modern economists to infer on a set of rules and norms on public budgeting. Prof. Lacasse, in this context, remarked as "The recent experience of budgeting and policy-making has left behind a substantial body of rules, norms and practices, which are routinely applied or pursued in most countries, because they are widely recognized as workable and reasonably efficient and are required by international organizations and/or financial markets". In other words, the budget norms are explicitly formulated; their compliance or non-compliance is easily observable and, often sanctioned by financial markets. Prof. Mikesell has also stated that "new budget reform techniques are consistent with the classical principles for appraising budgets". However, the main rules and norms for budgeting are:

(i) **Comprehensiveness:** The budget should include all receipts and outlays of the government. The single process would thus include all activities of the government.

(ii) **Unity:** All spending and revenue-collecting parts should be related to each other. Consistent evaluation criteria should be applied to any expenditure, regardless of the government area in which it is located.

(iii) **Exclusiveness:** Only financial matters should be in the budget. However, modern analysts recognized that almost every governmental action has financial implications.

(iv) **Specification:** The budget should be executed as it is enacted. Cavalier changes should not be made during the budget year.

(v) **Annularity:** The budget should be prepared every year for the next year of agency existence.

(vi) **Accuracy:** Forecasts should be as reasonable as possible and the document should be internally consistent.

(vii) **Clarity:** The budget should describe what is proposed in understandable fashion. The document, in an effort to encompass all, should not bury policy intent in line-item detail.

(viii) Publicity: The budget in a representative democracy should not be secret. The budget contains the expenditure plan as well as the revenue estimates of the government. It is clearly contrary to the underlying principles of a democracy that such important choices are made without complete public consideration.

According to Lacasse, there are three most important budget related rules. These are: (i) comprehensiveness and a multi-year perspective in budget elaboration, (ii) the capability for monitoring implementation, and (iii) the accountability and timely adjustments. These issues in budget office-centre relations all fall under the three categories of harmonization, complementarity and co-responsibility, as discussed above. On the other hand, Wildavsky and Caiden argue that to understand what was happened to budgeting in our time consider the radical changes in the norms of desirable behaviour that used to guide budgeters. According to them, budgets emerged at the beginning of the nineteenth century as the result of reforms that replaced centuries of muddle and mismanagement with expenditure control based on norms of annularity, comprehensiveness, legislative appropriation, audit and balance. Public budgets today are evaluated against their long-term implications, they consist of many different kinds of spending, and they are unbalanced, uncertain and dependent on circumstances beyond their control.

5.1.5 Techniques of Budgeting

Budgeting is a policy process, related to organizing, managing, controlling and administrating of public revenue, expenditure and debts, that aims at achieving economic goals in a financial year as well as in long-run. Similarly, techniques of budgeting refers to the methods of budgeting to achieve the goals or objectives of budget. These are:

(i) Methods of Balancing and Unbalancing Budgeting: (a) Balanced Budget: The government budget said to be balanced when the public revenue and expenditure are equal. Balanced budget is advocated by classical economists who the opinion that the government should have limited activities limited to civil administration, police and defence so financial resources should collected through levying taxes to that extent which is just enough to meet the expenses of these activities. Under balanced budgeting, public debts are not included in public receipts and expenditure. Classical economists advocated technique of balanced budgeting to both developed and underdeveloped or developing countries. The balanced budget concept can be expressed as:

At full employment level. $Y = C + I + G$, i.e. national income is equal to total expenditure of private and government.

Y = National income, C = Total Consumption, Total Investment and G = Government Expenditure

Hence, on income-side $Y = Y_d + T$ or $Y_d = Y–T$........ (1)

Y_d = Disposal Income, T = Tax

Since disposal income is divided into consumption-spending and savings, $Y_d = C + S$ .... (2)

On expenditure-side, $Y= C + I + G$ .... (3)

By substituting the value Y of equation (3) from equation (1) it is found:

$$Y = C + I + G \therefore Y_d + T = C + I + G, \text{ since } Y_d = C + S$$
$$C + S + T = C + I + G$$

Since $Y = C + S = C + I$, the equation will be:

$$Y + T = Y + G$$

$\therefore$ $Y – Y + T= G$, hence, $T = G$, it implies that tax revenue is just equal to government expenditure. Classical economists said that the balanced budget has neutral effect on the economy so they disagree with the unbalanced budget policy or technique.

(b) Unbalanced Budget: The government budget said to be unbalanced when the public revenue and expenditure are not equal. The unbalanced budget may be 'surplus budget' or 'deficit budget'. It is said to be 'surplus budget' when public receipts are greater than public expenditures. Similarly, it is said to be 'deficit budget' when public receipts are less than public expenditures. Modern economists like Keynesians advocated the unbalanced budget as a fiscal policy instrument to achieve pre-determined objectives. They said that balanced budget is not always suitable for the economy because it fails to control economic distortions like inflation and deflation.

The 'surplus-budget' instrument can be devised to control inflation. During inflation, the profiteer class enjoys huge benefits in form of high-prices but common people and fixed-income groups would be the sufferers. The technique of surplus-budget helps the government to levy additional taxes on people who are benefited by inflation; it reduces excess purchasing power of the people by levying taxes and borrowing from money market thereby to control excess aggregate demand, on the one hand and on the other hand, it reduces unproductive or unnecessary public expenditures to reduce supply of money to fight inflation. To fight inflation, in brief, government uses surplus-budget by following the measures like imposing taxes, reducing public expenditures, borrowing from money market and postponing of repayment of public debts. The choice of these measures depends country's economic conditions.

The 'deficit-budget' instrument can be devised to control deflation or depression. All economic activities are at low ebb during depression for instance, low level of employment, income, output, consumption, investment, etc.: it is total mass discontentment period. To create budgetary deficit, the choices before government are (a) increasing public expenditure on public works, social security schemes, etc., (b) reducing and removing taxes, and (c) repayment of public debts. Deficit financing is the right technique, as recommended by J.M. Keynes, to finance the deficit budget. Under this method, government borrows from central bank of the country that issues new money or currencies which leads to increase in supply of money in the economy thereby the effective demand will be increased that will lead to increase in all economic activities, thus, economy will be recovered from depression.

In brief, the techniques of budgeting are very closely related with fiscal policy.

(ii) Methods of Budgeting in Boom and Depression: Boom and depressions are the economic situations deviated from full employment equilibrium phase. They mainly happen in advanced economies, particularly industrial economies. Classical economists have belief in market mechanism forces such as demand and supply that definitely correct these deviations in long run automatically through self-adjustment so to them budget has no role to play in these situations also. But the 'Great Depression of 1930s had falsified this classical belief and gave room to Keynes to advocate 'deficit financing policy' to recover from said depression. It mean the modern economist had the belief that the unbalanced budget is the suitable fiscal instrument to correct these deviations from full-employment equilibrium.

Boom in form of prosperity makes happening of many discontentment in the economy such as hyper-inflation, unemployment, poverty, etc. To fight the boom 'surplus-budgeting' is the appropriate fiscal instrument so government have to take measures like imposing additional taxes, reducing public expenditures borrowing from money market and recovery of debts to check increasing prices and abnormalities in economy.

Depression is also curse to the economy because it lowers the levels of all economic activities and creates mass discontentment. Deficit-budget is being used as fiscal instrument to fight the depression through measures like removing and reducing taxes, increasing public expenditures on social security schemes and autonomous investments, repayment of internal public debts and deficit financing or issuing new money in circulation.

In brief, surplus-budget technique is suitable to control boom and deficit-budget technique is suitable to control depression.

(iii) Method of Budgeting for Redistribution of Income and Wealth: According to R.A. Musgrave, distribution of income is one of the major functions of budget. The budgetary instruments like taxation policy and public expenditure policy are used to undertake redistribution of income and wealth among the people. Taxes collect funds from the rich business men and other profiteer and renter classes and public expenditure use them for benefit of poor class, it is nothing but redistribution of income and wealth. The business and investor classes gain more benefits during inflation or in other favourable situations like developmental programmes but the losers are the poor and consumers so budget is being used as a measure to redistribute income and wealth in the society.

(iv) Method of Budgeting for Economic Growth and Development: Economic development and growth are the basic issues of the modern economies. Since the modern states are committed to welfare programmes for their subjects, they have to go for deficit budgeting techniques wherein the public expenditures can be raised for capital building plants, investment activities and infrastructural development activities in commodity and service sectors. Moderate taxation and public debt policies are used on revenue side to encourage developmental activities.

Developing countries need huge funds for developmental programmes so deficit budgeting is the suitable technique, for instance, India financed its developmental programmes of five year plans by deficit-budget.

(v) Method of Budgeting for Stabilization: R.A. Musgrave argued that 'stabilization service' is another major function of budget. He further said "It is the function of this branch (in conjunction with other means of stabilization such as monetary and debt policy) to maintain an appropriate level of aggregate demand". The task of the budget is to measure the inflationary or deflationary gap and then to decide what level of taxes or transfers is required to close it. Of course budgeting for stabilization has many complications but suitable tax-policy, appropriate public expenditures and public debt policies could help to control economic distortions and maintain stability.

(vi) Method of Budgeting for Political and Social Objectives: Budget depends upon economic, social and political decision-makings. The objectives and functions of budget are decided by political and social system of the country. The democratic government budgets are different from communist governments. Since political institution is part of structure of budget, its technique depends on political decisions. Public health, public education, subsidies, social security schemes, etc. programme related budgeting depends upon political decisions related to social commitments.

5.1.6 Principles of Budgeting

Principles of budgeting are also known as 'Canons of Budget'. Budgeting is heart of administrative management; as a powerful tool it avoids duplications, wasteful and unnecessary activities, it controls costs and funds. Planning and programmes are accurately designed and materialized by budgeting. Since it is pre-audit, it disciplines and streamlines administration. Budgeting must be an effective tool of administrative management, thus, it must be governed by certain principles. Prof. Harol D. Smith has set out eight canons of budgeting. These are:

(i) **Executive Programme:** The budget is chief executive's programme. The chief executive must have adequate powers, facilities and discretions in budgetary matters. This work programme of chief executive reflects all political, economic and social responsibilities and activities of the government. Budgeting and programming are the two sides of same coin, thus, it must be under the supervision of chief executive for instance, Bureau of Budget is the chief executive and in UK, India the Finance Minister.

(ii) **Executive Responsibility:** It is the responsibility of chief executive to see that the departmental programmes are being implemented as per legislative intention with the possible minimum costs.

(iii) **Reporting:** The preparation and execution of budget are based on the reports from various departments of the government regarding revenue-receipts, expenditures on programmes and projects, work progress, etc. Budgeting without such reporting is blind and arbitrary.

(iv) **Adequate Tools:** The chief executive must have adequate administrative tools such as direct-supervision over budget, sufficient powers to execute legislative intentions in most economical way and the authority to undertake allocations monthly or quarterly.

(v) **Multiple Procedure:** Modern government performs various functions such as day-to-day administration, construction and development of long-run projects, quasi-commercial operations like buying and selling of goods, banking operations, etc. it is essential to reflect all these functions in budget. Thus, methods of budgeting differs from government's activity to activity for instance budgeting for industrial development programmes is different from that of social security schemes' programmes.

(vi) Executive Direction: The budget document must contain information of legislature and guidance of executive. It means there must be detailed guidelines concern to allotment and utilization of funds on approved projects and programmes. Meanwhile, the executive must have discretionary power to choose suitable means of operation to achieve budgetary goal.

(vii) Flexibility in Timing: The budget must have provision to permit the executive to undertake immediate adjustments to suit changing economic conditions. For example, if the budget allotted sum fund for completion of a project for the period of five years but the executive must be permitted either to increase or decrease this period as the changing conditions warrant.

(viii) Two-way Budget Organization: There should be coordination among all the departments of the government and each department must have its own budget office. So, there must be cooperation and coordination between central office and departmental offices. Budgeting and programming are joint responsibility of the both, thus, it is two-way traffic street.

5.1.7 Performance of Budgeting

(a) Meaning and Definition: 'Performance Budgeting' is a recent origin concept as it is warranted by increase in volume of public fund operations under modern context due to increasing functions and responsibilities of government. Generally, performance budgeting refers to system of presentation of public expenditure in terms of functions, programmes, performance units like projects, activities, etc. that reflecting primarily the government output and its costs. In budgetary context, the terms 'programmer or programmes budgeting' and 'performance budgeting', are more or less, inter-changeable. US Bureau of Budget defined performance budget as "As performance budget in one which present the purpose and objective for which funds are required, the cost of the programmes proposed for achieving those objective and quantitive data measuring the accomplishment and work performed under each programme". In brief, performance budgeting is a process that consists the technique and a new approach to budget formation and execution.

Under performance budgeting system the overall budget is divided into functions based on the major purpose of government and then sub-divided into programme and activities, funds are granted for doing a specific quantity of work.

However, the success of performance budgeting system depends upon the conditions discussed below:

***(i) Installation of Work Measurement and Application of Performance Standards*:** It is the first condition for the success of performance budgeting. There is no single yardstick to measure activity or performance standard, some agencies use workload and unit-cost or some other descriptive measures. The agencies must be encouraged to devise suitable methods for given performance and to determine the standards based on nature of work and past records.

***(ii) Record Keeping along Functional Lines*:** It is second condition for success of performance budgeting. Records must be kept along functional lines. An ideal reporting system must cover volume, quantity, time-extended and cost of each programme or activity accomplished or done. These records give the picture of variance between budgeted costs and actual costs and enable the executive to check off the work accomplished and work assigned. The size of such variance tells the degree of improperness in utilization of equipment, personnel, operations, etc. Some variances are remediable and some other are irremediable.

***(iii) Integration of Budgeting and Accounting Classification*:** The adequate and proper accounting support is the third condition for success of performance budgeting. Budgeting and accounting should be integrated, accurate accounts should be maintained under double entry book-keeping principle or method wherever appropriate.

***(iv) Organization for Programme Management*:** The improved organization is required for the success of performance budgeting. It should be the constant endeavor of the organs of the executive to evolve new methods, procedures, technique of operation, internal audit, etc. The programme management needs data from performance reporting.

***(v) Proper Classification of Public Expenditure*:** There are various expenditures in performance budgeting so they must be classified on the basis of their nature for instance, capital-outlay, current operational outlays, etc. They appear under different heads based on activities. They are authorized and justified separately under each major programme.

(b) Advantages of Performance Budgeting: The work-performance of budget can be measured in some areas like construction activities, education, etc. and it cannot be measured in some other areas like diplomacy, etc. Performance budgeting serves as convenient tool of management. The main advantages are:

- (i) It helps the administrators to prepare their budget on the basis of the work to be completed.
- (ii) It serves both as a tool of reviewing the efficiency of existing operations and a system of data for future programmes.
- (iii) It helps to upgrade budget decision-making on the basis of information on cost and accomplished work of the programme.
- (iv) It makes budget more meaningful in all respect and enable the taxpayers to understand it.
- (v) It is excellent instrument for translating long-term plans and programmes into reality.
- (vi) It helps for rational choice of programmes in terms of cost-benefit considerations.

(c) Difference between Programme Budgeting and Performance Budgeting: There are differences between 'programme budgeting' and 'performance budgeting'. These are:

- (i) Programme budget is a comprehensive budget and it includes several performance units whereas performance budget concentrate on the efficiency of input-output relationships in order to attain a particular budgetary goal.
- (ii) Programme budget relates to broad programmes and assist policy-making decision at top level government machinery whereas performance budget is useful for efficiency control within a particular government agency.

(iii) Programme budgeting is forward looking so it related to ex-ante plans and projects whereas performance budgeting is looking backward so it related to ex-post analysis of efficiency of action already done.

However, the objective both budgeting is to increase efficiency in decision-making.

5.1.8 Incremental and Zero Base Budgeting

These are two approaches of budgeting. They can be discussed as below:

(a) **Incremental Budgeting:** Public sector budgets in many advanced and backward countries like US, UK, India, typically rely on the incremental approach to budgeting. Under 'incremental budgeting', the previous year's budget for a department or division is carried forward for the next annual budget. It is adjusted for known factors such as new legislative requirements, additional resources, service developments, anticipated price and wage inflation and so on. It is known as incremental budgeting because the process is mainly concerned with the incremental or marginal adjustments to the current budgeted allowance. A key characteristic of the approach is that the budget preparation is a process of negotiation and compromise. The Chartered Institute for Public Finance and Accounting, Ireland (CIPFA), defined, thus it as "Incremental budgeting is therefore based on a fundamentally different view of decision-making than more rational approaches". This is because negotiated settlements between interested parties require a willingness to compromise. If consensus breaks down, compromise cannot be reached and the incremental process becomes invalid. Hence, according to CIPFA, the use of this model, therefore, requires a relatively stable form of representative government. The process incremental budgeting has the following key stages:

*(i) **Establishing the Base**:* First the committed expenditures should be decided and then the adjustments could be made to reflect unavoidable changes such as (a) full-year effects of staff appointments, (b) full-year effects of the capital programme, (c) salary increments, (d) non-recurring items which should be removed, (e) external factors, e.g. changes in legislation or

government funding regimes; changes in price levels for labour, goods and services.

(ii) Additions: Required additions could be to the implications of the development budget to reflect proposed savings and growth.

(iii) Preparation of New Budget: New budget could be prepare after aggregating all changes and additions.

However, the incremental budgeting has 'pros and cons'. These are:

(a) Advantages of Incremental Budgeting: The incremental budgeting approach has the following advantages:

- *(i)* *Easily Understood*: As it is retrospective and easily understood, the marginal changes can be done and agreement can be secured through negotiation.
- *(ii)* *More Economical*: Since it is administratively straightforward, it needs low cost.
- *(iii)* *Importance to Key Areas*: It allows policymakers to concentrate on key areas of change. Ministers, elected representatives and senior officials are not required to study long and detailed budgetary documents.
- *(iv)* *Useful in Difficult Areas*: It is useful particularly in those areas where outputs are difficult to define or quantify.
- *(v)* *Gradual Changes*: It is stable, therefore, the changes are gradual.

(b) Disadvantages of Incremental Budgeting: Despite several advantages, it suffers the following demerit:

- *(i)* *Backward Looking*: It focuses more on previous budget than future operational requirements and objectives.
- *(ii)* *No Scope*: It does not allow for overall performance overview.
- *(iii)* *Ignores Budgetary Slack*: It does not help managers identify budgetary 'slack'.
- *(iv)* *Inconsistency*: It often underpinned by data or service provision which is no longer relevant or is inconsistent with new priorities.

(v) *Inertia*: It encourages systemic inertia and 'empire building'.

(vi) *Reactive*: It tends to be reactive rather than proactive.

(vii) *Assumption*: It assumes existing budget lines are relevant and satisfactory.

To resume, it is believed by the government departments that the incremental budgeting system fits quite well into the overall public finance system. Departments and their agencies are often large and complex and fulfil a range of functions in different policy areas. Decisions can, however, sometimes be made very quickly. It can be easier to accept the distribution of most expenditure as given and to concentrate on deviations from the existing pattern. This approach, therefore, reduces the need for Ministers and senior officials to frequently spend large amounts of time dealing with reviews of budgets. However, the biggest difficulty is that it can be problematic for managers and Ministers to get an overall picture of performance. Also, the potential for inertia is a source of possible concern; the inefficient and ineffective use of resources can be perpetuated and creative thinking could be stifled.

(b) Zero-based Budgeting: It is another approach to budgeting. Unlike the incremental approach, 'Zero-based budgeting' starts from the basis that no budget lines should be carried forward from one period to the next simply because they occurred previously. Instead, everything that is included in the budget must be considered and justified. CIPFA defined zero-based budgeting in its purest form as "involves the preparation of operating budgets on the assumption that the organization is starting out afresh in the new planning period—it as is the life of the organization exists as a series of fixed-term contracts". The approach relies upon the involvement of all executive managers. It requires the organization's objectives to be clearly stated—as with any budget process—but also considers and assesses different ways of delivering those objectives before the budget is allocated. It is, therefore, less 'how should we deliver this service with the money available' and more 'here's what we have to achieve, different options for achieving it and the budget required for each of those options'.

The process requires specification of minimum levels of service provision, the current level, and an 'incremental' level—either between the minimum and the current or an improvement over the current level. Options for delivering at each level can then be evaluated and a justification put forward along with the request for resources.

This is essentially a process of providing business justification for each activity undertaken by an organization. According to CIPFA, "the analysis should also extend to considering the benefits of the activity, alternative courses of action, how to measure performance, and the consequences of not performing the activity". Activities are then ranked in order of priority and this is where resources are focused.

Like incremental budgeting, zero-base budgeting too has several merits and demerits that are discussed as under:

(a) Advantages of Zero-based Budgeting: The main advantages of zero-base budgeting are:

- *(i) Challenge*: It allows questioning of the inherited position and challenge to the status quo.
- *(ii) Focus*: It focuses the budget closely on objectives and outcomes.
- *(iii) Operational Involvement*: It actively involves operational managers rather than handing them down a budget from above.
- *(iv) Adaptive Nature*: It can be adaptive to changes in circumstances and priorities.
- *(v) Better Allocation:* It can lead to better resource allocation.

(b) Disadvantages of Zero-based Budgeting: Though it has several merits, yet it suffers several disadvantages that are discussed as under:

- *(i) Time-Consuming*: It is more time consuming than incremental budgeting that is it may become overly bureaucratic and produce excessive paperwork.
- *(ii) Need Skills*: It needs specialised skills and training.

(iii) *Difficulties*: The difficulties can arise in the identification of suitable performance measures and decision or prioritisation criteria for instance if there is insufficient information in some areas ranking them could also be problematic.

(iv) *Demotivation*: The specification of a minimum level of service provision, if below the current level, may demotivate managers.

(v) *Threatening*: The questioning of the inherited position can be seen as threatening to organisations and their people.

(vi) *Uncertainty*: It may be difficult to cost and estimate resource requirements for options different from the current practice that leads to greater uncertainty.

Despite demerits, CIPFA argued that the key benefit of a zero-based approach is that it focuses attention on "the actual resources that are required in order to produce an output or outcome, rather than the percentage increase or decrease compared to the previous year". CIPFA further argues that the technique is usually used most effectively when applied to activities that are wholly or mainly discretionary in nature—and therefore can be ceased. In many areas of public-sector activity, this will not be the case because of legislative and regulatory obligations. But CIPFA also cautions that "it is very easy to fall into the trap of assuming that something is non-discretionary for no other reason than the activity has been carrying on at a similar level for a number of years".

So, there is a need to identify first what the discretionary areas are. Then there is a need to define in measureable terms the outputs and outcomes that are required. There are parallels here with the debate over the efficiency-savings agenda. The public sector traditionally has difficulty in focusing on outcomes rather than inputs.

CIPFA recommends a phased introduction to a zero-based approach. Initially, focus should be on the less complex areas—this is to allow for budget practitioners skills and experience to be built up. Secondly, the approach should be contained to activities that are truly discretionary. Thirdly, it is suggested that the approach should be adapted so that it "becomes a consideration of the impact on service delivery of step changes up or down in resource provision".

Given the current focus on efficiency savings and the difficulties associated with establishing service-delivery baselines against which to measure the impact of proposed savings, it seems that more widespread use of zero-based budgeting techniques could be helpful. There seems to be considerable cross-over between the requirements of the budgeting approach and the requirements for proper efficiency delivery plans. For example, part of the zero-based budgeting process requires the identification of activities with clearly measurable inputs and outputs which should then be ranked in terms of priority. This is similar to the need to prioritize activities to establish where efficiency savings could be made in the lower-priority programmes.

5.1.9 Qualities of a Good Budget

The classical economists had opinion that budget does not matter or have no effect on economy. Modern economists disagree with this classical thought, to them, budget does matter or influence on economy: it is an effective instrument to control economic distortions such as inflation, depression, recession, etc. and to achieve development and growth with stability; besides, it controls problems like unemployment, poverty, etc. Hence, a sound budget should possess the following qualities or characteristics or features:

(i) Responsibility: There should be a well-defined government authority to prepare budget. In UK and India, Finance Minister is the authority to prepare budget but cabinet as a whole is responsible for it; in US Bureau of Budget prepares budget under the direction of President who is ultimately responsible for it.

(ii) Comprehensiveness: Budget should prepared in broad details that must show the entire financial position of the government and it must have explanatory statement of all sort so it can give clear picture to understand by any one.

(iii) Flexibility: A good budget must have certain degree of flexibility and should avoid too much rigidity regard to its detailed allocations. The authorities have some scope to use their discretions.

(iv) Reliability: Budget should be prepared on the basis of reliable information as much as possible. These information must be collected from reliable competent government authorities.

(v) Integrity: A good budget assures the implementation of fiscal programmes successfully through creating integrity among the various authorities concern.

5.1.10 Components of Budget

Generally, the budget contains three sets of figures. These are:

(i) The actual figures of revenue and expenditure of the previous year.

(ii) The revised estimates of revenue and expenditure of the current year.

(iii) The estimates of revenue and expenditure of the coming financial year.

The budget is prepared in two parts, namely (a) revenue budget and (b) capital budget. The components of these budgets are:

(a) Revenue Budget: It consists of the revenue receipts and revenue expenditures of the government. The details of these components are:

***(i) Revenue-Receipts*:** It is also called revenue income. It contains various sources of government income. They are broadly classified into (i) tax revenue, and (ii) non-tax revenue. The revenue collected by government through levying various taxes on people is called 'tax revenue'. Income-tax, corporate-tax, wealth-tax, death-duties, expenditure-tax, service-tax, excise-duties, customs-duties, etc. are the taxes levied on people, commodities and services by government. The revenue collected from other than taxes by government is called 'non-tax revenue'. The non-tax revenue sources are interest on loans, dividends on investment, profits of public sector undertakings, central bank of the country, fees and receipts for various government departmental services such as judicial service, revenue services, education, post and telegraph, etc.

***(ii) Revenue-Expenditures*:** The expenditure that does not create asset and the grants given to regional or state and local bodies are called revenue expenditures. The government have to spend on its day-to-day functioning through its various departments and various services offered to the people, to pay interest on borrowings and to pay subsidies, grants, etc. to people; these all constitute the total revenue-expenditures of the government.

If revenue receipts fall short of revenue expenditures, it will be 'revenue-deficit budget' or if revenue receipts exceeds the revenue expenditures, it will be 'revenue-surplus budget'.

(b) Capital Budget: It is different from 'revenue budget' means it consists of only 'capital receipts' and 'capital expenditures'. Government receives capital receipts from sources like public borrowing from the sources within the country such as household savings, money-market, central bank of the country, disinvestment of public sector undertakings, provident funds, deposit schemes, etc. and the sources from foreign countries such as foreign governments, institutions, money-market, international financial institutions, etc. The loan recoveries and borrowing loans by government also constitute the capital receipts.

The capital expenditures refer to government spending on acquisition of assets such as land, machineries, equipment, etc., purchase of shares, lending loans to regional or state governments, local bodies, public sector undertakings, investments, etc.

If capital receipts fall short of capital expenditures, it will be 'capital deficit budget' or if capital receipts exceeds the revenue expenditures, it will be 'revenue surplus budget'.

5.1.11 Theories on Budget

There are certain difficulties of applying economic theory to budgeting. Prof. Fozzard concluded "After a search of sixty years for a comprehensive theory of budgeting that would resolve the basic budgeting problem, it is somewhat disappointing to arrive at a conclusion that no such theory exists and it is unlikely that such a theory can ever be formulated [...] nevertheless, considerable progress has been made in the development of analytical techniques that support the appraisal of public expenditure decisions. Individually these techniques do not provide a satisfactory basis for resource allocation decisions, though they are more powerful when combined so that spending decisions are subject to an analysis of the underlying rationale for public intervention, the relative costs and benefits of alternative interventions and the distributional impact of spending." If, then, economic theory is imperfect in resolving the budgeting problem, what remains is to look at different approaches that have been used in the public sector and consider the advantages and disadvantages of different models. However, the attempts have been made to give appropriate economic theory to budgeting. Some of the theories and approaches are discussed as under:

(a) Normative Theory and Descriptive Theory: There are two theories in budgeting, namely (i) normative theory and (ii) descriptive theory. Irene S. Rubin gave the brief account of these theories as "Descriptive theory is based on close observation or participation in public sector activities. Theorists describe trends, sequences of events, and infer causes, paying attention to local variations as well as uniformities across cases. Normative theory advice may be based on a much narrower range of observations than descriptive theory and its proposed solutions may be based on values rather than observations. If the explanatory power of the descriptive theory is too weak, or if the advice of normative theory is not adopted by public officials or is adopted and abandoned because it does not work, the gap between theory and practice may become unacceptably wide." These theories are discussed in detail as under:

***(I) Normative Budget Theory*:** Wildavsky, Aaron and Naomi Caiden, in their book *The New Politics of the Budgetary Process*, defined normative budget theory as "...a normative theory of budgeting would be a comprehensive and specific political theory detailing what the *government's action ought to be* at a particular time. Given that the budget represents the outcome of political struggle, a normative theory of budgeting suggests the elimination of any such conflict over the government's role in society. Such a theory, therefore, is utopian in the fullest sense of the word: Its creation and acceptance would mean the end of politics." Normative budget theory is the result of budgeting debates of the economists. The theorists individually differ on particulars, but the executive budget reform proposals were generally based on a federalist model of government. Reformers looked longingly back at Hamilton's financial authority and across at the political systems of England, Switzerland and Germany. They wanted a stronger, more independent executive, more like the Prime Minister in a parliamentary form of government, and less role for parties and party caucuses; generally they sought a smaller role for legislators. These proposals led to debate on the role of the budget process in a democracy. While many reformers were concerned to limit the growth of government and the access of special interests, it mattered to them how it was to be done. They looked at the evolution of line-item controls that legislative bodies had devised to control machines and they argued that although effective in achieving their purpose, they hamstrung the executive and created less efficient government. It was not only spending control the reformers were after, but efficient government.

Public accountability was an important theme in this reform literature, and it could only be achieved by improving the quality of budget information and publicizing that information. The public as well as the legislature should understand what the government was doing and how much it was spending to achieve particular goals. These reformers did not argue that new services should not be included in the budget, only that the cost for doing so should be the lowest possible commensurate with the quality of services demanded. They therefore advocated cost accounting and detailed performance budgets based on unit costs. The assumption was that when such information was made public, there would be an outcry if one city's park services cost much more than another's.

The budget reformers at the turn of the century also emphasized the role of planning in the budget. They argued that budgets must contain a work plan and provide funding for future as well as current needs. Some of there formers went further and argued that budget planning was a way of finding and responding to unmet needs in the community. Prof. Otho Cartwright argues that members of the public should be allowed to present their case to the proper government authority. He envisioned civic societies that would advocate particular policies, such as more industrial safeguards or better sanitation in the school houses.

Some of these formers explicitly linked planning and budgeting, arguing that poor planning for growth cost more money in the end and were inefficient.

Budget planning meant at the least choosing particular target levels of service by activity and figuring out inadvance what it would cost in personnel and supplies to accomplish those specific goals. They were convinced that there was much waste in government and that expenditures could be cut back without losing much in the way of services. They did not think that changes could be implemented only at the margins. They told stories of cutting departmental budgets in half while improving services. Paralleling these early budget reformers were the public economists, who advocated some of the same kinds of reforms, but from a different theoretical perspective. While the budget reformers emphasized both the need to run government like a business and the constitutional basis for their reforms, the public economists based their arguments on what they perceived as rational choices and optimization of decision-making. Both groups emphasized the need to get the most from each unit of money, but the public economists were less concerned with cost accounting and management and more concerned with choices between options, laying out the options carefully and choosing between them on carefully specified grounds. Over the years, many specific budget reforms have been formulated and advocated, then adopted, rejected, or modified. Many of these reforms have the same goals or purposes as those of the reformers of the early 1900s. Programme budgeting, for example, and its explanation of what government is trying to accomplish at what cost, addresses specific concerns raised by the early reformers; the linking of planning to programming in the Planning Programming, Budgeting System (PPBS) was also foreshadowed many years earlier. Performance budgets, with their varied emphasis on measuring demands and workloads or efficiency and unit costs, also reflect earlier concerns. The idea of determining desired service levels, associating costs with each one, and budgeting for only desired levels of service is the heart of Zero-based Budgeting (ZBB) and Target-based Budgets, but it was also part of the early reformers' attempts to judge what was needed versus what was wanted and to get out of the budget waste that had accumulated over the years. Current models of budgeting for outcomes perfectly express the activist, efficiency, and accountability goals of the early reformers.

Normative Theory Practice: The success of normative theory and its specific evaluations of budget reforms, both specifically and generically, have often been negative. The reformers urged wide public participation in budgeting, with open hearings, advertisements, public presentation of budget exhibits, and budgets that were explanatory to the average person. Such participation was either short lived or did not materialize. Specific reforms such as Management by Objectives (MBO), Planning Performance Budgeting (PPB), and Zero-based Budgeting (ZBB) have been evaluated and declared to be failures. More generically, the increment a lists argued that many reforms required comprehensive evaluation of programmes and specific delineation of spending for specific purposes, which would have negative effects. A great number of programmes could not be compared at one time, and the effects of making spending clearer would undoubtedly be more conflict. They disapproved of the idea of bringing the public more into the budgeting process for fear of increased and conflicting demands. They argued that budgeting should not be reformed.

A review of the literature suggests that budgeters have underestimated the success of normative theory for a variety of reasons discussed as under:

(i) The first reason is that once a reform has been widely adopted, people tend to forget the role of normative theory in bringing the changes about. The idea that budgets should be tools for public accountability, and therefore should be easy to read, has been widely accepted and often inventively implemented. Even more recent and controversial recommendations for budget reform like zero-based budgeting, programme budgeting, management by objectives, and performance budgeting have been far more successful than many people in public administration have thought. Some studies suggested that many budget reforms had few or no lasting effects; in some cases they changed the budget formats but not the decision-making.

(ii) The second and final reasons that success with normative budgeting has been underestimated are that evaluators looked too quickly to find consequences and tried to find the innovation in the exact form in which it was introduced. Many of the innovations were clumsy when introduced, so that public administrators adopted and then adapted them, piecing together parts of reforms that suited their environments. The reforms were often oversold, leading to the inevitable claim that they could not deliver. "In order for major reform legislation to become law, exaggerated claims are made for its future performance." If one claims that a budget reform will reduce the federal deficit and the federal deficit remains, the reform appears to have failed, even if a variety of more modest improvements were made. Evaluations that examine the evolution of goals over time and evaluate outcomes on a scale of achievement have found budget innovations moderately successful.

Need for Improvement in Relationship between Normative Theory and Practice: The relationship of normative budget theory and practice can be improved as:

(i) A better understanding is needed of what the budget process and format can and cannot do so that reform proposals will be realistic. Greater clarity is required about the difference between being idealistic, asking for budgets to be completely transparent, for example, and suggesting budget reforms as solutions to broader problems that such reforms may influence only marginally. The former is an important part of public administration; the latter at best makes budget reform look impotent, and at worst, detracts attention from more likely solutions.

(ii) Reconsideration is needed to what accountability means and how to achieve it in budgets that allocate multiple resources on a multiple year basis. One does not want to add tax expenditures to outlays, they are different kinds of numbers and they do not meaningfully add. One does not want to include the balances in trust funds to offset the deficit, as the United States Government now does, when those funds can never be spent to reduce that deficit. So some parts of the budget should remain separate; full consolidation in the context of different types of expenditures and expenditure restrictions should not be a goal.

(iii) The openness and clarity of presentation are more urgent in the context of multiyear and multisource budgets than they were when budgets were simpler. The completeness of the budget takes on increasing importance. Are the costs of tax breaks adequately represented? How are the costs of loans presented? Are various subsidies reported? How? What about the shifting of costs through regulation of the economy? How are unfunded liabilities being reported, where, and with what accuracy? In short, what is not in the budget that should be? This avenue of budget reform needs to be continued and applied more widely at state and local levels. The appropriate level of budgetary secrecy must be re-examined. Openness of budget decision-making to the public also opens the budget process to interest groups. What level of secrecy is justified and at what potential and actual cost? The tendency has been to create budget systems that are closed on the executive side and open on the legislative side; as budget power has shifted overwhelmingly toward the executive branch, what has been the impact on public accountability and democratic government? Is the trend toward greater balance between the legislature and the executive gradually solving the problem of accountability, or is the legislature going to become more isolated or insulated as it regains more budget power?

(iv) Indicators are needed to give early warning when various processes or interests are getting out of balance, with potentially serious and unwanted consequences on the budget. Perhaps indicators need to flash a warning when the budget estimates have become too rosy. Governments need to avoid the extremes of centralization or decentralization, of executive or legislative dominance, of openness and secrecy. Perhaps a need exists to measure and monitor the swings, to give early warning of needed adjustments. It would also be useful to monitor the budget process itself for signs of excessive strain and potential future collapse. How much stress can the process take? How much delay is too much? What does failure of the budget process look like?

(v) Balance needs to be struck between pre-controls and post-controls in budget implementation. How effective have various measures to evaluate programmes been with respect to the budget? Are programme audits or even financial audits used in the preparation of new budgets? Is there a way to make such audits more useful, more accessible to more people? Varied controls are at government's disposal now, but how many are too many?

(vi) The increment a lists' model argued that no major changes in budgets from year to year and hence that few choices of policy consequence were being made in the context of the budget. These assumptions may have seemed more descriptive in the 1960s much autonomy. This is too much autonomy. The entitlement programmes had been was a problem that bothered the early created during the Great Depression reformers. If ways can be recommended to improve accountability in complex budgets, the link between taxpayers and public makers can be strengthened—If ways can be recommended to public officials to explain what they are doing and how well they are doing it, perhaps the anti-government flavour of tax revolts can be moderated.

The match between theory and practice may also be improved if budgeters learn to give conditional rather than absolute advice. It is necessary to learn when particular reforms are likely to work and when they have outlived their usefulness. If reform can be reconceptualized, reaching for a new set of ideals beyond reducing the deficit and even beyond traditional goals of increased efficiency and fiscal control, budgeters will have a better chance of affecting the future of budget practice.

***(II) Descriptive Budget Theory*:** The present and future of normative theory look gloomy without major fresh ideas because the world of budgeting has changed and many traditional reform ideas have outlived their usefulness. Descriptive theory has traditionally been weaker, but it has improved in recent years and will probably do well in the near future.

If, in normative theory, budgeters were more successful than they knew, in descriptive theory, scholarly evaluation may have been overly optimistic. Incrementalism, which was intended not only as a normative theory but also as a descriptive theory, was dominant and in many ways inadequate. It prevented many budgeters from seeing the changing budget reality in front of them and theorizing about it. As a result, theory and practice grew unacceptably far apart. Prof. Aaron Wildavsky's well-known study, *The Politics of the Budgetary Process*, emphasized the role of agencies in the budget process, assumed their desire for growth, and discussed their strategies in dealing with the congressional review process, especially the appropriations committees. The incrementalists' model left out these features, and others did not fill in the blanks for years. The 1960s and 1970s were periods change and reform in budgeting, but the incrementalists seemed ignore of it.

These studies were followed for many years with quantitative studies of budgetary outcomes that seemed to reaffirm that budgets changed little and did not involve policy choices. These models focused attention on the difference between last year's budget and this year's and the size of the increment for different departments or programmes. They made assumptions about the definition of the base budget, because the theory divided all budgets into unquestioned bases and sometimes superficially examined increments. Zero-based budgets and in fact any kind of budget trade-offs were explicitly rejected by the incremental modellers. Even those who wished to disprove the incrementalists' assumptions and conclusions followed the incrementalists' hypotheses in order to disprove them. Though there have always been a few dissenters, incrementalists theory dominated budgeting literature for close to two decades, and it focused attention away from phenomena that did not fit the theory. Only when something dramatic happened such as a constitutional crisis or a major reform, did attention shift to describing what had happened. For example, incrementalism postulates a decentralized budget process, which focused attention away from the actual level of centralization and coordination of the budget process.

Descriptive Budget Theory and Practice: The various studies on theory on budget brought a fact that the level of centralization of budget processes varies, and that theory needs to describe and explain that variation. The various most believable aspects of descriptive budget theory and the practice are dealt as:

(i) In incrementalist model, budgeters did not focus for many years on the role of the budget office as a policy formulator. Incrementalism argued that budgeting does not really deal with policy that dealt with somewhere else. Incrementalism assumes that moderate revenue growth will create a positive increment to be distributed among the departments and agencies. It did not deal with the possibility of frozen or declining revenues. One conclusion was that budgeting was both top down and bottom up, and the balance changed over time in response to environmental changes. More broadly, it meant both that the level of resource availability affected budgeting and that budget behaviour was conditional and not absolute. It also meant the budget base was not inviolable and that cuts were often not across the board.

(ii) Incrementalism had been static, arguing that changes in budgeting were few. The theory examined changes from one year to the next, down playing major historical changes. That mould has now been broken, and budgeting has a much more self-conscious concern with change. Similarly, incrementalist theory directed attention away from issues of budget trade-offs for many years. When the issue was finally addressed, it tended to be at least initially by non-budgeters, many of whom were outside public administration completely. This literature was primarily quantitative, often comparative, and generally at the national level. Many authors tried to prove statistically that trade-offs had to occur in the budget process. Even at the local level, where the level of discretion in spending is often small, budget trade-offs occur over time. At the local level, the lack of adequate descriptive theory has been acute. The most important omission has been the neglect of the linkage between municipal policy making and budgetary decisions.

(iii) Incrementalism blocked the view for many years by asserting that policy issues were not dealt with in the budget process. Recent observation suggests otherwise. Most major policy issues decided involve budgetary decisions, and most are made in the context of budgetary decision-making. Will the poor or the "well to do" bear the greater burden of taxation? What range of services will be provided, and to whom? What work will be done on what projects, and how much money will be allocated to the capital as opposed to the operating budget? How to deal with requests for grants, loans, or subsidies from social service providers, builders, or merchants? These issues routinely come up in the budget process. They do not always come up directly in the hearings between the departments and the budget office, however, which may have misled incrementalists into thinking that such decisions were not part of the budget process. The tax increase that was decided on was regressive and grouped ear marked capital funding with social services as the beneficiaries of the tax. It is difficult to imagine a more far-reaching discussion on the priorities of the definitions of need, equity, and balance between group interests. Again, this is a common policy issue raised in the context of the budget, requiring resolution in the budget through choice of projects and funding alternatives. Other policy-laden decisions occur at intervals or at periods of growth or decline. The time span of the observer has to be long enough to see these events, or the observer has to be lucky enough to come across them.

(iv) The issue that has been relatively ignored, because of the incrementalists' focus on departmental autonomy and legislative budgets, is the amount of centralized executive review of the budget proposal, the amount of policy input from the executive and the legislature in the formation of the proposal, and the level and timing of the involvement of the legislation in decision-making. In many countries, the budget process begins with a meeting between the executive and the legislation to discuss budget priorities. These priorities are then reflected in the budget that the executive proposes. Such a model implies that the departments are given guidance on what to emphasize in their proposals, and that the departments follow such guidance. This is not the only model of the budget process, but it is an important one, and, with its emphasis on central control and cooperation between the legislature and the executive, it is outside the realm of much budget theory. The budgeting looks incremental only in the sense that revenues tend to increase slowly, and most changes occur at the margins. Reorganizations-shifting and merging functions, emphasizing some tasks at the expense of others occur with considerable frequency but are not easily detected in an incremental analysis of budget totals. Detection requires a perspective that goes inside the departments. In short, many non-incremental decisions are part of the budget process and have been relatively unexplored.

Need for Improvement in Relationship between Descriptive Budget Theory and Practice: The history of the relationship between descriptive theory and practice in budgeting suggests a worsening of the relationship from the middle 1960s until the early 1980s, followed by a rapid improvement. The main needs be required to improve relation between descriptive budget theory and practice are:

(i) A moredescriptive theory is needed: A continued accumulation of good descriptive studies is needed to encourage budgeters to theorize about trends and causation.

(ii) The openness and variety should be the guiding principles: Exploration of everything that might be relevant is necessary. In other words, there is need for the exploration of the relationship between budgeting and society and the link between budget processes and democracy.

(iii) Need to look at the trends over time: There is need for effort to link changing environmental conditions (private and public sectors), budget processes, and budget outcomes.

However, budget theory has been too restrictive about what is important for too long period. The work of budgeting is complex, thus, no simple theory will ever be adequate to describe it.

Conclusion: The reviews on recent budgeting thoughts laid down the conclusion that "The relationship between budget theory and practice has been different, depending on whether one was looking at normative or descriptive theory. On the normative side, budget theory has generally been more successful than imagined; that is, it has set attractive goals that have often been a guide for behaviour. On the side of descriptive or even predictive theory, budget theory has been much weaker, often unable to see the phenomena in plain view to theorize about their meaning." They further argued that the projecting to the near future, successes in normative theory may be limited unless budget theory can formulate some recommendations that address the complexity of modern multifunction, multisource, multiyear budgets; by contrast, descriptive research has improved enormously in recent years, and the near future for descriptive theory looks bright. The budgeters have regained the ability to see the thing before them that are beginning to recapture the ability to theorize from what in fact is there. The field is poised for a mushrooming of descriptive theory over the next few years. The match between descriptive theory and practice will almost certainly improve over the next decade. According to these reviews, unfortunately, recent proposals for reform have often been attempts to curb the deficit or curb the level of national spending. The result has been a series of unrelated, and sometimes worn-out proposals, many of which have little potential for success. But perhaps the growth in descriptive theory will suggest some useful reforms.

(b) Classical Balanced Budget Theory: Classical economists much believed in deep-rooted belief "Principle of Sound Finance". They assumed laissez-faire policy, perfect competition, full-employment, automatic adjustment between market forces and free-play of market mechanism. Principle of sound finance means "the best government spends least and imposes the lowest amount of taxes". So they advocated "Principle of Balanced Budget". Wherein the government has limited role or functions to play such as defence, administration, internal law and order maintenance. The social and economic services or activities are out of government's purviews. So, to them, the balanced budget does not matter or no influence on the economy. The surplus or deficit budget is unnecessary because, for example, under surplus budget the additional taxes transfer the money from private sector to government thereby reduces private expenditures on goods and services on the one hand, on the other, the government expenditure on unproductive activities increase that disturbs the economy. Besides, the public borrowing for the purpose of public expenditures make the government irresponsible and extravagance.

Classical economists advocate the balanced budget policy or theory because it has the following advantages:

(i) It maintains the balance between government income and expenditure, it is sign of solvency.

(ii) It has capability of self-adjustment between economic forces in long-run so needs no imbalance budget policy.

(iii) It has neutral impact on economic system so it initiate neither boom nor depression.

(iv) The annually balanced budget is politically desirable and could discipline the politicians' tendency and control extravagance.

(v) It is fully consistent with the classical assumption of full-employment equilibrium so no deviations from it.

The classical budget theory was in practice till outbreak of '1930s Great Depression'. Moreover, the theory had some limitations that are summarized as:

(i) Its neutral effect on economy is objectionable: Classical assumptions such as automatic adjustment, full-employment, etc. are unacceptable in reality. The expansionary effects of balanced budget takes the economy to boom wherein the increased income, prices, profits, etc. raises tax revenue even at unchanged tax rates thereby it results into surplus in budget. So the balance budget has no neutral effect as such.

(ii) It has destabilizing effect on the economy: The disturbances in market forces due to changes in endogenous or exogenous factors may result into either inflation or deflation. To correct these distortions the balance budget either increase or decrease tax rates and public spending but that too further destabilize the economic situations.

(iii) It creates economic inequalities among nations: Gunnar Myrdal has pointed out that when free play of market forces are uncontrolled it creates income inequalities within the country and between the nations.

(iv) It is unsuitable to underdeveloped and developing countries: For development these countries depend upon investment efforts of the government.

(c) Optimal Budget Theory: The optimum budget theory is propounded by Prof. Richard A. Musgrave. This theory is also known as 'Normative Theory' or 'Theory of Optimal Budget Policy' or 'Multiple Theory'. For need of this theory R.A. Musgrave states "The requirement is obvious, but it is not easily met. For one thing, the nature of budget policy is too heterogeneous to permit a unitary explanation. Various functions must be distinguished and dealt with separately, even though they are part of an interdependent system. For another, certain aspects of the problem lead us into the thin air of welfare economics, where as yet the oxygen has been prone to give out before the peak was scaled." Further, he observed "while operations of public household involve money flow of receipts and expenditure, the basic problems are not issues of finance. They are not concerned with money, liquid or capital markets. Rather, they are problems of resources allocation, the distribution of income, full-employment, price level stability and growth". In a nutshell, budget policy is both positive and normative science since the process of public expenditures have socio-economic effects. In approaching the design of a multiple budget theory Prof. Musgrave distinguish between three major budget functions. These include (i) the function of providing for the satisfaction of public wants (service-branch), (ii) the function of providing for adjustments in the distribution of income (distribution-branch), and (iii) the function of contributing to stabilization (stabilization-branch). Further, functions are also added in the discussion of the theory. He assumed that the fiscal department of government is divided into three branches, viz. service-branch, distribution-branch and stabilization-branch, to deal with these functions respectively. He shown how the sub-budgets of the various branches are determined as parts of an interdependent system and how a consolidated budget is derived by a clearing process. The functions of these branches achieve the main three objectives of budget-policy, viz. allocation of resources and social services, distribution of income and economic stability, through fiscal instruments such as taxation, public spending and borrowing. These are discussed as:

***(i) Allocation of Resources and Service Branch*:** According to Prof. Musgrave, the main objective of this branch to take optimal allocation of resources to satisfy public wants. Hence, he said "Its function is to decide just what public wants should be satisfied, how much of such want satisfaction should be provided for, and who should bear the cost". These objectives will be met by the operation of the other two branches. The problem, then, is to provide for the satisfaction of public wants free of direct charge, and paid for out of general tax revenue.

While discussing the distinction between public and private wants, Prof. Musgrave emphasized on an essential similarity between the both that is both are individual wants; but the fundamental difference between the two is that private wants of individuals are being supplied and satisfied by the varying amounts whereas the goods and services supplied in the satisfaction of public wants must be consumed in equal amount by all. Prof. Musgrave said that this has two implications:

(i) There is a difference in the competitive solution of market price of private and public (social) goods and services. A market demand schedule for goods and services supplied in the satisfaction of private wants could be derived by adding individual demand schedules horizontally. The competitive equilibrium price is determined at the point where this market demand schedule intersects the supply schedule. Depending upon their particular preferences, individuals will consume goods and services, varying amounts, at the same price according to their individual preference. For instance, 'A' consumes 10 kg and 'B' 5 kg and 'C' 1 kg of apple at price ₹ 120 per kg.

But in case of a market demand schedule for goods and services supplied in the satisfaction of public wants, individual demand schedules must be added vertically, as first noted by Prof. Bowen. It implies that all individuals must consume the same amount of public goods and services by paying different prices. For instance consumer 'X', 'Y' and 'Z' consume 10 kg sugar each at different prices respectively ₹ 40, ₹ 25 and ₹ 10 per kg.

(ii) The second and more important implication is the fact that this analogy between price determinations in the two cases breaks down once it is viewed as an operational solution. The demand schedules for the satisfaction of private wants are revealed in the auction process of the market but it is not so in case of the satisfaction of public wants. Since the same amount public goods and services will be consumed by all, individuals know that they cannot be excluded from the resulting benefits. This being the case, they are not forced to reveal their preferences through bidding in the market. Thus, 'exclusion principle' cannot be applied and the market mechanism does not work in case of public wants or goods and services.

Prof. Wicksell recognized this problem clearly and suggested a political process of decision-making as a measure to solve this problem. But the decision by voting is not unanimous so the result will not be optimal. However, the voting mechanism must be designed so as to approximate a true statement of preferences, and hence come as close as possible to that solution which would be obtained if the 'exclusion principle' and the forces of the market could be applied. The search for the best method of voting related to Prof. Arrow's recent work in welfare economics. The case for majority vote follows from Arrow's third condition that the result must not be influenced by the dropping out of 'irrelevant' alternatives. If this condition is adopted, the plurality or majority vote is disqualified. On the contrary, it seems that all alternative budget arrangements should be considered as relevant, so that the results of plurality or even point voting may well be superior to those of majority rule. Thus, it is the problem of the 'Service Branch' so its budget must be balanced and the function of taxation in this first context is to place the cost of public want satisfaction with those whose wants are being satisfied.

According to Prof. Musgrave, this approach relate to some of the earlier views on fiscal theory. There is a direct lineage or background to the benefit approach, more specifically to its basic proposition that public services should be related to the people's wants for such services. Similarly, Lindahl's formulation provides an optimal result and not as an operational solution. Lindahl's theory becomes a voluntary payment approach and overlooks the crucial fact that public wants are not subject to the 'exclusion principle'. Hence, public wants are not revealed on a voluntary basis and the proper solution cannot be found through the market. It can be approximated only through a political process and compulsion in applying the decision reached by vote. The 'ability-to-pay principle' has the initial advantage of viewing the problem as outside the market, but beyond this it is seriously defective and bears little relation to the approach. To Musgrave, ability-to-pay principle, including thoughts of J.S. Mill, Edgeworth and Pigou, have concerned themselves with the tax side of the problem only. In other words, they have disregarded the problem of the 'Service Branch' altogether. 'Least total sacrifice' as the basic criterion of tax policy is a principle in distribution rather than in selecting public services and allocating their cost. If it is to be accepted as the principle by which the cost of public services should be allocated, then the same reasoning points to a general rearrangement of the distribution of income, beyond the arbitrary limit set by the size of the 'service budget'. In other words, the ability-to-pay approach deals with matters pertaining to the 'Distribution Branch' rather than the 'Service Branch'. Multiple pricing in the context of the 'Service Branch' reflects differences in effective demands for the satisfaction of public wants, based on a given distribution of income. Thus, it should not be confused with distributional adjustments undertaken by the 'Distribution Branch'. Further Musgrave argues "A case for progression at the level of the Service Branch follows if the income elasticity of demand for public wants typically exceeds unity. It has nothing to do with the slope of income utility schedules, traditionally considered the determinant of the proper degree of progression".

(ii) Distribution of Income Branch: According to Prof. Musgrave, it is second important function and branch of public budget. The functioning of this branch is based on the assumption that the other branches will meet their objectives, i.e. that public wants are provided for and that full employment is maintained. Prof. Musgrave argued that the tax transfer mechanism of the public budget furnishes an efficient tool to accomplish society wishes to undertake distributional adjustments and one that provides least interference with the market. For the just adjustments, the 'least total sacrifice or maximum welfare approach' of the old welfare economics should be applied. However, the assumptions of equal and comparable utility schedules, underlying the Edgeworth Pigou type of analysis, are too dubious to permit objective conclusions, even if the goal of maximum total welfare is accepted. Prof. Musgrave said that the proper 'state of distribution' cannot be derived as a simple exercise in maximization from a given set of utility schedules; it is a problem of social choice. So it shifts the burden from determining the proper distribution of income to determining the proper distribution of votes.

A value judgement of some sort lies at the bottom of any solution to the distribution problem. However, it may be assumed for present purposes that the 'proper state of distribution' is to be determined by social choice, based on an equal distribution of votes and with due allowance for its effects upon economic efficiency and social structure. A tax transfer plan could be used for distributional read justments. In other words, the distribution-branch through its balanced budget instruments like taxes and transfers must achieve desired distributional corrections.

***(iii) Stabilization Branch*:** It is the third major function of budgetary policy. Prof. Musgrave agreed the reality that an uncontrolled free economy leads to drastic fluctuations in price, employment and other economic variables. Thus, according to Musgrave, there is need for designing the budgetary policy to achieve the goals such as price-stability, high employment, and soundness of foreign accounts and acceptable rate of economic growth. It is the function of this branch, in conjunction with other means of stabilization such as monetary and debt policy, to maintain an appropriate level of aggregate demand. The stabilization-branch must take this task with a given service-branch budget and a given 'proper state of distribution'. In other words, the task of the stabilization-branch is to determine the inflationary or deflationary gap in the absence of stabilizing action and to decide what level of taxes or transfers is required to close it, in spite of many complications. The budget of the stabilization-branch consists of either transfers or taxes. The function of taxes and transfers in this case is to check inflation or deflation. The budget of this branch is always unbalanced except for the very special case where a zero level of taxes and transfers is called for. Prof. Musgrave, further, argued that taxes or transfers will be distributed in line with the 'proper distribution of income' established by the distribution-branch, i.e. they will be proportional to income after adjustment by the distribution-branch but before taxes of the service-branch.

***(iv) Simultaneous Determination of Sub-budgets*:** Prof. Musgrave contended that the functioning of three sub-budgets shows how each branch pursues its objectives on the assumption that the others accomplish theirs. In other words, the three sub-budgets are determined as parts of a simultaneous system.

In the budget of the service-branch, it determines the satisfaction of public wants and their cost allocation on the basis of individual preferences. In other words, we have demand functions for such wants based on preferences, relative prices of goods supplied in the satisfaction of various public and private wants, and a given state of distribution. The state of distribution given for this purpose will include earnings plus distribution and stabilization-branch transfers, minus distribution and stabilization branch taxes. The service-branch budget will be usually balanced.

In the budget of the distribution-branch, it determines the distribution of earnings at full employment and decide what adjustments should be made to obtain the 'proper state of distribution'. The resulting tax-transfer system again leaves with a balanced budget.

In the budget of the stabilization-branch, it determines total earnings at full employment and current prices. The total demand will be determined in the absence of stabilization and the inflationary or deflationary gap that need be closed will be found-out. Given the marginal propensity to consume with the 'proper state of distribution', the necessary level of taxes or transfers is determined and distributed accordingly. The stabilization-branch budget, if operative at all, will consist of taxes or transfers only and hence has either a deficit or a surplus.

***(v) Consolidation of Sub-Budgets*:** Prof. Musgrave further advocates that after determination of three sub-budgets each might be put into effect by itself, but this would be a clumsy administrative procedure. The service-branch budget expenditures on goods and service must be carried out in such a way that the taxes or transfers of the 'Service, Distribution and Stabilization Branches' might be cleared against each other so that each individual will make one tax payment or will receive one transfer cheque only. The consolidated or administered budget should show a net deficit or surplus equal to that of the budget of the stabilization-branch.

The consolidation of the sub-budgets into a net plan facilitates administrative procedures but it must not overlook the facts (i) the consolidated budget merely an outcome of clearing and (ii) it hides the more important underlying policy objectives determined by sub-budgets. For instance, in case of the income elasticity of individual demands for public wants was typically unity then taxes of the service-branch must be allocated in a more or less proportional fashion; similarly the tax-transfer scheme of the distribution-branch must transfer income from high to low groups if it is held desirable to achieve a certain degree of equalization. The tax structure of the consolidated budget would then still be progressive but less than for the distribution-branch alone.

(vi) Advantages of Division of Functions: According to Prof. Musgrave, the division of budget-functions has several advantages that are discussed as:

(a) Advantage of separation of 'Service and Stabilization Branches': The budgets of both branches are planned on the basis of the assumption of full-employment so they give importance for optimal utilization of given resources. Thus, the separation of functions has the advantage that it rules out ditch digging to check a depression as well as curtailing teachers' salaries or essential public works to check a boom. In other words, the indicated separation helps to eliminate distortions in the politics of fiscal policy.

(b) It helps support fiscal measures to control depression or boom: It has the advantage of permitting the individual with low preferences for public wants to support fiscal measures against depression. Moreover, it has advantage of permitting individual with high preferences for public wants to support fiscal measures to check a boom.

(c) Advantage of separation of service and distribution branches: Prof. Musgrave said that if the two functions are distinguished properly, the two tax plans are free to follow different patterns, and more efficient budget determination becomes possible. For example, this division of functions has the advantage of permitting an individual with higher rate public

wants to vote for a large service-branch budget even though he does not favour income redistribution and *vice versa* for someone who favours distributional adjustments but opposes a large budget in the service-branch.

(d) Advantages of separation of stabilization and distribution branches: There are obvious advantages (i) if the appropriate use of fiscal policy as a stabilization device is not interfered with by fears or hopes that such changes will carry the by-product of distributional adjustments, and (ii) if distributional objectives can be formulated without having to allow for the possibility that one or another state of distribution may result in a higher or lower level of demand, in the absence of appropriate adjustments by the stabilization-branch.

(vii) Criticisms: Of course, everyone will agree that separation of three major branches to perform the budgetary-functions is good, but there are various objections have been raised to such a separation. These are:

(a) *Objections of a pragmatic sort*: It is associated with the separation of service and stabilization branches. Prof. Samuelson's argument is that the very occurrence of a depression is evidence of the fact that there results a shift in individual preferences from private to public wants. Since the want pattern must be related to the allocation of resources at full employment, any decline in expenditures for the satisfaction of private wants must be taken to reflect an increase in the demand for the satisfaction of public wants. This invalidates the basic proposition that resource use for the satisfaction of public wants should be planned in a full-employment context unless such special circumstances intervene.

(b) *Favouring of particular groups*: In separation of service and distribution branches the first fact is to be objected is that goods and service expenditures of government frequently involve programmes which are not distributionally neutral means they favour particular groups. For example, free hospitals for the poor or public subsidies to low cost housing programmes. As far as

free-hospital programme is concerned it is redistribution function so budget of the distribution-branch ought to be taken care of it. It is a transfer payment to low income people. Whereas in case of subsidies programme it is a quite different matter. Here as in the case of sumptuary taxes public policy aims at interference with individual preferences and, frequently, such interference carries redistributional implications, of course interference of this sort is not always bad. It may not result in an improved allocation of resources.

(c) *It endangers the essential content of budget schemes*: The separation of service and distribution branch is more serious and comes closer to endangering the essential content of budget schemes. It is noted that any concept of efficiency in resource allocation in response to given preference patterns must relate to a given state of distribution. If distribution is arbitrary, there is little point in adapting resource allocation to effective demands.

(d) *The separation of distribution and stabilization branch is contrast to stabilization policy*: 'Taxes ought to be progressive in the slump and regressive in the boom' is a matter of stabilization policy. The separation of distribution and stabilization branch is to be contrasted to stabilization policy. Possible effects of distributional changes upon the level of output at full employment are a different matter and must, of course, be taken into account.

To conclude the theory, Prof. R.A. Musgrave states: "In concluding, let me add that I do not recommend translation of this multiple budget plan into immediate legislative and administrative practice. While some practical applications may be possible, my primary concern here is with the components of a normative theory of the public household. The construction of such a theory, I believe, remains the heart of what is hopefully referred to as the Science of Public Finance; and it need be straightened out before we can go very far in being helpful on the practical level."

5.1.12 Differences between Public and Private Sector Budgeting

Generally, in broad terms, the objectives of a budget are the same in both public and private sectors but they operate under the different environmental conditions that leads to certain differences between them. These are shown in following Table 5.1:

Table 5.1: Differences between Public and Private Sector Budgeting

Private Sector	Public Sector
1. Budget will be prepared on the basis of private individual, institution or corporate body decisions depending on market conditions.	1. Budget will be prepared on the basis of political decisions. Acceptable level of taxation determined first and then total resources generated by taxation are rationed between services by political decision. Budgets largely fixed for the year once the political decision has been made.
2. Senior managers are accountable to shareholders for financial performance. Management is relatively free to determine details of budget, since profit that matters to shareholders.	2. Politicians are responsible for determining service priorities. The senior managers are accountable to politicians and other stakeholders for delivery. The process to budget creation includes political input.
3. The performance is defined by relating value of sales to financial inputs. There is control emphasis on profit.	3. Outputs are often non-financial. The control emphasis is upon keeping costs within budget and on the use of non-financial indicators of performance.
4. Resources influenced by market demand.	4. Resources controlled by government through grant settlements.
5. Need for flexibility	5. Fixed budgets
6. Profit oriented	6. Service/community oriented
7. Single or limited number of objective(s)	7. Multi (and often conflicting) objectives
8. Decisions made by:	8. Decisions made by:
• Shareholders	• Electorate
• Customers	• Service Users
• Workforce	• Employees
• Management	• Management
• Board	• Politicians

However, the above distinctions are a broad generalization. In the last three decades, the boundaries between public and private sectors have become blurred. Some public services have developed trading activities and have become more market orientated, hence to some extent moving towards the private sector model.

Nevertheless, these key differences will influence the approach which public sector bodies take to budgeting particularly in relation to the need for processes and procedures to be adapted to reflect the external environment in which they operate and translate this into the setting of budget requirements.

5.2 FISCAL POLICY

Before the Great Depression in the United States, the government's approach to the economy was laissez-faire. But following the Second World War, it was determined that the government had to take a proactive role in the economy to regulate unemployment, business cycles, inflation and the cost of money. By using a mixture of both monetary and fiscal policies governments are able to control economic phenomena. The formulation of fiscal policy and its mixture with monetary policy is depend upon the political orientations and the philosophies of those in power at a particular time, one policy may dominate over another.

The theory of fiscal policy owes much to North European economists such as Jan Tinbergen, Bent Hansen, Leif Johansen, and others who five decades ago developed it. In spirit, if not in geography, Richard Musgrave could be placed among this group. There were obviously also contributors from North America such as Alvin Hansen, Lawrence Klein, Abba Lerner, Robert Solow, Paul Samuelson, and others, but, in their writing, they focused mostly on the stabilization role of fiscal policy. The Keynesian stabilization policy is only a part, though an important part, of the modern theory of fiscal policy. In the conception of this theory, especially well developed in Musgrave's and in Johansen's treatises, the goals of fiscal policy extend beyond stabilization because fiscal tools can be used also for redistributing income and for reallocating resources.

5.2.1 Meaning and Definition

The term fiscal comes from the Latin word fiscalis which in turn comes from fiscus, i.e. a basket used for collecting money. In Italian 'il fisco' refers to the agency that collects taxes. Thus, 'fiscal policy' means policy related to taxes. The same is the case in Spanish, French, and Portuguese. In English, the expression 'fiscal policy' was apparently first used by Edwin R.A. Seligman, a prominent professor of public finance at Columbia University in the early part of the 20th century. He used the expression to criticize Adolf Wagner, a German economist, who had suggested that governments should engage in some redistribution of income through their budgetary activities. This seems to be the genesis of the 'redistribution branch' of the trilogy made popular by Richard Musgrave. The Keynesian revolution changed the meaning of fiscal policy moving it away from the tax or revenue side of the budget to include both revenue and spending. For the Keynesians, fiscal policy refers to the manipulation of taxes and public spending to influence aggregate demand. Thus, we had the genesis of the 'stabilization branch' in Musgrave's trilogy.

Moreover, some economists tried to give precise definition on fiscal theory and policy. The important definitions are as:

(i) **Prof. Arthur Smithies:** Prof. Arthur Smithies defines fiscal policy as "a policy under which the government uses its expenditure and revenue programmes to produce desirable effects and avoid undesirable effects on the national income, production and employment was practically unknown".

(ii) **Harvey and Joanson M.:** Harvey and Joanson defined fiscal policy as "changes in government expenditure and taxation designed to influence the pattern and level of economic activity".

(iii) **Maurice W. Lee:** Prof. Lee defined fiscal policy as "fiscal policy relates to the government decision-making with respect to (1) taxation, (2) government spending, (3) government borrowing, and (4) the management of government debt".

The very contents of the definitions state, in brief, that fiscal policy is the means by which a government adjusts its levels of spending in order to monitor and influence a nation's economy. It is the sister strategy to monetary policy with which a central bank influences a nation's money supply. These two policies are used in various combinations in an effort to direct a country's economic goals.

Fiscal policy involves the government changing the levels of taxation and govt. spending in order to influence 'Aggregate Demand' ($AD = C + I + G + X - M$) and therefore the level of economic activity. Fiscal policy is based on the theories of British economist John Maynard Keynes. Also known as Keynesian economics, this theory basically states that governments can influence macroeconomic productivity levels by increasing or decreasing tax levels and public spending.

5.2.2 The Purposes or Objectives of Fiscal Policy

Fiscal policy is one of the main ways in which government tries to influence overall economic performance of the country. It has fiscal instruments such as taxation, public expenditure, public borrowing and deficit finance to achieve its objectives. A sound fiscal policy encourages sustainable economic growth and prevents the wild deviations or distortions in the economy. Musgrave and other modern economists pointed out the various purposes or objectives of the fiscal policy as discussed under:

(i) Optimal Allocation of Resources: Prof. Musgrave contended that the optimal or efficient allocation of resources between private and public sector is the essential objective of fiscal policy. Fiscal policy aims at the satisfaction of public wants or social goods and services. The market mechanism has several failures and imperfections or inefficiencies such as uneven distribution of resources, neglect of public wants as they yield low returns, neglect of social-costs, inefficient firms, monopolism, etc. The fiscal policy uses its regulatory measures such as free entry of firms, tax-subsidies to decreasing-cost industries, etc., to remove market imperfections. Meanwhile the government withdraw resources from private sector through fiscal measures and spend for production of social goods and services by maintaining equality between cost of withdrawing resource from private sector and benefits of satisfaction of public wants.

(ii) Distribution of Income and Wealth: 'Fair and just' distribution of income and wealth is the important objective of fiscal policy. In market economy, the distribution of income and wealth depends upon factors like laws of inheritance, talents, availability of opportunities, social mobility and market structure that may often lead to uneven distribution on income and wealth. According to Musgrave, the fiscal policy should aim at improvement in economic efficiency means the economic condition of the individual 'A' should be improved through fiscal measures without disturbing or deteriorating economic conditions of other individuals 'B' and 'C'. In other words, taxes should be levied on persons according to their ability-to-pay and the tax revenue or revenue of the government should be spent on the programmes that improve the economic conditions of the poor. So fiscal policy undertakes the re-distribution of income and wealth among people through its measures leaving taxpayers position intact. It, thus, establishes economic equality or justice in the country.

(iii) Economic Stabilization and Full-Employment: To attain economic stability is the main concern of the modern economies. Fiscal policy is being used as a measure to control economic instability or distortions. Inflation, deflation, recession and recovery are the economic-distortions or instabilities. These instabilities create ups and downs or fluctuations in economic activities like employment, prices, income, investment, output, consumption, etc. in the economy. Fiscal policy is being devised to control these instability to maintain the stability of employment and price at possible high level. It all depends upon the type of economic instability. These are discussed as:

***(a) Inflation and Fiscal Policy*:** Inflation occurs due to various reasons, thus, accordingly the fiscal measures are to be devised. In case of inflation due to excess demand for goods and services, levy of taxes, raising of existing tax-rates, reducing government expenditure on unproductive activities, public borrowing, etc. fiscal measures are being used to fight inflation.

***(b) Deflation and Fiscal Policy*:** Deflation is the opposite economic situation of inflation. It occurs due to various reasons, thus, accordingly the fiscal measures are to be devised. In case of deflation due to deficiency in demand for goods and services, removal of taxes, lowering of existing tax-rates, increasing government expenditure on both productive and non-productive activities, redemption of public debts, etc. fiscal measures are being used to fight deflation.

***(c) Recession and Fiscal Policy*:** Recession is the economic situation where economic activities move downwards from full-employment equilibrium level. It takes economy to depression. To control recession the fiscal measures such as tax-reduction, increasing government expenditure, public debts redemption, etc. measures should be used along with monetary measures like reduction in interest rate, increase in supply of money, etc.

***(d) Recovery and Fiscal Policy*:** It is economic situation that recovering or reviving economic activities from bottom of depression and taking them to full-employment equilibrium level. The deflation control fiscal measures are to be further strengthened to take economy to the full-employment level. To maintain economic stability at full-employment level, the fiscal stabilizers are being used that are discussed as under:

(i) Automatic Fiscal Stabilizers: The fiscal measures, like taxation, public spending, public debts and deficit financing, inbuilt in such a way they work automatically as economic situation warrant:

- If the economy is growing with inflation, people will automatically pay more taxes such as VAT and income tax and the government will spend less on unemployment benefits. The increased tax and lower public spending will act as a check on aggregate demand.
- In a recession, the opposite will occur with tax revenue falling but increased government spending on benefits, this will help increase aggregate demand.

(ii) Discretionary Fiscal Stabilizers: This is a deliberate attempt by the government to affect aggregate demand and stabilize the economy, e.g. in a boom the government will increase taxes to reduce inflation.

(iv) Economic Development and Growth: The market economy failures have raised the importance of fiscal policy operations in modern economies. Economic development and growth with stability have become the main objective of modern economies. Public spending is used to supply public or social goods that has encouraging the development of both private and public sectors as they function side by side in countries like India. Infrastructural development, mass-education, public health programmes, etc. by public spending have raised national income and output as well as improvement in quality of life of the people. India and other countries have been achieving higher rate of economic growth because of pragmatic role being played by the fiscal policy instruments or 'Fine-Tuning'.

5.2.3 Evaluation and Criticism of Fiscal Policy

Fiscal policy is the use of government spending and taxation to influence the level of economic activity. In theory, fiscal policy can be used to prevent inflation and avoid recession. But, in practice, there are many limitations of using fiscal policy. The evaluation and criticism of fiscal policy are discussed as under:

(i) Middle Class is being Affected Much: Unfortunately, the effects of any fiscal policy are not the same on everyone. Depending on the political orientations and goals of the policy-makers, a tax cut could affect only the middle class, which is typically the largest economic group. In times of economic decline and rising taxation, it is this same group that may have to pay more taxes than the wealthier upper class. Similarly, when a government decides to adjust its spending, its policy may affect only a specific group of people. A decision to build a new bridge, for example, will give work and more income to hundreds of construction workers. A decision to spend money on building a new space shuttle, on the other hand, benefits only a small, specialized pool of experts, which would not do much to increase aggregate employment levels.

(ii) Disincentives of Tax Cuts: Increasing taxes to reduce aggregate demand may cause disincentives to work, if this occurs there will be a fall in productivity and aggregate supply could fall. However, higher taxes do not necessarily reduce incentives to work if the income effect dominates.

(iii) Side Effects on Public Spending: Reduced government spending to increase aggregate demand could adversely affect public services such as public transport and education causing market failure and social inefficiency.

(iv) Poor Information: Fiscal policy will suffer if the government has poor information. For example, if the government believes there is going to be a recession, they will increase aggregate demand, however, if this forecast was wrong and the economy grew too fast, the government action would cause inflation.

(v) Time Lags: If the government plans to increase spending this can take along time to filter into the economy and it may be too late. Public spending plans are only set once a year. There is also a delay in implementing any changes to spending patterns.

(vi) Budget Deficit: Expansionary fiscal policy, cutting taxes and increasing government spending, will cause an increase in the budget deficit which has many adverse effects. Higher budget deficit will require higher taxes in the future and may cause crowding-out.

(vii) Other Components of Aggregate Demand: If the government uses fiscal policy its effectiveness will also depend upon the other components of aggregate demand, for example, if consumer confidence is very low, reducing taxes may not lead to an increase in consumer spending.

(viii) Impact of Fiscal Policy Depends on Multiplier: The multiplier effect may the change in injections to circular flow of income. Therefore, the size of the multiplier will be considered as significant factor in influencing economic activities.

(ix) Crowding-Out: Increased government spending to increased aggregate demand may cause "Crowding out". Crowding-out occurs when public spending increase results in decreasing the size of the private sector. For example, if the government increase spending it will have to increase taxes or sell bonds and borrow money, both method reduce private consumption or investment. If this occurs aggregate demand will not increase or increase only very slowly.

(x) Decline Economic Welfare: Classical economists argue that the government is more inefficient in spending money than the private sector, therefore, there will be a decline in economic welfare.

(xi) Pressure on Interest-Rate: Increased government borrowing can also put upward pressure on interest rates. To borrow more money the interest rate on bonds may have to rise, causing slower growth in the rest of the economy.

(xii) Monetarist Critique: Monetarists argue that in the long-run aggregate supply is inelastic therefore an increase in aggregate demand will only cause inflation to increase further. Fiscal policy was particularly used in the 1950s and 1960s to stabilize economic cycles. These policies were broadly referred to as 'Keynesian' in the 1970s and 1980s governments tended to prefer monetary policy for influencing the economy.

There are the many factors which make successful implementation of fiscal policy more difficult in practice.

To sum-up, one of the biggest obstacles facing policymakers is deciding how much involvement the government should have in the economy. Indeed, there have been various degrees of interference by the government over the years. But for the most part, it is accepted that a degree of government involvement is necessary to sustain a vibrant economy, on which the economic well-being of the population depends.

5.2.4 Types of Fiscal Policy

Fiscal policy is one of the main ways in which government tries to influence overall economic performance in the modern economies. The two main types of fiscal policy are expansionary and contractionary policy. Both involve the use of the government's budget and its ability to levy taxes.

(i) Expansionary Fiscal Policy: Expansionary fiscal policy uses increased government spending, reduced taxes or a combination of the two. The chief objective of a fiscal expansion is to increase aggregate demand for goods and services across the economy as well as to reduce unemployment. Governments often enact expansionary measures during an economic recession, when unemployment rises and output decreases. By boosting its own purchases of goods and services, government tries to stimulate the economy. During the 1930s, the U.S. Government used expansionary fiscal policy to combat the effects of the Great Depression.

According to Professor Gregory Mankiw, a Harvard economist and former White House adviser, the 'expansionary fiscal policy' has a multiplier effect, in which each unit of money spent by government generates additional demand across the economy, for example, if the Defense Department orders additional parts and equipment from a defense contractor, those purchases raise production and employment at the contractor. The firm's employees increase their spending on consumer goods, illustrating the multiplier effect resulting from a fiscal expansion.

(ii) Contractionary Fiscal Policy: When government policy-makers cut spending or increase taxes, they engage in contractionary fiscal policy. Governments may enact contractionary measures to slow an economic expansion and prevent inflation. In addition, governments may enact contractionary policy for ideological reasons. These include reducing the overall size and scope of government activity or lowering budget deficits, in which the government spends more money than it collects. Besides, the contractionary policy reduces aggregate demand in the economy by lowering inflation. But it may also lead to higher unemployment.

Economic fluctuations independent of policy actions by government often affect the level of tax revenues, forcing elected officials to alter fiscal policy. For example, economic recessions reduce output and employment, resulting in reduced revenue for government. This often forces policymakers to consider contractionary measures, such as increasing revenues by raising taxes or cutting government spending.

5.2.5 Classical vs. Modern Concept of Fiscal Policy

Fiscal policy has undergone revolutionary developments in recent years. All the recent innovations and developments have been with reference to advanced economies. The concept of fiscal policy can be studied under classical and modern contexts as:

(a) **Classical Concept of Fiscal Policy:** 'Laissez-Faire Policy' was the strong belief of classical economists so they believed in market economy where free play of demand and supply automatically, through self-adjustments, establishes full-employment equilibrium in long-run. This belief is based on J.B. Say's 'Law of Market' that is "supply creates its own demand" so there are equalities between demand and supply, income and expenditure, savings and investment in the free capitalist economy. There is no unemployment problem; even if it appears due to misbehaviour of producers or over production, it is temporary in nature so it can be corrected by wage-cut policy. Hence, there is no need of government interference in the economic system.

Classical economists assigned limited role or functions to government in economic system. They think government expenditure is unproductive so its interference in working of economic system creates instabilities. In other words, the role of fiscal policy in economic system is nil or it is non-functional. Prof. Hansen, therefore, put the classical concept of fiscal policy as "the classical concept of sound fiscal policy corresponds to the maxim of a neutral fiscal policy and it called for two things: (i) the reduction of public expenditures to the utmost possible limit, and (ii) a tax structure which disturb the pricing system as little as possible, including the pricing of factors of production, thereby leaving intact the relative distribution of income as it would be in a tax free society". Thus, classical economists propounded two principles related to fiscal policy, namely (i) Principle of Sound Finance, and (ii) Principle of Balanced Budget.

(i) Principle of Sound Finance: According to classicals, the least spending and the lowest amount of tax imposing by government is called 'Principle of Sound Finance'. Under this principle they laid down:

(a) A government should tax the least and spend as little as possible.

(b) More tax adversely affects production.

(c) Government expenditure is unproductive.

(d) Government should not borrow because if it borrows, government has to impose tax to collect revenue to pay debt-services but such taxation affects adversely on production and economy.

(e) Government should follow balanced budget otherwise public expenditure could result into inflation.

(ii) Principle of Balance Budget: Classicals advocated principle of balanced budget fiscal policy because of the following reasons:

(a) Public expenditure make the government irresponsible and insolvent.

(b) Economic system is capable to correct itself automatically.

(c) Since balanced budget has neutral effect on economy, it could not initiate boom or depression.

(d) It could discipline the politicians' tendency.

(e) It is consistent with classical assumption of full-employment equilibrium.

This classical neutral fiscal policy theory was discarded during 1930s Great Depression period because of its failure.

(b) Modern Concept of Fiscal Policy or Functional Finance: Lord J.M. Keynes, A.P. Lerner and other modern economists discarded the classical theory of neutral fiscal policy; they believed in that the government must have positive role in economic system and it should regulate and control economic activities through its fiscal tools like taxation, public expenditure, pubic borrowing and deficit finance. So they called this 'principle of functional finance'. It is called functional finance because it corrects inflation or deflation through financial activities.

Classicals assumes there is always full-employment at point of equilibrium in free capitalist or market economic system; there is no problem of involuntary unemployment in the economy, even if it occurs in short-run, it will be corrected by market forces through automatic-adjustment between them in long-run. But Keynes out-rightly discarded this classical employment theory and presented a 'General Theory on Income and Employment' that contends that the effective demand plays a vital role in determination of income and employment in the economy. The deficiency of effective demand creates unemployment problem in economic system. Savings and Investment are equal by definition ($S = I$) but functionally they are not equal ($S \neq I$) thus if $S > I$ it leads to depression or deflation because of under consumption or if $S < I$ it leads to boom or inflation because of excess effective demand. Thus, to maintain income and employment at the present level, it is necessary to offset the effects of increase or decrease in effective demand through public expenditure tool for instance Keynes suggested deficit finance as method of correcting or controlling 1930s Great Depression.

Hence, the modern fiscal policy is a technique or method to attain and maintain full-employment by manipulating public expenditure and revenue in such away so as to keep an equilibrium between effective demand and supply of goods and services at that time in the economy. It is nothing but the application of the principle of functional finance.

Tools of Functional Finance: The concept of 'Functional Finance' was first introduced by J.M. Keynes then it developed by A.P. Lerner. According to A.P. Lerner, functional finance refers to the way of working of fiscal measures in economic system. Its central ideas is that the government's fiscal policy involves government spending, taxing, borrowing loans, issue of new money and withdrawal of money from circulation should be viewed with the consideration of their impact upon the national income as a whole, unlike classical doctrine of principle of sound finance. Hence, the main tools of functional finance are:

(a) Government spending
(b) Taxation policy
(c) Public borrowing
(d) Issue of new money and
(e) Withdrawal of money from circulation

Rules of Functional Finance: The basic logic behind the functional finance is to produce desirable effects and to avoid undesirable effects on economic system through fiscal policy measures. Moreover, the main objective of it is to attain economic stability. Prof. A.P. Lerner has suggested the following rules for government activities under functional finance.

(i) The first rule is that the first responsibility of the state is to regulate spending to absorb the goods and services at the current price. It means the government spending amount should not be either excess or short of the amount of available goods and services at current price otherwise if excess it leads to inflation or short it leads to deflation that results into unemployment, for instance it is exactly what is happening in India. The government spending is on five elements, viz. individual consumption and investment, government consumption and investment and business-investment. The government spending on these elements make up the total spending on currently produced goods and services for attainment of full-employment.

(ii) The second rule is that the purpose of borrowing is not raise money but to make the public hold more bonds and less money. It means government should borrow only when it desires that people should have less money and more government bonds so that their purchasing power is reduced thereby to control inflation. It is exactly opposite when government desire to control deflation.

(iii) The third rule is that the purpose of taxation is never to raise money but to leave less money in the hands of taxpayers. According to Lerner, a tax has two-fold effects, namely (a) it increases the money in the hands of government, and (b) it decreases the money in the hands of the people. The first effect is unimportant because government may get money easily by printing currency-notes. The second effect is important because it directly effects on taxpayers spending. So government should levy tax only when it desires that the taxpayers spending should be reduced to control inflation. In contrary situation it is vice versa. As a general rule the volume of taxation and rates of taxation should reduce during depression and increase during inflation and this is true for both direct and indirect taxes.

(iv) The fourth rule is that any excess of government money outlays over the current money revenue of the government it can be met by deficit financing or printing of new money but not by public debt. This is required to control depression but to control inflation the destruction of money measures should be used. This rule points out the importance of deficit and surplus budget to maintain economic stability with full-employment in economic system.

***Role of Functional Finance in Economic Stability*:** Generally, economic instability refers to occurring of inflation and deflation so there is need to control them by fiscal measures.

(a) Inflation and Functional Finance: Inflation, generally, occurs due to excess private expenditure so to control it the following measures are suggested:

(i) by reducing the spending, (ii) by imposing new taxes and raising existing tax rates for transferring resources from private use to government use, (iii) by increasing government borrowing, (iv) by raising interest rate for discouraging consumption and encouraging savings, and (v) by increasing selling of goods and services through government.

(b) Deflation and Functional Finance: Deflation, generally, occurs due to deficiency in the private expenditure so to control it the following measures are suggested:

(i) by encouraging consumption through tax-rate reduction, (ii) by increasing government expenditures on social security schemes like unemployment allowance, old-age pension, etc., it encourages consumption, (iii) by reducing rate of interest to encourage private investment and business, (iv) by taking public works programmes like construction of roads, bridges, public utilities etc., (v) by giving grants and subsidies to backward and poor sectors, and (iv) by repaying public debts.

Thus, functional finance controls deflation and inflation to maintain economic stability and to achieve full-employment in the economic system.

Limitation of Functional Finance: Functional finance is an instrument to achieve economic stability but is doubtful because it assumed certain rate of economic growth but there is possibility of higher rate of growth. It also ignored that increased aggregate spending have effect on investment that further stimulates propensity to consume. The theory of functional finance set-rights the cyclical fluctuations in short-run but it neglects long-run problems.

5.3 DEFICIT FINANCING

There is no precise definition on the term 'Deficit Financing'. The 'principle of deficit financing' was first introduced by J.M. Keynes who suggested it as measure to lift economies from 1930s great depression. It is usually used as method of financing budgetary deficit. Now it has been playing a holistic role in regulating economic activities to achieve goals like stability, growth, development, employment, etc. in both developed and developing countries.

5.3.1 Meaning and Definition

The term 'Deficit Financing' is wider than the term 'Budget Deficit'. The definition of 'budget deficit' is not same in Western industrial economies and the developing economies like India. In

Western advanced countries 'budget-deficit' is defined as "loan financing of all excess government outlays over revenue receipts". But in India it is defined as "the net increase in Treasury bills and withdrawal from cash balances". Similarly, the methods of financing deficit budget is not same in these countries. In Western countries, budget deficit are financed out of market borrowings. Loans from public and commercial banks are not treated as government income-receipts but any government expenditure excess over current income is financed by borrowing from the public and commercial banks is called 'deficit financing'. Whereas in underdeveloped countries where transactions are carried out through common money deficit financing means borrowing from 'Central Bank' on the country; the simple mechanism of borrowing is that the government hands over its securities to the central bank, on backing of which the central bank issue paper currency. Hence, Planning Commission of India has defined deficit financing as "the term deficit financing is used to denote the direct addition to the gross national expenditure through budget deficits whether the deficits are on revenue account or capital account".

In brief, the term 'deficit financing' or 'deficit spending' is generally used to mean any government expenditure which is in excess of its current revenue. Thus, deficit financing implies an excess of expenditure incurred by the government over its current revenue and the deficit in the budget so incurred could be financing either through public borrowings or through the creation of new currency by the government; both the methods would result in deficit financing.

5.3.2 Methods or Techniques of Deficit Financing

Prof. Eli M. Remolona conducted a study on the methods of deficit financing wherein it is examined that how the deficits were financed in the past and proposes a rule for financing them in the future. Further Prof. Remolona argued that the size of the deficit itself seems to have been managed for stabilization purposes, but little attention has been paid to the way it has been financed in spite of the enormous amount of resources involved and the far-reaching implications on economic efficiency. To prof. Remolona, "In the first instance, of course, the national government finances its deficit by issuing debt. But it makes a great deal of difference who ends up holding suchdebt".

According to Prof. Remolona, there are four basic methods of financing a budget deficit, those are:

(i) *By Creating New Money*: The creation of currency, when the Central Bank holds part of the newly issued debt, thereby monetizing it, and it ends up in the hands of the public as freshly printed money or in bank vaults as excess reserves.

(ii) *By Raising Reserve Requirements*: When banks are made to hold additional required reserves in the form of cash, balances with the Central Bank, or eligible government securities.

(iii) *By Borrowing from Domestic Money Market*: Domestic open-market borrowing by government is another suitable method of financing budget deficit. When government debt is voluntarily held by the banks or the public for the interest it pays.

(iv) *By Foreign Borrowing*: The national government borrows from abroad or foreign sources for deficit financing purpose.

According to Prof. Romolona's contention (a) the first method (i) increases supply of money causing inflationary effects, (b) the second method (ii) reduces credit creation power of commercial banks that reduces supply of money, (c) the third method (iii) too reduces supply of money but it influences on savings and interest rate, and (d) the fourth method (iv) affects adversely on balance of payment position of the country. However, the choice of the optimal mix of these methods or instruments could be done for maximizing the welfare of a representative households subject to financing a given budget deficit; ultimately it depends on the prevalent of economic conditions in the country.

5.3.3 Objectives of Deficit Financing

It is during the post-1930s Great Depression period the deficit financing method got greater significance in public finance. It is mainly use to serve the basic objects that are discussed as under

(i) To Finance War Expenditure: It is used to help the government to get fulfilled its financial needs during the time of war. It is very difficult to raise funds by using normal methods such as taxation, etc.

(ii) For Economic Stability and Full-employment: Lord J.M. Keynes the first man who advocated 'principle of deficit financing' as a suitable method to recover the economies from Great Depression when other measures failed to do so. Now both advanced and developing countries are using this method to protect or preserve the economic stability through controlling inflation and deflation and attaining of higher possible level on output, income and employment.

(iii) For Financing Economic Plans: The underdeveloped countries have no adequate fund to finances their developmental plans and programmes. These plans and programmes are inevitable on part of government due to failure or inefficiencies of private sector.

(iv) For Mobilization of Resources: Under the deficit financing government borrows from people and institutions that helps for mobilizing of surplus, idle and unutilized fund to flow to the sectors where needed in the economy.

5.3.4 Role or Importance of Deficit Financing

The role or importance of deficit financing has been discussed in the context of the achievement of its major objectives. These are:

(i) It is Suitable Method to Finance War Expenditures: During the time of war, the government have to bear the burden of expenditure on fulfillment of war requirements like purchase weapons, wages of military forces, vehicles, etc. Government cannot meet these expenditures out of its regular revenue nor does it raise additional income by using normal methods. Thus, the deficit financing through borrowing or issue of new money is the easily available method to finance war expenditures. Nowadays the fear of war and defence balance on the border or in the regions make the governments to spend more on defence through deficit budget policy, for instance US, India and other countries spending more than 25 per cent of its revenue on defence expenses. The very bad effect of it is that such public spending increase purchasing power of people thereby the inflation occurs.

(ii) It Improves Employment Level in the Economy: Deficit finance is used to meet the government spending on employment generation activities like investments in public works, public sector industries, irrigation, etc. Directly, first, they create direct employment opportunities and then due to generating of income in people's hands it increases effective demand thereby, indirectly, generates further income and employment and solve unemployment problem in the economy; it is based on logic of Keynes' general theory of employment and investment multiplier theory. But its success depends upon fulfillment of the propositions such as Marginal Propensity to Consume must be less than unity (MPC<1) and there should not be any excess capacity in the economy.

(iii) It Helps to Implement Development Programmes: All types of economies need development activities such as development of agriculture, industries, infrastructure, science and technologies, etc. Comparatively with other sources of financing government expenditures deficit financing is more preferable because under this method government gets funds easily through borrowing from central bank, money market and foreign sources. They have advantages like controlling of inflation or deflation or possibility of achievement of growth with stability, for instance India practicing it since its third five-year plan. As an instrument of development deficit finance plays three important roles:

(a) It mobilizes surplus, idle and unutilized resources through public borrowing.

(b) It creates new resources means it transfers funds from private use to public uses that, on the one hand, reduces private consumption and on the other hand, public investment boosts economic development process. The transfer of resources from private to government is called 'forced savings'. In such case, there is no fear of inflation.

(c) It is engine of development of developing economies. Poor or developing countries have insufficient resources to spend on their developmental programmes meanwhile private sector is disinterested in national importance developmental activities. Deficit finance enables the government implement the developmental programmes.

5.3.5 Effects of Deficit Finance

As a practical method or instrument of fiscal policy deficit finance has both good and bad effects on the economy but they depend upon the prevalent economic conditions, the purpose to be achieves and efficiency and honesty of the government. These are:

(i) It creates irresponsibility in government. When government have easy way to get money for its spending it makes the government extravagant. It gives scope for misappropriation of funds. It encourages corrupt practices in the country, for example, self-employment and wage-employment programmes in India.

(ii) Deficit financing is both pro-inflationary and anti-inflationary measure. It is pro-inflationary because it increases the supply of money thereby rise in prices. It is anti-inflationary because through public borrowing it reduces supply of money thereby reduces prices.

(iii) It generates income, output and employment. Both advanced and developing or underdeveloped countries using this method to generate income, output and employment. Advance countries use it to recover the economy from recession and depressions whereas developing countries use it take their economy to prosperity and solve unemployment and under-employment problems. It helps them to achieve growth with stability or controlling of business cycles.

(iv) It encourages prolonged heavy deficit in budget that increases the burden of taxation, depreciation of value of money, debt burden on next generation. It may put the national into 'debt-trap'.

In conclusion, the deficit financing is suitable method to achieve budgetary goals if it would be used in honest and efficient way otherwise it would be a dubious and dangerous weapon.

5.4 MODEL QUESTIONS

(a) Questions each needs answer in 2-3 sentences (2 Marks each)

1. What is budget?
2. Name any two features of budget.
3. What is balanced budget?
4. What is unbalanced budget?
5. Name any two types of budget.
6. Name any two objectives of budget.
7. What do you mean by Service Branch?
8. Name any two rules of public budgeting.
9. Give the difference between methods of balanced and unbalanced budgeting.
10. What is method of budgeting for distribution?
11. Name any two principles of budgeting.
12. What do you mean by 'Performance Budgeting'?
13. What do you mean by 'Program Budgeting'?
14. Give the meaning of 'Incremental Budgeting'.
15. State the meaning of 'Zero-base Budgeting'.
16. Give the meaning of public debt burden.
17. Name any two qualities of good budgeting.
18. What is 'Revenue Budget'?
19. What is 'Capital Budget'?
20. Mention any two theories of budgeting.
21. Give the statement of normative theory on budgeting.
22. Give the statement of descriptive theory on budget.
23. Give the statement of classical theory on budgeting.
24. Give the statement of optimal budget theory.
25. Mention any two differences between private and public budget.
26. What is fiscal policy?
27. State any two purposes of fiscal policy.
28. Give any two criticisms on fiscal policy.

29. Name any two tools of functional finance.
30. What is deficit financing?
31. State any two methods of deficit financing.
32. Name any two objectives of deficit financing.

(b) Questions each needs short-note type answer (5 Marks each)

1. Give a brief account of meaning of budget.
2. Write a note on types of budget.
3. Discuss in brief the functions of budget.
4. Write a short-note on rules of public budgeting.
5. Explain in brief the methods of balancing and unbalancing budgeting.
6. Write a note on principles of budgeting.
7. Write a note on performance budgeting.
8. Discuss in brief incremental budgeting.
9. Write a note on zero-base budgeting.
10. Write note on qualities of a good budget.
11. Discuss in brief the components of budget.
12. Discuss briefly normative theory of budgeting.
13. Narrate in brief the descriptive theory of budgeting.
14. Write a note on classical budget theory.
15. Give a brief account on the differences between private and public budgets.
16. Write a note on objectives of fiscal policy.
17. Discuss in brief the types of fiscal policy.
18. Analyze in brief classical concept of fiscal policy.
19. Explain in brief the objectives and methods of deficit budgeting.
20. Write a note on role and effects of deficit budgeting.

(c) Questions each needs essay type/long answer (10/15 Marks each)

1. Define public budget, explain its various types.
2. Define public budget, explain its various objectives and rules.

3. Define public budget, explain the various methods of budgeting.
4. Define public budget, explain its various principles.
5. Explain performance budgeting.
6. What is incremental budgeting? Explain its merits and demerits.
7. What is zero-base budget? Explain its merits and demerits.
8. Explain the normative theory of budgeting.
9. Discuss the descriptive theory of budgeting.
10. Analyze the optimal budget theory.
11. What is fiscal policy? Explain its objectives and criticisms.
12. Discuss functional finance in detail.
13. What is deficit financing? Explain its objectives and methods.
14. What is deficit financing? Explain its importance and effects.

6

Public Finance of India

6.1 INTRODUCTION

Since India is a socialist secular democratic republic state, one of the biggest democratic countries of the world, and having second largest populous country in the world, she has more responsibility to establish socio-economic justice to her people within the framework of her constitution. Accordingly, India formulated her public economy.

The Indian Government structure has three-tier system; at the centre union government, state level government and local level local bodies or governments. Moreover, India followed mixed economy model, an exemplary model in the world. Accordingly, the taxation, public expenditure, public dent, fiscal policies and distribution of financial resources policies are formulated and subsequently amended and reformed as per the recommendation finance commission.

Since independence public expenditure gained a significant place in the country to pull the economy out of its terminals. Public expenditure regulates the economic activities and helps to attain the long-run and short-run socio-economic objectives. This is the reason for continuous upward trends in both revenue and expenditure of the Indian Government. Actually, the government has been widening the scope of its activities in social and economic spheres to bring economic growth as early as possible. To achieve this, it has been accelerating the speed of modernization, especially in backward and developing areas.

But the serious threat to the economy is uncontrolled growth of public debt as well as deficit inbudget. Internal and external debts have created many problems such as heavy debt services, deficit balance of payments, excess supply of money, exchange-depreciation, hyper-inflation, market instability, etc. So there are series of challenges to be faced and pre-determined goals to be attained before the country.

6.2 CENTRAL GOVERNMENT BUDGET

The central budget gives the complete picture of the estimated receipts and expenditures of union government of India for the specific financial year. In fact, the budget document is a complete action plan depicting three sets of figures, viz., the actual figures for the previous fiscal year, revised estimates for the current year and budget estimates of the coming years.

The budgetary fiscal year starts every year from April 1 to March 31. The budget of the next financial year will be presented on the last day of February of the current financial year by the Union Finance Minister before the parliament. In case of state governments, the budget is being presented before the state legislatures by their respective Finance Minister. The entire budget speech of the Finance Minister is broadly classified under two parts, viz., part A and part B. Part A of the speech covers the broad allocation of funds for various sectors and sub-sectors, initiation of new schemes, and focus areas of the government. This part is more concerned about the development issues at macro level. On the other hand, Part B covers the specific tax proposals in the economy. It has direct bearing over household and manufacturing/service providing unit. Therefore, it deals with the micro aspects of the economy. After the budget is presented by the Union Finance Minister before parliament, the members of parliament debate on it. The demands of various ministers are discussed and suitable amendments are made thereon. There is scope in the budget session for discussion on the working, efficiency or otherwise of each ministry or department. After the budget proposals of receipts and disbursements are passed through the critical analysis of the members' parliament as the case may be, and voting will be done on the demands and amendments, thereby a 'Finance Bill' is passed to approve the proposals to raise proposed taxes and incur proposed expenditure; an 'Appropriation Bill' is passed to authorize the expenditure for the year. The Public Accounts committee and the Estimates Committee of the parliament examine the expenditures of the government.

The budget documents is are divided into two parts, viz., revenue account and the capital account. The revenue budget deals with receipts from taxation and non-tax revenues like earning from public enterprises, fiscal services, interest and dividends, etc. on the one hand; and disbursements on the heads of expenditure on both development and non-development activities on the other hand. The revenue budget comprises of the following main heads of receipts and expenditure.

Table 6.1: Revenue Budget Model of India

Receipts items	Disbursement items
Total Revenue (A+B)	**Total Disbursement (A+B)**
(A) Gross Tax Revenue (a+b+c) minus States share = Centre's share	**(A) Development expenditure (a+b+c+d)**
(a) Taxes on income and expenditure.	(a) Social services.
(b) Taxes on property and capital.	(b) Economic services.
(c) Taxes on commodities and services.	(c) Grant in aid to States and UT's.
	(d) General services.
(B) Non-tax Revenue (a+b+c)	**(B) Non-development expenditure (a+b+c+d+e)**
(a) Fiscal service.	(a) Interest payment.
(b) Interest receipts.	(b) Administrative services.
(c) Profits and others.	(c) Grants to States and UT's.
	(d) Collected of taxes and others.
	(e) Defence expenditure.

The capital budget is the statement of all capital receipts such as savings and provident funds, etc. and of all capital expenditures like expenditure on defence, loans and advances, general services, development investments, grants, etc. The capital budget comprises the following heads of receipts and expenditures.

Table 6.2: Capital Budget Model of India

Receipts items	Disbursement items
1. Market loans (net)	1. Defence expenditure
2. External loans (net)	2. Loans and advances
3. Recoveries of loans and advances	3. Other non-development expenditures
4. Small savings (net)	4. Development expenditure (a+b+c)
5. Provident funds	(a) Social Services
6. Others	(b) Economic Services
	(c) General Services

Union Government Budget for 2012-13: Union government budget for the year 2012-13 is referred for the study. The characteristics and trends of the union government budget is discussed in detail.

Table 6.3: A Glance on Union Government Budget 2012-13 (₹ in Crore)

Details	2010-11 (Actuals)	2011-12 (Budget Estimates)	2011-12 (Revised Estimates)	2012-13 (Budget Estimates)
1. Revenue Receipts (net of States' share)	788471	789892	756193	935685
2. Capital Receipts	408857	467837	542251	555240
3. Total Receipts	**1197328**	**1257729**	**1298444**	**1490925**
4. Revenue Expenditure	1040723	1097162	1140915	1286109
5. Capital Expenditure	156605	160567	157529	204816
6. Borrowing & Other Liabilities	373591	412817	509731	513590
7. Total Expenditure (3-7)	**1197328**	**1257729**	**1298444**	**1490925**
8. Revenue Deficit	252252	307270	384722	350424
9. Fiscal Deficit	373591	412817	509731	513590
10. Primary Deficit	139569	144831	237276	193831

Source: Union Budget documents and Controller General of Accounts.

Actuals: Based on Provisional Actuals for 2010-11.

6.2.1 Budgetary Trends

Since India has been following incremental budgeting method, the receipts, expenditures and various deficits have been increasing continuously. The developments and growth in union government budget can be studied as under:

(a) Rising of Total Revenue and Expenditure: The total revenue and expenditure on both the revenue and capital accounts have the rising trends.

The total receipts increased from ₹ 414162 crore in 2002-03 to ₹ 1298444 crore in 2011-12. It was estimated to be increase to ₹ 1490925 crore 2012-13. The total receipts increased many times because of the following reasons:

(a) Increments in tax revenue (Central Share)
(b) Increments in non-tax revenue
(c) Recoveries of loans
(d) Borrowing and other liabilities.
(e) Other receipts like provident fund, special deposits, small savings, etc.

Similarly, the total expenditure of the Central Government has been increased from ₹ 414162 crore in 2002-03 to ₹ 1298444 crore in 2011-12. It is estimated to increase to ₹ 1490925 crores in 2012-13. The total expenditure has been increased due to the following reasons:

(i) Increase in non-plan expenditure like defence, interest payments, civil administration, economic and social services, etc., and

(ii) Increase in plan expenditure like central plan, central assistance to state governments, etc.

The notable trend in the Union Government Budget is that the total expenditure is increased much more than the total receipts and the trends of rising still continued in recent years.

(b) Deficit in Budget: The Union Government Budget is based on Keynes' principle of deficit finance. The deficit budget is often being used as method to achieve economic goals. The expenditure is always in excess of its receipts. Deficits have become the regular feature of Indian budget; every year Finance Minister promise of reducing the deficits while presenting the budget for discussion and approval but it is not yet done. There are four types of deficits usually found in Union Government Budget. These are:

***(i) Budgetary Deficits*:** The budgetary deficit refers to the difference between government total expenditure (revenue expenditure and capital expenditure) and total receipts (revenue receipts and capital receipts). In other words, budgetary deficit is the excess of total expenditure over total receipts.

***(ii) Revenue Deficits*:** It appears on revenue accounts. The revenue deficit appears due to excess of revenue expenditure over revenue receipts. Revenue deficit decrease from ₹ 107880 crore in 2002-03 to ₹ 99860 crores in 2003-04. But it was increased to ₹ 252252 crore in 2010-11 and further, it was estimated to go up to ₹ 350424 crore in 2012-13.

A most notable point related with central budget is that initially from 1951 to 1975 revenue surplus policy was adopted to finance economic development but after 1975, due to increased non-plan expenditure there is chronic deficit in revenue accounts and it is being used to finance developmental programmes in the country.

(iii) Fiscal Deficit: Fiscal Deficit (Df) is the budgetary deficit (TR–TE) plus market Borrowings and other Liabilities (B), i.e. Df = TR – TE + B, where TR = Total Receipts and TE = Total Expenditure.

The Fiscal deficit decrease from ₹ 145072 crore to ₹ 132103 crore in 2003-04 but in 2010-11 it was increased to ₹ 373591 crore. It was estimated further may go up to ₹ 513590 crore in 2012-13. The fiscal deficit in terms of Gross Domestic Product (GDP) was 6.3% in 2008-09, 6.8% in 2009-10, 5.1% in 2010-11 and 6.1% in 2011-12.

(iv) Primary Deficit: Primary Deficit (Dp) refers to fiscal deficit (Df) minus interest payments (Ip), i.e. Dp = Df–Ip. Primary Deficit was declined from ₹ 27268 crore in 2002-03 to ₹ 7548 crore of in 2003-04 but in 2010-11 it was increased to ₹ 139569 crore. It was estimated to increase to ₹ 193831 crore in 2012-13.

The persistent chronic deficit in budget has created inflationary situation in the country. It became hurdle to sustainable economic growth and effective implementation of poverty eradication programmes. Equally, it shows lack of political will to curb inflation through effective fiscal policy measures like curbing unproductive expenditures and wage-reductions.

(c) Contribution of Taxation: Central Government imposes two types of taxes, viz. (i) Direct Taxes and (ii) Indirect Taxes. The magnitude of these taxes are very effective on economy. India is practicing multiple taxation system that found the common people have bearing heavy tax burden. The indirect taxes have created hyper-inflationary situation in the country recently. The total tax revenue (centre's share) increased from ₹ 541864 crore in 2007-08 to ₹ 788471 crore in 2010-11 and further, it was estimated to increase to ₹ 771071 crore in 2012-13. About 84% of tax revenue was being collected from indirect taxes before 1990 but it declined to 43.68% in 2011-12; however, it is merciless tax burden on common people and regressive tax system.

(d) Slow growth of Non-Tax Revenue: The total non-tax revenue is increasing very slowly. It was ₹ 102317 crore in 2007-08 which was 23% of tax revenue. It was increased to ₹ 218602 crore in 2010-11 which was 38% of tax revenue. But it was declined to ₹ 124307 crore in 2011-12 that was 19.6% of tax revenue. Some wrong policy associated with disinvestment in public sector undertakings, decline in profits and earnings of departments, etc. are the main causes for slow growth of non-tax revenue.

(e) A Continuous Rise in Revenue Expenditure: This component of total expenditure has been increasing continuously since 1951; it is because of uncontrolled increase in interest-payments and major subsidies, defence expenditure is also mounting that is necessary for maintaining defence balance in the region. On and average Indian Government have to pay daily ₹ 120 crore towards interest payments. The revenue expenditure increased from ₹ 594433 crore in 2007-08 to ₹ 1140915 core in 2011-12 meanwhile interest-payments increased from ₹ 171030 Crore to ₹ 272455 crore.

(f) The Mounting Borrowing and Other Liabilities: Since the central government is using deficit finance as easy method of covering its excess expenditure, it has been borrowing heavily from sources like money market, banks, etc. This government borrowing is tune or extent of mounting fiscal deficit. The borrowing and other liabilities have been increased from ₹ 126912 crore in 2007-08 to ₹ 509731 crore in 2011-12. If, at all, government wants to control the deficit, it should minimize its dependence on easy borrowing and reduce unproductive expenditure.

(g) Plan and Non-Plan Expenditures: The plan expenditure deals with the new initiatives of government. It includes the central plan expenditure and the central assistance to state and union territory plans. Plan expenditure has the budget heads of revenue plan expenditure and capital plan expenditure. The plan expenditure has been increasing since 1951 to achieve the budgetary goals related to five year plans. It was increased from ₹ 205082 crore in 2007-08 to ₹ 413513 crore in 2011-12 and it was estimated that it may increase to ₹ 521025 crore in 2012-13.

Unlike plan expenditure, non-plan expenditure deals with the past commitments of the government. Non-plan expenditure has the budget heads of revenue non-plan expenditure and capital non-plan expenditure. Compared to revenue non-plan expenditure, the share of non-plan capital expenditure is much lower. Within the capital component of non-plan expenditure, the largest allocation goes to defence. The total non-plan expenditures was increased from ₹ 507589 crore in 2007-08 to ₹ 884931 crore in 2011-12; and it was estimated that it may increase to ₹ 969900 crore in 2012-13.

The point to be noted here is that non-plan expenditure is always higher than plan expenditure so that is the inflationary ineffect.

(h) Relief and Welfare Measures: To impose personal income tax, the income slabs are reduced to four slabs. Personal income tax exemption limit is also raised and tax reliefs are given on income of certain investments. Social Security Schemes are introduced to help the unorganized and poor class of the society. Self-employment, wage-employment, poverty eradication programmes, woman empowerment programmes, etc. received higher priority in central budget. Since Tenth Five-Year Plan, women is considered as budget-component thence more funds are allocating for women development activities. This concept is called 'Gender Budgeting'.

Of course, every time, Union Govt. budget focuses on attention of development of infrastructure, generation of employment and poverty eradications. However, the overall effect of central budget is hyper inflation, rather than giving more reliefs to the poor.

6.3 CENTRAL GOVERNMENT REVENUE

The Central Government receives revenue from various sources. It needs revenue to meet its various expenditures on activities like administration, defence social, economic and general services. Public revenue provisions are made in government budget.

6.3.1 Sources of Public Revenue

Central Government collects its revenue from two types of revenue namely (I) revenue receipts and (II) capital receipts; these are:

(I) Revenue Receipts: Revenue receipts can be broadly classified into two sources namely (a) Tax Revenue and (b) Non-Tax Revenue Sources. The revenue from these sources has been increasing that is shown in the following table:

Table 6.4: Central Revenue on Revenue Accounts (₹ in Crore)

Sources	2010-11 (Actuals)	2011-12 (BE)	2011-12 (RE)	2012-13 (BE)
Tax Revenue (Centre Share)	569869	664457	631886	771071
Non-Tax Revenue	218602	125435	124307	164614
Total	788471	789892	756193	935685

Source: Union Budget Documents and Controller General of Accounts 2012-13
Actuals: Based on Provisional Actuals for 2010-11.

***(a) Tax Revenue Sources*:** The revenue raised from levying of tax by government is called 'tax revenue'. Central Government levy taxes on income, expenditure, property, services, commodities, capital transactions, etc. Some tax-proceedings are shared between centre and state governments, e.g. income tax, as per recommendations of finance commission of India. The main tax revenue sources of Central Government are:

(i) Direct Taxes: Central Government imposes various direct taxes on individuals, companies and others. They can be studied as:

(a) *Personal Income Tax*: It is levied and collected by Central Government but it is shared between centre and state government. It is levied on annual income of individual or joint family. It is based on 'ability-to-pay principle'. At present there are four slabs of income; the first slab is tax exemption limit, i.e. ₹ 2 Lakh as per 2.12-13 budget, it is 0% tax-rate slab; the second 10% slab; the third 20% slab and the fourth 30% tax-rate slab. Previously a tax on tax-proceeds means 'Surcharge' was in practice but now it is abolished.

In India 'Income Tax' was introduced by Sir James Wilson in 1860 to finance the expenditure incurred due to 'Sepoy Mutiny of 1857'. The British Government passed the first Income Tax Act in 1886, then, a series of amendments and acts were passed by British Governments but they were replaced by 'Income Tax act 1961' passed by Indian Government after independence. Till 1975 there were nine income slabs and highest tax rate was 97.25% but due to 'Justice Wanchoo Committee' recommendations these income slabs are reduced to four and maximum tax-rate to 30%. Tax revenue from this source was ₹ 90 crore in 1951. Now it has been increased from ₹ 5371 crore in 1990-91 to ₹ 120566 crore in 2010-11. According to 11th finance commission recommendations the state governments share in income tax revenue increased to 80%.

(b) *Corporate Tax*: The tax levied on profits of companies is called 'Corporate Tax'. It was first time introduced in India during First World War Period. The tax structure has been changed from time to time. In 1994-95 the corporate tax rate was fixed as 40% on net profits of domestic companies and 55% on net profits of foreign companies in India. The corporate tax rate on domestic companies reduced to 30% in 2005-06 and 10% surcharge was introduced on income exceeding ₹ 100 million that is reduced to 5% in 2011-12. Now the Minimum Alternate Tax (MAT) arte is 18.5%, in 2011-12. The revenue from this tax increased from ₹ 5335 crore in 1990-91 to ₹ 2,96,377 crore in 2010-11.

(c) *Others*: Wealth tax, gift tax, interest tax, expenditure tax and estate duties are the other types of Central Government direct taxes. The wealth tax is imposed on accumulated wealth or property of individuals, families and companies if it exceeds more than exemption limit. Gift tax is levied on the gifts presented in various occasions to the individuals, it has exemption limit. Interest tax is levied on gross interest earned by commercial banks and credit institutions. Expenditure tax is imposed on expenditure incurred in hotels where per day room charge is above ₹ 400. Estate or Death Duty is levied on the legal heir while transferring property of deceased man to legal heir. Some of these are not economical and their entire tax-proceeds are shared by states.

The total direct tax revenue has been increased from ₹ 11,024 crore in 1990-91 to ₹ 4,38,500 crore in 2010-11 meanwhile its share in total tax revenue increased from 19.15% to 56.32% in 2011-12; it is one of the reasons of inflation in the country.

(ii) Indirect Taxes: Indirect taxes are also called 'Commodity and Service Taxes'. Central Government levies various indirect taxes. They are discussed as:

(a) Central Excise Duties: Central Government levies taxes on all commodities, except liquors and narcotic drugs, produced within the country. Certain commodities, used by all or public goods like life saving drugs, controlled clothes, etc., are exempted from it. The tax revenue from it is shared between centre and states, though it is levied and collect by Central Government. According to 11th Finance Commission recommendation 50% of its revenue is shared by state governments. The revenue from this source has been increased from ₹ 20,644 crore to ₹ 1,31,800 in 2010-11.

(b) Custom Duties: Custom duties are of two type, viz., Import Duty and Export Duty. Import duties are levied on imported goods and export duties on exported goods. These duties are very important from revenue and trade control points of view. Central Government revenue from this source has been increased from ₹ 24,514 crore in 1990-91 to ₹ 1,37,263 crore in 2010-11.

(c) Service Taxes: Central Government imposes taxes on services like telephones, insurance, brokerage, etc., every year new services are brought under tax net. The revenue from this source has been increased from ₹ 2,613 crore in 2000-01 to ₹ 69,400 crore in 2010-11.

Besides, central sales tax is also imposed on sales transactions and collected in Union Territories. Moreover, the total indirect tax revenue has been increased from ₹ 45,158 crore in 1990-91 to ₹ 3,38,463 crore in 2010-11; its share in total tax revenue declined from 80.85% in 1990-91 to 43.64%, really its regressive nature is declining.

(b) Non-Tax Revenue Sources: In addition to tax revenue Central Government collects revenue from various sources without imposing taxes, that is called 'Non-Tax Revenue'. The non-tax revenue of the Central Government is shown in the following table:

Table 6.4: Non-Tax Revenue of Central Government (₹ in Crore)

Sources	2010-11 (Actuals)	2011-12 (BE)	2011-12 (RE)	2012-13 (BE)
Non-Tax Revenue	218602	125435	124307	164614

Source: Union Budget Documents and Controller General of Accounts, 2012-13

The non-tax revenue has actually declined from ₹ 218602 crore in 2010-11 to ₹ 124307 crore in 2011-12. The main sources of Central Government non-tax revenue are discussed as under:

(a) Revenue from Fiscal Services: It includes income from currency, coinage, mint, penalties, etc. Reserve Bank of India (RBI) earns profits from its note-printing press, mintage of coins, etc. Central Government collects revenue in form of penalties due to violation of Acts like Foreign Exchange Regulation Act, Forfeiture of Property Act, etc. They all constitute income to Central Government.

(b) Interest-Receipts: It is an important source of non-tax revenue of Central Government. Union government gives loans to state governments, Union Territories' governments, railways-department, postal service departments, public enterprises, etc. It receives interest on these loans that forms its revenue.

(c) Dividends and Profits: Indian Railways, RBI, Post and Telegraph, Nationalized Banks, Life Insurance, Public Sector Undertakings (PSUs), etc. are owned and controlled by Central Government. It invests fund for their developments; the profits and dividends earned by them go to revenue accounts of Central Government.

(d) General Services: Central Government renders various administrative services to the public through its various departments such as public service commission, police, jails, supplies and disposals, public works, etc.; it receives fees, price, etc. form of receipts as returns to these services. Unclaimed postal certificates, deposits and market loans are also comes under this category.

(e) Social and Community Services: Union government renders various social and community services to the public such as education, art, culture, medical and public health, family-welfare, sanitation, water supply, housing, urban development, information and publicity, labour and employment, social security, etc. social and community services; as returns to these services it receives income from them.

(f) Economic Services: Central Governments carries out various economic services such as agriculture and allied services, irrigation and flood control, energy, industries and minerals, transports and communications, science and technology, environment, foreign trade, civil supplies, etc. It earns income these services.

(g) Gifts and Grants: Gifts are voluntary contributions from domestic and foreign governments and private individuals or non-government donors to the government fund for specific purpose such as relief fund or defence fund during a war or an emergency some part may contribute to the government funds for specific purposes. Gifts have some significance, especially during wartime, Floods, drought or emergency periods. India receives cash grants and commodity from counties like Denmark, Japan, USA, UK and others.

(II) Capital Receipts: Central Government borrows loans from RBI, money market, sales of treasury bills, etc. within country and from outside country. It borrows short, medium and long-term loans. India borrows loans from International Monetary Fund (IMF), World Bank and other international financial institutions. Recovery of loans given to States, Union Territories (UTs) and others, disinvestment of equity holdings, state provident fund, special deposits, etc. are also included in capital receipts. These capital receipts can be classified into two sources namely (i) internal borrowings and (ii) external borrowings. The revenue from capital receipts to Central Government increased from ₹ 408857 in 2010-11 to ₹ 542251 in 2011-12 and it was estimated to increase to ₹ 555240 in 2012-13.

6.3.2 Trends in Central Government Revenue

The trends in Central Government revenue through lights on various aspects and problems of the Indian economy. These are:

(i) The Total Revenue has been Increasing Continuously: The total revenue of Central Government has been increased from ₹ 406 crore in 1950-51 to ₹ 1298444 in 2011-12, it is increased by more than three thousand times; meanwhile GDP (Gross Domestic Product) at current price increased from ₹ 10036 crore to ₹ 8353495 crore which increased by 832 times that is less than the increment of Central Government's total revenue. It indirectly indicates that there is no control over public expenditure thereby prolonging of inflationary situations in the country. There are several reasons for the continuous rise in total revenue such as, increase in national and per capita incomes, raising of existing tax-rates and levying of new taxes and increased non-tax revenue.

(ii) Central Government becomes more Important than State Governments: Central Government plays important role in imposition and collection of taxes. It is because (a) it imposes productive taxes like corporate tax, customs duties, income taxes, excise duties, etc., (b) it has effective machinery to collect taxes, and (c) it collects taxes from whole country.

(iii) Increasing Importance of Income Taxes: The share of direct taxes in total tax revenue was decline from 36% in 1950-51 to 26% in 1996-97 but after that it started rising; in 2011-12 it increased to 56.32%; it is because the share of corporate tax revenue is increasing.

(iv) Share of Indirect Taxes Declining: Before tax reforms the commodity-taxes were the important tax revenue source of Central Government. It share in total tax revenue increased from 64% in 1950-51 to 74% in 1996-97 but after that it declined to 43.68% in 2011-12; it shows the direct taxes have become less regressive tax system. However, a persistent inflationary situation has disappointed the common people in the country.

(v) More Tax-Proceeding Shares to State Government: According to the recommendations of finance commission some tax revenue proceeds are being distributed between centre and states governments. 80% of income tax revenue and 52% of central excise duties' revenue are shared by states.

(vi) Increasing Importance of Non-Tax Revenue: The non-tax revenue of Central Government was increased from ₹ 49 crore in 1950-51 to ₹ 67790 crore in 2000-01; further, it has been gone-up to ₹ 124307 crore in 2011-12; it has been increased by more than 2500 times during 1950-2012. It has been increasing continuously because of Central Government's investment in public sector undertakings, loans, etc. activities brought more income to it on one side and on the other the profits, dividends, fees, etc. incomes are increasing.

(vii) Uncontrolled Growth of Capital Receipts: The borrowing became unseparated part of Central Government because deficit finance method is being used to finance the developmental activities and to cover unproductive expenditures too. Central Government is paying more to its income and borrowing on debt-services; there is fear of debt trap.

6.4 CENTRAL GOVT. EXPENDITURES

Since India is a socialistic secular democratic republic state, it has various responsibilities to be shouldered and multifarious duties to be discharged in the best interest of to be kept up the socio-economic justice promise given to its people by its Constitution. Hence, the Central Government has been rendering various services such as civil administration, law and order, defence, social, economic and general services. It has been giving grants and loans to states, UTs, PSUs, etc. for their developmental activities. Thus, it spends huge amount on these activities out of its total revenue. These expenditures provisions are approved in the Union Government Budget every financial year. The total Central Government expenditures are shown in the following table:

Table 6.5: Central Government Expenditures (₹ in Crore)

Year	Revenue Expenditure	Capital Expenditure	Total Expenditure
1950-51	350	180	530
1980-81	14540	9630	24170
1990-91	735165	24756	98272
2000-01	272696	46914	319610
2010-11	1040723	156605	1197328
2011-12	1140915	157529	1298444
2012-13 (BE)	1286109	204816	1490925

Source: Compiled Data

The total expenditure of Central Government increased much during 1950-2013; it shows that the tax burden and supply of money both are increasing in the country that pose various challenges before the government while it is struggling to fight inflation in the country.

6.4.1 Heads of Central Government Expenditure

Central Government total expenditure is broadly classified into two types namely (A) Revenue Expenditure and (B) Capital Expenditure. These are studies as:

(A) Revenue Expenditures: Revenue expenditure refers to the expenditure incurred by government out of its current revenue for day-to-day administration and for maintaining social, economic, defence, etc. services. The revenue expenditure of Central Government has been increased from ₹ 350 crore in 1950-51 to ₹ 1140915 crore in 2011-12 and it was estimate to increase to ₹ 1286102 crore in 2012-13. The main heads of Central Government's revenue expenditure are discussed as:

***(a) Interest Payments*:** For to cover budgetary deficits, balance of payment deficits, to finance developmental programmes, etc. purposes Central Government borrowed huge loans from internal and external sources so it has been paying interest payments thereon. It increased from ₹ 37 crore in 1950-51 to ₹ 272455 crore in 2011-12 and estimated may increase to ₹ 319759 crore in 2012-13.

***(b) Major Subsidies*:** Food, fertilizer, export promotions, etc. are the major subsidies have been being given by Central Government. It increased from ₹ 12550 crore in 1995-96 to ₹ 146951 crore in 2011-12 and further estimated may increase to ₹ 179554 crore in 2012-13.

***(c) Defence*:** For protection national boundaries, wealth, resources, people from external aggressions and internal disorder, the defence force must be maintained so incurring expenditure on them is must. Defence expenditure is constantly increasing in recent years because of reasons like to purchase of the modern warfare instruments, technology and weapons to maintain defence-balance in the region; to maintain more defence forces like Army, Navy and Air Force. The revision of pay scales, dearness allowance, pension, etc. of these forces raised the Central Government expenditure. The defence expenditure increased from ₹ 18835 crore in 1995-96 to ₹ 102827 crore in 2011-12 and it was estimated to increase to ₹ 113828 crore in 2012-13.

(d) Civil Expenditure and Grants: The other important heads of Central Government revenue expenditure are civil administration and grants to States, UTs and foreign governments. The Central Government civil services mainly comprise of the following services:

(i) General Services: It includes organs of government, tax collections, external affairs, police, pension, etc. are the general services being rendered by Central Government.

(ii) Social Services: It includes education, health, broadcasting etc. social and community services are being rendered by Central Government.

(iii) Economic Services: Central Government renders economic services like agriculture, industry, power, transport, communication, science and technology, etc.

In addition to these services, it gives grants to States, UTs and foreign governments; it gives two types of grants to State and UTs governments, viz. (a) Statutory Grants would be given as per recommendation of Finance Commission of India and (b) Development Grants would be given as per recommendation of Planning Commission of India. Central Government gives grants to foreign governments during the time of natural calamities occurred in their countries.

The total revenue expenditure incurred under the heads of civil administration and grants increased from ₹ 10679 crore in 1995-96 to ₹ 618683 in 2011-12; it was estimated to increase to ₹ 672968 in 2012-13.

(B) Capital Expenditure: Capital expenditure incurs on creating permanent revenue yielding assets. It consists of capital expenditure on development of agriculture, industry, transport, communication, irrigation, power, development projects of State and UTs (Grants), defence sector and repayment of long-run public debts. The capital expenditure would be met out of fund raised by public loans. The total capital expenditure increased from

₹ 31165 crore in 1995-96 to ₹ 157529 crore in 2011-12 and it was estimated to increase to ₹ 204816 crore in 2012-13.

New Classification of Public Expenditure: Central Government has adopted new classification of expenditure from 1987-88 as (i) Non-plan expenditure and plan expenditure. Non-plan expenditure divided into 'Non-Plan Revenue and Capital Expenditures'. Non-plan revenue expenditure further divided into different heads like interest payment, defence, major subsidies, civil administration services and grants to States, UTs and foreign governments; Non-plan capital expenditure includes defence capital expenditure, loans to PSUs, States, UTs, foreign governments for non-plan purposes, etc. Plan Expenditure too divided into 'Plan Revenue and Capital Expenditures'. Central Plan Revenue Expenditure classified as agriculture, rural development, irrigation, flood control, energy, industry, minerals, transport, communication, science and technology, environment, social services, etc. Central Plan Capital Expenditures refers to central financial assistance to States and UTs like economic development, social and community development, general services, etc.

The total Non-Plan and Plan Expenditures are shown in the following table;

Table 6.6: Central Government Plan and Non-Plan Expenditures (₹ in Crore)

Year	Plan Expenditure	Non-Plan Expenditure	Total Expenditure
2007-08	205082	507589	712671
2010-11	379029	818299	1197328
2011-12	413513	884931	1298444
2012-13 (BE)	521025	969900	1490925

Source: Compiled Data

Both plan and non-plan expenditures have rising trends but non-plan expenditure is greater than plan expenditure.

6.4.2 Trends in Central Government Expenditure

Since independence, public expenditure gained significant place in the development of our country as well as to pull the economy out of its turmoil. Public expenditure regulates economic activities and helps to attain the long-run and short-run objectives of economic development. This is why there is continuous upward trend in both revenue and expenditure of the Indian Government. With the growth population Central Government has been widening its activities in general, social and economic spheres to bring economic growth as early as possible and as much as possible at sustainable high rate. Hence, its expenditure on both development and non-development activities have been increasing continuously since 1950-51 or during Five-Year Plans period. The major trends of Central Government expenditures can be discussed as:

(i) **A Continuous Rise in Central Government Expenditure:** The total spending by central government increased from ₹ 530 crore in 1950-51 to ₹ 1298444 crore in 2011-12, it is increment of 2450 times in the time span of 61 years; it is still rising, a symptom of persistent of uncontrollable inflationary situation in the country.

(ii) **Revenue Expenditure Increased much more than Capital Expenditure:** Central Revenue expenditure rose up from ₹ 350 crore in 1950-51 to ₹ 1140915 crore 2011-12 meanwhile central capital expenditure increased from ₹ 180 crore to ₹ 204816 crore; the former rose up by 3260 times and later by 1138 which is less than the former. Revenue expenditure share in total expenditure increased from 66% to 88% during the said period meanwhile capital expenditure share declined from 34% to 12%. Such situation makes the inflation grow wilder.

(iii) **Non-Development Expenditure still continue to be a Large Proportion of the Total Expenditure:** Non-development expenditures comprises the expenditure on tax collection, debt-services, grants and aids to local bodies like municipalities, panchayats, etc. and civil administration like police, judiciary, etc. Development expenditure refers to expenditure on social, community, economic services and grants-in-aid to States and UTs for development purposes. Even today 65% of central total expenditure constituted non-development expenditure.

(iv) **Non-Plan Expenditure is more than Plan Expenditure:** It is always the size of non-plan expenditure is greater than plan expenditure, for example, in 1995-96 non-plan and plan expenditures were respectively ₹ 134320 crore and ₹ 48685 crore;

in 2011-12 they were respectively ₹ 884931 crore and ₹ 413513 crore. But a point to be noted is that during 2007-13 period plan expenditure increased by 148% which is greater than the increment of non-plan expenditure by 91%. It is little relief from inflation as well as protection from debt-trap. However, defence, civil service and debt service expenditures remained the main component of non-plan as well as total central expenditure.

(v) Interest Payment is the Single Largest Item of Central Expenditure: Interest payment is the single largest head of Central Government expenditure. It share in total revenue expenditure was 11% in 1950-51 but now it increased to 23.8%, in 2011-12. It has become the chronic feature of central budget and endorses that the Indian economy is very close to debt-trap.

(vi) Defence Expenditure: It is next to interest payments. It was 47% of the total central expenditure in 1950-51. Of course, the defence expenditure on revenue account has been increased from ₹ 18835 crore in 1995-96 to ₹ 102827 crore in 2011-12 but its share in revenue expenditure declined to 9% in 2011-12. In the context of growing terrorism inside and outside the country and need for maintaining regional defence balance comparatively with China and Pakistan, the present defence-spending is less.

6.4.3 Reasons for Increase in Central Government Expenditure

India being the second populous and one of the biggest democratic developing country in the world, its Central Government expenditure has been increasing continuously. She has lot of constitutional promises to be kept-up and duties to be discharged so various development and non-development activities are being organized since the day of independence. The Central Government expenditure has been increasing much; the reasons for its increase are discussed as under:

(i) Increment in Development Activities: Since 1st April, 1951 the epoch of five year plans being started in India to implement various developmental programmes in agriculture, industry, infrastructure, socio-economic overheads, etc. for to achieve the well defined and pre determined socio-economic goals as well as to solve economic problems like poverty, unemployment, illiteracy, etc. It has widened the role and responsibility of Central

Government that led to continuous increase in Central Government expenditures.

(ii) Strengthening of Defence: India fought wars with China and Pakistan to protect her people, territory and resources from their aggressions. There is cold war between these countries compelled India to spend more on defence services and industries meanwhile the salaries and dearness allowances, pensions, etc. are also revised that lead to increase in defence expenditure of Central Government.

(iii) Inflationary Situation: India has been facing inflationary situation since the beginning of second five-year plan because it used deficit financing method to finance the developmental activities such as industries, etc. that led to excess supply of money in the country; besides, the population growth and failure of rainfall too resulted into inflation in the country. The inflationary situation mounted up burden of public debt and size of public expenditure. Salary scales, dearness and other allowances of civil servants were revised from time to time due to inflation, thus, it increased the Central Government expenditure in many times.

(iv) Incidence of Democracy: The political party in power compelled to spend on many unproductive programmes to please the voters of their respective constituencies. Sometimes they spent more than requirements; sometimes unsuitable projects are being implemented to please their voters; the benefits from project would be less than cost. It is burden of democracy on Central Governments.

(v) Increased States' Activities: There are 28 states and 6 UTs in India and they have a good number of both developmental and non-developmental activities. In recent years the competition between State and Central Governments to please the voters has increased expenditure of both the governments.

(vi) Government Extravagance: The strength of ministers and number of departments increased in many-fold. The number of government employees also increased in greater number; the duplication works took place in various forms. The Travelling Allowance, Dearness allowance, facilities and monetary benefits extended to these ministers and government officials, etc. extravagances have raised the Central Government expenditure.

(vii) Mounting Debt-Services: The burden of payment of interest on borrowed loans and repayment of their principal loan has been increasing continuously due to inflation on the one side and mounting deficit finance on the other side. More or less India is in debt-trap.

(viii) Increased Non-Plan Expenditure: The heads of non-plan expenditure are increased in number as well increment in their size. Subsidies, payment of interest, general services, unproductive expenditures, etc. are rising continuously which the main components of Central Government expenditures are.

(ix) Corruption and Red-Tapism: Everywhere there is corruption in the country that is the main cause for failure and delay in completion of various developmental programmes in the country. Government has implemented various programmes such as subsidy giving programmes, employment programmes, industrial development programmes, etc. programmes but major part of the programme—cost go to government officials pockets in form of bribe. A peon in revenue department drawing monthly salary in thousands is the real owner of crores of rupees property, it is because of corruption; same is true with all government officials and ministers. In other words, about 30%-40% Central Government total expenditure go directly to ministers and government officials in form of corruption. It is the bad mischief being played by these ministers and government officials the total government expenditure is increasing continuously.

6.5 PUBLIC DEBT OF INDIA

Under Article 292, the Constitution of India is also empowered union government to borrow on the security of its consolidated fund under certain conditions determined by the parliament from time to time. Central Government borrows loans from both internal and external sources; the internal loans are 'Rupee-Loans' and external are 'Foreign Currency Loans' such as Sterling-Loans, Dollar-Loans, etc. Central Government borrows loans to finance budgetary deficit because taxation is not a suitable method to finance budget-deficit as it is inflationary in nature as well burdensome on public. However, the public borrowing means substituting of future taxation for current taxation, because public debts would be generally repaid out of tax revenue in future dates.

Public debt arises when the government floats loans and borrows from public. The instruments of public borrowing are in the form of government bonds and securities such as Treasury bills, rural development bonds, etc.

6.5.1 Components or Types of Public Debt

Generally, public debt of India can be classified in three groups as under, they are also called components.

(a) **Permanent or Funded Debt:** The tenure of permanent or funded debt is atleast of twelve months and repayable after this period from the date of issue. Since it repayable after twelve months from the date of issue, it is also called 'currency'. Sometimes, permanent or funded debt is for specified period, to be paid at the will of the government; but the debt can be repaid at any time after giving short notice.

If it has time limit, it will be called 'Terminable Funded Debt' or if it is at government's will, it will be called 'Interminable Funded Debt'. Funded debts cover loans raised in the open market by sale of securities, etc.

(b) **Temporary or Floating Debt:** This type of debt is of purely temporary in nature and repayable within twelve months of the date of issue. It consists of the loans as the 'Ways and Means Advances' from Reserve Bank of India and Treasury Bills, etc. Generally, ways and means advances are taken from Reserve Bank of India for three months only. Treasury bills are also issued to the public that have currency of three, six, nine or twelve months. It also includes non-interest bearing securities issued from International Monetary Fund (IMF), International Development Association (IDA), Asian Development Bank (ADB) and World Bank (IBRD).

(c) **Unfunded Debt:** There is no difference between unfunded debt and floating debt in many countries but in India unfunded debt is used in special sense. Unfunded debt has certain interest bearing obligations of central government such as Small Savings Scheme, Post Office Savings, National Defence Certificates, Provident Fund Deposits, etc.

New Classification: Central Government has classified public debts into three major groups as under:

(i) Internal Debt: Internal debt consists of market borrowing or market loans raised in the open market. It was previously called permanent or funded debt. Internal debt also includes treasury bills issued by the Government of India to the Reserve Bank and other financial institutions. These loans were formerly called temporary loans or floating loans.

(ii) External Debt: External debt includes loans taken by the Government of India against the non-negotiable, non-interest bearing securities issued to international financial institutions like IMF, IBRD, IDA, ADB, etc. It also includes Central Government's borrowing from foreign individuals, institutions and governments.

(iii) Other Outstanding Liabilities: The Government of India is liable to repay its outstanding liabilities against to various small saving schemes such as Public Provident Fund, Compulsory Deposits, and Income Tax Deposit, super-tax deposits of Local Funds and Civil Deposits and other reserve funds of government departments like Post and Telegraphs, Railways, etc. These were earlier termed as unfunded debt.

6.5.2 Magnitude of India's Public Debt

India's total debt has been increased much in recent years. It has become inevitable to the Indian government to use public debt as a method on financing both covering public expenditure and development programmes. Its dependency on foreign debt too increased much because of need for foreign capital, technology, defence requirements, etc. increased much. The magnitude of India's public debt is shown in the following table:

Table 6.7: India's Public Debt. (₹ in Crore)

Years	Internal debt	External debt	Other liabilities	Total debt
1950-51	2022	32	811	2865
1980-81	29008	1116	18398	58723
1991-92	172749	36948	144963	354661
1992-93	193034	41217	162229	396481
2010-11	2667115	157639	1114020	3938774
2011-12	3202411	167950	1098353	4468714
2012-13 (BE)	3743658	178098	1103616	5025372

Sources: Compiled Data & Economic Survey, 2012-13

The total public debt of India increased from ₹ 2865 crore in 1950-51 to ₹ 5025372 crore in 2012-13 (BE), it is almost increased by 1754 times. The Table 6.7 helps to find out the trends in growth of India's public debt in the span of 62 years after independence. These trends are:

(i) Overall Growth of Public Debt: Being had three components the total public debt increased by 2827% average annually during 62 years due to increment in size of these components. This annual growth rate is much higher than GDP annual average growth rate of India; it is symptom of fall in debt trap.

(ii) Uncontrolled Growth of Internal Debt: The internal debt increased from ₹ 2022 crore in 1950-51 to ₹ 3743658 crore in 2012-13 (BE); it is increased average annually by 2985% during 62 years, it is more than total public debt growth rate. Market loans is the main component of internal debt. Market loans and bonds and securities sale method not only helps the government to mobilize financial resources from surplus to deficit areas but also helps to fight inflation. However, the uncontrolled growth of internal debt shows unscientific expenditure by government and heavy future tax burden.

(iii) Growing External Debt: External debt has been playing a significant role in economic development of India. It fills important gaps like foreign exchange-gap, technology-gap, balance of payments gap, etc. It includes long-term and short-term loans. The total external debt of India increased from ₹ 32 crore to ₹ 178098 crore in 2012-13 (BE), it is increased average annually by 8975% during 62 years. It also helped to control inflation in the country.

(iv) Other Outstanding Liabilities: It is an important sources borrowing of the government. The total debt from this source increased from ₹ 811 crore in 1950-51 to ₹ 1103616 crore in 2012-13 (BE); its average annual growth is 2193% in 62 years. It too helped to control inflation in the country.

6.5.3 Causes for the Growth of India's Public Debt

The total public debt of India increased average annually by 2827% during 1950-51 to 2012-13. There are several causes for continuous increase in public debt of India. These are:

(i) Expansion of Government Activities: The Government expands its activities in all directions including economic service, general services and social and community services to achieve development.

(ii) Increase in Defence Requirements: The external aggressions compelled India to spend more on defence services including purchase of arms and ammunitions. The terrorist activities and maintaining defence balance in the region have resulted into increase in public debt.

(iii) Increase in Unproductive Activities: The Government expanded its unproductive and consumption expenditures in recent years. Interest payment, subsidy programmes, social security schemes, revision of pay scales, etc. have raised public spending that is more than the revenue capacity of the government so public borrowings has been increasing continuously.

(iv) Increasing External Debt: There is rapid increase in external debt of India due to following reasons:

(a) Our Constitution does not permit States to borrow from abroad so the Central Government raises all external loans on their behalf. Since the States needs towards foreign capital increased, the Central Government's external borrowing increased much.

(b) There are huge imports by government to supply the needs of defence department, industry and agricultural sectors, infrastructure sector and essential consumption goods.

(c) Recently, under the new economic reforms the government policy is encouraging direct foreign investment that has encouraged borrowing from abroad for purpose of inputs.

(d) The foreign loans raised for production activities have not been used to generate adequate export earnings. The cost of debt servicing has been increasing an account of growing of external indebtedness. Out of borrowed \$100, India using \$65 for external debt services.

(v) Uncontrolled Growth of Internal Debt: In this case, the basic reason for growing internal indebtedness lies in recurring and mounting fiscal deficit of the centre. The internal debt has been increasing because of the following reasons:

(a) The growing commitments by the political party in power have been raising internal debts. For example, food subsidies and other subsides, self employment programmes, etc.

(b) Public sector undertakings are running in losses due to excess intervention by politicians, inefficient management, etc. These loss suffering industries are being fed by public borrowing funds.

(c) Avoidable and wasteful public expenditure on numerous functions, activities and other heads are increasing continuously.

(d) Borrowings from RBI, particularly non-negotiable and non-interest loans, have encouraged the government to get more loans.

(e) The phenomenon of increase in other liabilities of the centre is partly explained by the causes mentioned earlier. The growing financial needs of the government encouraged it to explore all possible ways of raising additional resources. Naturally the government is exploiting this source of funds to the full extent. The resource pooled by means like tax incentives and legal obligations wherein the savings of the economy were forced to flow into government hands in the form of small savings, provident funds and deposits, etc.

(vi) Inadequate Revenue Source: It is not possible to government, or even desirable, to raise all needy fund resources through taxation only; it would be more burdensome on the people. The government departments and its PSUs to earn more income to meet government expenditures.

6.5.4 Limitations of Public Borrowing

In India, one of the prime tasks of the government is to stimulate the growth of the economy with stability. For the purpose of rapid development of the economy, certain minimum conditions are essential such as abundant natural resources, skilled enterprises, trained man power and dedicated civil services, etc. At the same time, fundamental factor to determine development is the capital formation or resource mobilization. Therefore, the most vigorous efforts are being made to mobilize the financial resources to achieve the higher rate of economic growth with stability.

The capital accumulation or resource mobilization can be raised through taxation, borrowing and deficit financing at domestic level. Domestic savings are very limited. Household sector alone contributes 75 per cent of domestic savings. The propensity to save is very poor in India; a large size of population falls in low income groups. The situation is further worsened as a longer part of it goes to unproductive channels like hoarding, purchasing of property and precious metals and jewellery, etc. In other words, the scope of public borrowings, taxation is not much wide due to the following several constraints:

(i) Since majority of population lives at the subsistence level, it results in low ability of savings of these people.

(ii) There is lack of saving habits among the people. Even if they save, it will be spent on ceremonial consumption such like wedding, birth and death ceremonies, religious ceremonies, etc.

(iii) Lack of banking facilities, investment opportunities, fear of heavy taxation compel them too hoard savings.

(iv) There are money market imperfections and unorganized sector. It is difficult to float government loans in money market.

(v) Inflationary situation has been taking away the savings of the people in form of rising prices.

(vi) There is uncontrolled growth of population in India. It has affected adversely on propensity to save.

(vii) A large number of people are ignorant of investment in government securities.

These limitations of financing, economic development with domestic resources leads us to consider the role of public borrowings as means of mobilizing financial resources.

On the other hand, external borrowing become more burdensome and problematic because the value of Indian Rupee is declining continuously in foreign exchange market.

6.5.5 Role of Public Borrowing

Public borrowing has accelerated the speed of economic development in India. It has been helping the country in the following ways:

(a) It helps to increase in real per capita income and output.

(b) It helps to provide the necessary institutional framework for the effective implementation of fiscal as well as monetary policies.

(c) It acts as an anti-inflationary measure for mobilizing resources in the hands of the people.

(d) It promotes saving and investment which in turn can be utilized in the risky industrial ventures.

(e) It strengthens the money and capital market on sound fooling.

(f) It influences social, cultural and institutional factors to a greater extent that helps to economy directly and indirectly.

(g) It is an essential medium to bring changes in socio-economic scenario of the country.

(h) If the public external borrowings are to be more productive, it accompanied with technology and innovations.

Like western countries, India has too initiated pro-developmental activities with the assistance of both internal and external debts.

6.5.6 Problems of Public Debt

The problems of public debt depend upon factors such as the sources of loan funds, the purpose for which borrowing is done, the terms and conditions which the debt is floated, and the volume of the existing public debt, the interest rates, the types of loan employed and the general economic conditions of the community. These are discussed as:

(i) Problems of Public Debt and the Sources of Borrowing: The government may barrow from individual investors, financial institutions, commercial banks, and central bank of the country and from abroad. The domestic borrowing are quite different from that of foreign borrowing. In internal borrowing, there is no increase in the total quantity of resources available for the use; rather, it is a method to enable the government to command more domestic resources. Borrowing from individuals and financial institutions is simply a transfer of resources from private to government use thus it does not create any expansionary effects on the economy. However, it creates expansionary effects only when government activated individuals' idle savings. Besides, borrowing from the commercial banks and the central bank will also produce such an effect due to increase in additional purchase in power, as a result of credit expansion.

(ii) Problem of Public Debt and the Purpose of Borrowing: The problems of public debt also depend on the purpose for which the debt is created. If borrowing funds are used for waste full expenditure, they will not create any social assets; but such borrowing is indispensable welfare expenditures. Further, these borrowing too influence on interest rates thereby upon the banking system, individual and corporate investment and economic conditions in general. Higher the interest rate on borrowing funds, stronger the pull on funds from competing investments. If the governments attach the feature of tax exemption to their loans, this will tend to encourage the purchase of their securities that affects adversely on the private borrowings. Hence, it can be said that the government's credit policies may affect private enterprises and individuals investments adversely.

(iii) Problem of Public Debt and the Amount of Loans Obtained: The problem of public debt also depends on the amount of loans obtained and the term on which the loan is floated in the market. The larger the public loan more the problems on the economic system. If government employs borrowed funds for more productive purposes than private enterprise do, the social income will be increased, but if they used this fund for less productive activities then the social income suffer. However, it is to be kept in view that the volume of the existing debt or creation of new debt alone does not create the problem. The composition, maturity pattern and ownership have their own parts of public debt play a vital role in creation of problems, general economic conditions should also be taken into account. Heavy government borrowing during boom period may create inflationary effect, while borrowing at the end of the depression or at the beginning of recovery may help to promote recovery.

6.5.7 Effects of the Public Debt on the Economy

Through its associated problems public borrowing has various effects on Indian economy. It has both revenue associated and expenditure associated problems that directly and indirectly influence on the budget of the people. The consumption, savings and investment activities are to be changed by raising public borrowing. The economic effects of public debt are as follows:

(i) Effects on Consumption: When people purchase government securities, it reduces past savings as well as present consumption. People buy government securities, generally, out of their present income to avail high rate of interest opportunity that reduces present consumption expenditure.

(ii) Effects on Production: Generally, public borrowing diverts resources from available to private investment to government use thereby private sector production declines but its overall effects depend upon purpose of utilization of these funds; if used on more productive activities there are no adverse effects on production, otherwise it reduces production in the economy.

(iii) Effects on Distribution: In India, the purchasers of government securities are mostly rich people. But the burden of taxes imposed for raising of money to pay interest payments fall on the poor classes. Therefore, the general tendency of public debt is to increase the inequalities of income and wealth in the country.

(iv) Effects on Private Sector: In India, public debt encouraged the private sector development through supporting higher demand for its goods and services directly and indirectly. If the government utilizes the borrowed money in purchasing goods and materials produced in the private sector, the demand for goods and services produced in the private sector may increase to the extent of the government spends borrowed funds for this purpose.

(v) Effects on the Cost of Production: In India, the spending of public borrowing on infrastructural facilities development has reduced the cost of production of private sector. The cost of production depends upon the prices of raw materials and other factors used in production. The government utilizes the borrowed funds to supply raw material to the producers at reasonable rates and to provide transport and training facilities. The government also utilizes these funds for promoting industrial research or giving subsidies to enterprises. In all these cases, the spending of public debt by government reduces the cost of production.

(vi) Effects on Investment: Government spending on public sector undertakings and subsidies to the private industries have encouraged much investment activities in the country. Moreover, it provides extra purchasing power to the community that raises the aggregate demand.

(vii) Effects on Working of the Money Market: Government through its public debt policy controlling the interest rate and transactions in the money market of India. It floats more of its bonds and securities in money market. It is controlling credit creation activities of commercial banks.

(viii) Effects of Foreign Loans: External borrowing, of course, helped a lot to boost the development of Indian economy during 1950s, 1960s and 1970s. It helped much to import the basic needs of agriculture and industrial development in the early years of five-year plans. It effects both the consumption and investment favourably. But the worst part of it is continuous deficit in balance of payment position and decline in exchange rate.

6.5.8 Public Debt Policy

Public debt policy is also known as public debt management policy. The overall objective of the government debt management policy is to meet Central Government's financing need at the lowest possible long-term borrowing costs and also to keep the total debt within sustainable levels. Additionally, it aims at supporting development of a well functioning and vibrant domestic bond market. Moreover, the methods of borrowing funds and repayment of loans should help to maintain economic stability: it should reduce inflationary or deflationary effects on the economy as well as it should make needed funds available to the government. The management or repayment of public debt is concerned with refunding, floating or retirement of public debt, etc.

The public debt policy, fiscal policy and the monetary policy are closely connected with each other for the determination of economic policy, and therefore, they should work in co-ordination with each other. Various principles of public debt management are as follows:

(i) Minimization of Interest Cost: The Interest Cost of Public Debts must be minimized. According to this principle, the government must be in a position to create and redeem public debts at a minimum interest cost. This should be an important objective of public debt management. It should be kept minimum because the government has to pay it out of tax revenue; for this purpose either the additional taxes have to be levied or the existing tax rates have to be raised by the government. If the interest cost is minimum, the government will have to impose smaller amount of additional taxes, it means future tax-burden will be lesser on public. The Reserve Bank of India should keep bank rate at low level through its monetary policy to reduce interest cost burden on government.

(ii) Satisfaction of the Needs of Investment: It is always argued that public debts should be managed in such a way that the needs of the investors with regard to the types of the government securities and the terms of issues are satisfied. The government may find it difficult to manage the public debts, if the investors' needs are not satisfied. For instance, if government desires to fund its short-term debt into a long-term debt, it will have to offer attractive forms on the long-term securities such as higher interest rates on them. Or the government may offer to the security holders to convert long-term securities into cash without any loss for the purchase of new securities issued by the government.

(iii) Funding of Short-Term Debt into Long-Term Debt: It is argued that the public debt management or repayment should help to fund as much as of the short-term debt into long-term debt to the possible extent but it should be done in such a way that the economic stability is not disturbed. This policy would tend to raise the long-term rate of interest because the demand for long-term funds will have to be increased but this will also increase the budget expenditures in future. Simultaneously, it should reduce the short-term interest rates because the demand for short-term funds will fall.

(iv) Public Debt Policy must be Co-ordinated with Fiscal and Monetary Policy: The co-ordination of public debt policy with fiscal and monetary policy is essential to maintain economic stability as well as to promote economic growth. For instance, if the government forces the Reserve Bank of India to follow a low interest-rate policy in order to keep the cost of interest payment on public debt at low, it may create inflationary condition and may result in economic instability. Hence, such an economic instability should be avoided by a proper co-ordination between the public debt policy and monetary policy.

(v) Maturity, Distribution and Kinds of Debt Holders: If a large proportion of the total debt is short-term debt and a high proportion of the total debt is held by banks, there can be a high degree of liquidity which may contribute to an inflationary pressure at a time when an anti-inflationary policy may be desirable. Thus, high liquidity of debt makes the control of inflation difficult.

It is thus, obvious, from the study of these facts that it may not be possible to achieve all the objectives of the public debt management. For instance, the policy of keeping the interest rate low may contribute to an inflationary condition, while the funding of the short-term debt into long-term debt may cause recession and unemployment.

However, there are two options for the Central Government while preparing its road map for debt reduction in the coming years. These are (a) to have larger than the recommended deficit by the 13th Finance Commission and yet achieve the prescribed target of debt at 45 per cent of GDP; or (b) fulfil the commitments for fiscal consolidation made in terms of reduction in fiscal deficit and target for even lower debt level by 2014-15. While designing a debt reduction strategy for the period 2010-11 to 2014-15, it is suggested to follow the second option under which the commitment made in the Medium Term Fiscal Policy Statement of the government, as presented in the Budget 2010-11, regarding reduction in fiscal deficit would be honoured. It is projected that the fiscal deficit would be reduced to 3 per cent of GDP by 2014-15 and accordingly debt as percentage of GDP would come down from 50.5 per cent in 2009-10 to 43 per cent in 2014-15.

6.6 INDIAN DEFICIT FINANCING

In Indian as per normal practice, deficit financing means the filling of the budgetary deficit or gap caused by the excess of government total expenditure over its total receipts through either increasing Treasury bills and withdrawal of cash balance of the government or borrowing from Reserve Bank of India that creates of new currency into circulation or both. However, the external borrowing, market loans, deficit budget and other liabilities are the main methods of financing fiscal deficit in India; it is regular practice to finance budgetary deficit in India. The following table shows the recent trends in financing fiscal deficit:

Trends in Financing Fiscal Deficit: The Table 6.8 shows the various trends in Central Government methods of financing fiscal deficit as under:

(i) The size of total fiscal financing increased from ₹ 37606 crore in 1990-91 to ₹ 400998 crore in 2010-11; it is increased by 1066.3% during 20 years, the average annual growth rate is 53.3%. Financing of fiscal deficit by Central Government is still higher in India that created difficult situation to get rid of the inflation situation.

(ii) The share of external finance in total fiscal deficit finance has been declined from 8.5% in 1990-91 to 5.6% in 2010-11 meanwhile, however, its size increased from ₹ 3181 crore to ₹ 22264 crore that is increased by 699.9%; it is increased at average annually by 35%.

Table 6.8: Financing of Fiscal Deficit of Central Government

Year	External Finance (₹ Crore)	Market Borrowing (₹ Crore)	Budget Deficit /Draw down of cash balances (₹ Crore)	Other Liabilities (₹ Crore)	Total (₹ Crore)	External Finance (% of Total)	Market Borrowing	Budget Deficit /Draw down of cash balances (% of Total)	Other Liabilities (% of Total)	Total (% of Total)
1990-91	3181	8001	11347	15077	37606	8.5	21.3	30.2	40.0	100
1995-96	318	33087	9807	7041	50253	0.6	65.9	19.5	14.0	100
2000-01	7505	72931	-1197	39577	118816	6.3	61.4	-1.0	33.3	100
2005-06	33366	103374	-20888	30583	146435	22.8	70.6	-14.3	20.9	100
2010-11	22264	355414	-15000	38320	400998	5.6	88.6	-3.7	9.6	100

Source: Compiled Datafrom Union Budget Documents

(iii) The size of market borrowing for financing fiscal deficit has been increased from ₹ 8001 crore in 1990-91 to ₹ 355414 crore in 2010-11; it is increased by 4442.1% during 20 years or increased average annually by 222.11%. The share of market borrowing, meanwhile, increased from 21.2% to 88.6%; however, it is being used to control excess supply of money from circulation to fight inflation.

(iv) The budget deficit/withdrawing of cash balances of the government was ₹ 11347 crore in 1990-91 but it was reduced to ₹ 15,000 crore in 2010-11 so it changed by 132.2% during 20 years but average annual declining rate is 6.6%. Central Government committed, under Fiscal Responsibility and Budget Management (FRBM) Act 2003, to control the budgetary deficit less than 3% of GDP.

(v) Financing through the funds of other liabilities has been increased from ₹ 15077 crore in 1990-91 to ₹ 38320 crore in 2010-11 but its share in total deficit finance, meanwhile declined from 40% to 9.6%; so it has increased by 254.2% in 20 years and its average annual growth rate is 12.7%. This is also helpful to control inflation.

Among all the sources of financing budgetary deficit market borrowing is the major source and it is the suitable measure to fight inflation.

6.6.1 Role of Deficit Financing

There is need for deficit financing in economic development of India as well as providing of social justice. Its need and role in overall development of country are discussed as under:

(i) For Financing Five-Year Plans: India started five-year plans since 1951, 1st April to achieve economic development thereby attaining the socio-economic justice goal. It had no adequate fund to finance developmental activities during plans so since the beginning of the First Five-Year Plan itself the government has been using 'deficit-financing' method as the source of finance to developmental programmes. The volume of deficit financing has been increased during the various plan periods. It has been increased from ₹ 232 crore during first plan to ₹ 1421711 crore in eleventh plan. As a result of it the production in both commodity and service sectors increased much. In fact, Indian planners have justified it as a legitimate means of mobilization of unemployed resources for productive purposes.

(ii) For Establishment of Socialistic Pattern of Society: The Constitution of India in its preamble promises its people to provide them socio-economic justice thus government has been spending on subsidies, public distribution systems, education, social security schemes, public health, etc. programmes so as to establish socialistic pattern of society in India. Deficit financing has been empowering the government to carry-out these programmes successfully.

(iii) To Cover Defence Expenditure: The growing terrorism and regional defence imbalance demanding more money to meet growing defence expenditure, particularly in recent year. Import of most sophisticated defence technology, weapons, equipment and other requirements have become inevitable on part of government. A good defence of the country protects its people, territories and resources. These defence expenses are being met by both current revenues and deficit finance.

(iv) To Fill Savings-Investment Gap: There is always gap between savings and investment in India. The level of savings is always less than the level of investment by more than 1 per cent. This gap is being filled by deficit financing.

(v) For Utilization of Resources: India is rich in natural resources, including human being. Lack of adequate fund, backward technology, etc. are the main reasons for under utilization of these resources. Deficit financing has filled these gaps and helped for better utilization of these resources. Development plans being financed by deficit financing have put these resources to best uses.

(vi) To Develop Social and Economic Overheads: Private sectors are unable to take development of social and economic infrastructure such as transport, power, education, health, etc. So it is government that has been developing these overheads with the help of deficit financing.

(vii) Easy Means to Raise Fund: Taxation and borrowing levy burden on people, they even create inflation and discourage investment activities; they even need more efforts to gather fund. But deficit financing is easy means of raising funds. Reserve Bank of India supplies fund simply by issuing new money. Government need not worry about repayment of principal amount and payment of interest thereon.

6.6.2 Merits and Demerits of Deficit Financing

Of course deficit financing is most acceptable method by both developed and underdeveloped countries to attain economic stability with growth. It is boon to Indian economy because economic development was totally impossible without it. However, it has both positive and negative effects on the economy.

(a) Merits: Deficit financing has the following positive effects on economy or merits.

***(i) Best use of Resources*:** Deficit financing helped lot for making the best use of un-utilised and surplus resources. Moreover, for the development of several projects, it creates the funds.

***(ii) Helpful to Create Fund*:** In India, the government finds it as difficult to create resources through taxation. It is because there is always opposition from the public against increasing taxation. Voluntary borrowing has also a limit. For these reasons deficit financing remains necessarily alternative to create extra resources.

***(iii) Additional Purchasing Power*:** A small dose of deficit financing helps to increase the money supply and push up aggregate demand. This naturally adds to the purchasing power with the public. Furthermore, it boosts up the demand for goods and services, which in turn leads to increase in production, income and employment.

***(iv) Helpful despite Inflationary Nature*:** Generally, it is argued that deficit financing leads to inflation, which is against poor masses. But it is not a permanent feature. Since developmental activities are financed through it, they start yielding production as soon as the projects are completed. This leads to flow of goods and services into market so prices also start falling automatically.

(b) Demerits: The expansion or creation of money with the help of deficit financing has ugly side also. It is self-destructive in nature. However, the evil-effects of it are summarised as below:

***(i) Rise in Prices*:** It is truly admitted that deficit financing leads to rise in prices. It is due to the fact that deficit financing increases the supply of money and therefore, raises the aggregate demand for goods and services on the other side, the aggregate real output is not rising at the same speed as the supply of money, resulting in rise in prices. If prices go on increasing the value of money will decrease. India has been experiencing inflation since second plan due to mounting deficit financing.

***(ii) Increase in Money Supply*:** Deficit financing results in the direct addition to gross national expenditures. In other words, creation of fresh purchasing power in the hands of the government. This addition in money supply in an easy way upsets price level that suffers the weaker section of the society. In India, poverty alleviation became difficult task because of mounting inflation every year pulling poor down to below poverty line.

***(iii) Adequate Speculative Activities*:** With the help of deficit financing policy, the Reserve Bank of India and commercial banks found themselves with larger cash reserves to create larger amounts of credit in the economy. As a result, the Indian market is always flooded with the surplus of bank money which could be avoidable for any purpose. This has given further rise to the phenomenon of speculation, hoarding of essential commodities.

***(iv) Adverse Effect on Savings*:** Another evil effect of deficit financing is that it has adverse effects on savings. As there is rapid rise in prices of the essential commodities, the income and savings are being taken away from people in form of higher price. So savings are being affected adversely.

***(v) Less Investment*:** There are certain avenues of investment that are being much encouraged by inflation such as inventory holding, luxury items, urban construction and foreign assets. In fact, they are not necessarily the best avenues of investment from the angle of development. Rising money incomes greatly favour big producers and not persons with fixed income, salaries and wages groups. Thus, deficit financing led inflation has encouraged only those types of investment activities which are not desirable for the development of the Indian Economy.

(vi) Unequal Distribution of Income and Wealth: The deficit financing created inflation usually creates unequal distribution of wealth and income in the country. The richer are able to maintain their consumption at higher and higher level but the weaker find it difficult to be stayed on the old position. During such inflationary situation the rich will have more opportunity to harvest the fruits of development but the poor are the losers and victims of such situation.

6.7 INDIAN FISCAL POLICY

Indian fiscal policy refers to the policy of government regarding its revenue, expenditure and borrowing decisions. Its aim is to produce desirable effects and avoid undesirable effects on the national economy. Indian government has formulated various economic policies such as price policy, monetary policy, fiscal policy, etc. to have control over economic activities so as to channelize them to achieve its pre-defined socio-economic goals that would provide socio-economic justice to all. The execution of fiscal policy is being accompanied with monetary policy; fiscal policy is helping the effective implementation of monetary policy in the country. Fiscal policy is being executed by the Central Government in support of Reserve Bank of India's monetary policy that both could achieve aims like price control, economic stability with growth, control of supply of money, etc. The Indian Fiscal Policy could be studied as:

(a) Objectives: Fiscal policy is being used as instruments to achieve the following objectives:

(i) Rapid Economic Development: India is a backward country. India has 'social control' operated economic system. It needs government interference in productive investments in both private and public sector. Tax reliefs, concessions, and subsidies, infrastructural facilities, etc. by the government could encourage productive activities in private sector. Public expenditure on socio-economic overheads, direct investments in public sector undertakings, etc. could encourage public sector development. Public borrowing supplies more investable funds. Thus, fiscal

policy encourages rapid economic development. Today's higher rate of economic growth is the outcome of the fiscal policy.

***(ii) Removal Poverty and Unemployment*:** Unemployment and poverty are the major burning problems of India since the days of British Rule. Private sector is not enough efficient to generate more employment opportunities through investment activities. It is the deficit-financing oriented public expenditure supported much investment activities both in public and private sectors; these efforts put more men and materials to best use. Alleviation of poverty is another aim of fiscal policy. Food subsidies, public distribution system, self and wage employment programmes, etc. public expenditure have aimed at reduction of poverty.

***(iii) Socialistic Pattern of Society*:** There is socio-economic inequalities in the country. Fiscal measures like taxation and public expenditures are being used to establish socialist pattern of society in the country. The rich are taxed according to their taxable capacity and so collected tax-revenue is being used for the betterment of the poor. The ownership of income and wealth is de-centralized through the development of public sector development in every economic field.

***(iv) Reduction of Regional Imbalance*:** The economic status of all states and union territories is not same; only few states such as Punjab, Gujarat, Maharashtra, Haryana and Tamil Nadu are industrially advanced states and rest all are backward states. There is need for mobilizing of resources to these states could be made possible through fiscal measures like public investments, tax-reliefs, developmental grants, etc.

***(v) Re-distribution of Income and Wealth*:** The wealth and income are not distributed evenly among all people. The gap between haves and have-nots increasing much due to lack of effective fiscal measures. The investment and employment opportunities could be distributed among all. Taxation Policy has been used as instrument of re-distribution of income from rich to poor by diverting some portion income, taken in form of taxes, to poor in form of public expenditure on betterment programmes. Income and wealth are also re-distributed through de-centralization of industrial ownership by way of developing public sector undertakings.

(vi) Capital Formation and Mobilization of Resources: Less than 10 per cent of GDP was the level of savings and investment. The various methods of public borrowing and attractive interest rate in money market on the one side and ever increasing level of income due to development process on the other side took the level of savings more than 30 per cent of GDP in recent years. Meanwhile the mobilization of financial resources through fiscal measures took the level of investment above 31 per cent of GDP.

(vii) Control of Inflation: Inflation situation has been continued in the country since the beginning of second plan. Taxes to control excess demand, public spending on productive activities and raising of public borrowing have helped a lot to control inflation.

(b) Tools of Fiscal Policy: To achieve the objectives of fiscal policy government devised the following tools:

(i) Taxation Policy: Taxation is an important fiscal instrument to achieve fiscal policy objectives. Under this policy government has been imposing both direct and indirect taxes. The main objectives of taxation policy are (a) mobilizing of resources for financing development, (b) formation of capital through encouraging savings and investment, (c) re-distribution of income and wealth through progressive tax system, and (d) price stability. Now direct taxes constitute 56 per cent of tax revenue of Central Government. During the fiscal consolidation period, the tax-GDP ratio improved significantly from 9.2 per cent in 2003-04 to 11.9 per cent in 2007-08. This was achieved through rationalisation of the tax structure, moderate levels and a few rates, widening of the tax base and reduction in compliance costs throug him provement in tax administration.

(ii) Public Expenditure: Public expenditure has several effects on income, employment, output and price. It is another important tool to achieve the objectives of fiscal policy. It is inevitable to the government to spend its money on both productive and unproductive activities in which private sector is not or less interested but they have national importance such as irrigation, roads, railways, public health, education, core investment sector, defence, etc. The unproductive public spending is inflationary in nature. In recent years, Central Plan Scheme Monitoring System

(CPSMS) is an initiative towards establishing a suitable on-line management information and decision support system. It is proposed to expand the Scheme of Central Plan Scheme Monitoring System (CPSMS). This would improve the tracking of funds released by the Central Government and also ensure better utilisation of borrowed resources.

***(iii) Public Borrowing*:** Public borrowing is also important tool of fiscal policy. Government borrows funds from internal and external sources. Market borrowing is the main source. Public borrowing is used to finance budget deficit and to correct balance of payment deficit. It helps the government to get fund for its productive and unproductive activities. Government is committed to implement prudent debt management strategies so as to ensure that the public debt remains within sustainable limits and does not crowd out private borrowing for investment. The policy of the government is driven by the principle of gradual reduction of public debt to GDP ratio so as to further reduce debt servicing risk and create fiscal space for developmental expenditure. On the financing side, the government policy continues to remain anchored on the following principles, namely (a) greater reliance on domestic borrowings over external debt, (b) preference for market borrowings over instruments carrying administered interest rates, (c) consolidation of the debt portfolio and (d) development of a deep and wide market for government securities to improve liquidity in secondary market.

***(iv) Deficit Financing*:** In India deficit financing means injecting of new money in circulation through public borrowing from RBI. It seemed to be the best method of financing developmental programmes. But using this method to finance unproductive programmes would definitely lead to inflation. Today there is excess supply of money in the country due to deficit financing. To control inflation the fiscal deficit has to be controlled that can be done through reducing deficit-financing.

***(v) Budget Analysis*:** India has been using deficit budget as instrument to achieve its fiscal policy objectives. It helps the government to keep control on economic activities of the country. It helps to generate income and employment through investment activities.

(c) Fiscal Policy Evaluation: Fiscal policy and monetary policy are complementary to each other; both are two sides of the same coin. Since Reserve Bank of India has implemented 'controlled expansion' and 'growth with stability' approaches aiming to achieve economic development with higher growth rate and economic stability through controlling price level, the fiscal authorities have formulated suitable fiscal policy to make the monetary policy successful. Budget is being used as instrument of fiscal policy to attain its goals. The fiscal policy has several merits and demerits that are discussed as under:

***(a) Merits*:** The fiscal policy has empowered the government to regulate economic activities to attain desirable results such as high economic growth rate, increase in employment, price control, social justice, etc. The main merits of the policy are:

(i) Increased Central Government Plan Expenditure: The Central Government has under taken various developmental programmes such as agriculture, irrigation, energy, transport, communication, research and development, etc. with the help of its revenue and capital resources, for instance, budget 2011-12 raised plan expenditure to ₹ 413513 crore; really such expenditure could take the economy to higher and higher growth rate.

(ii) Tax Benefits: Various tax reliefs, concessions and benefits are being given to all class of people that could encourage savings and investment activities in the country. Now the level of both savings and investment are more than 30 per cent of GDP.

(iii) Socio-Economic Justice: India has been following progressive tax system. Fifty-six per cent of total tax-revenue is being collected by levying direct taxes like personal income tax, corporate tax, etc. So the tax burden on poor is low. Tax-revenue from indirect taxes is declining in recent years. Government is spending more on public health, education, drinking water, social security schemes, employment guarantee schemes, food and fertilizer subsidies, Bharath Nirman, etc. The size of population below poverty line also declined to 19 per cent in recent years. So the gap between haves and have-nots is narrowing down.

***(b) Demerits*:** Despite of the various merits, fiscal policy has suffered many demerits that are discussed as under:

(i) Mounting Non-Plan Expenditure: Central non-plan expenditure such as civil administration. Defence, subsidies, interest-payment, etc. are unproductive expenditures. It is ₹ 969900 crore in budget 2011-12. It has created huge fiscal deficit and inflationary situation in the country. Central Finance Minister has prepared the strategy to control non-plan expenditure.

(ii) Growing Fiscal Deficit: The fiscal deficit of Central Government increased from ₹ 126912 crore in 2007-08 to ₹ 509731 crore in 2011-12; it is 4.6 per cent of GDP in 2011-12. The growing huge fiscal deficit taken the resort of deficit financing that has raised excess supply of money in the economy and it made inflation control very difficult.

(iii) Low Tax Revenue: The tax-GDP ratio is always at low level. It was ₹ 569869 crore in 2010-11 and increased to ₹ 631886 crore in 2011-12. It constitutes low percentage in total revenue of Central Government. This compelled the government to take more help from deficit financing.

To rundown, budget 2011-12 was presented against the backdrop of robust revival of growth in Indian economy. Indian economy was estimated to grow at 9 per cent over the then estimated growth of 8.5 per cent in 2010-11. However, after budget presentation, happenings around the globe including hardening of 27 global crude prices and sticky high inflation scenario in the domestic economy, forced the government to make necessary changes in policy during 2011-12 to address the emerging challenges.

Fiscal deficit which was estimated at 4.6 per cent of GDP in BE 2011-12 has increased to 5.9 per cent of GDP in RE 2011-12. This increase in deficit could be attributed to moderation in growth, which impacted direct tax collection and high inflation necessitating additional expenditure on food, fertilizer and petroleum subsidies. In the budget 2012-13, government is addressing the two main reasons of slippage by controlling rise in subsidy related expenditure and improving tax receipts as percentage of GDP through 'Additional Resource Mobilisation' measures (ARM) in indirect taxes. With ARM from indirect taxes, coupled with estimated receipts of ₹ 40,000 crore from telecommunication spectrum auction and disinvestment proceeds of ₹ 30,000 crore, the fiscal deficit for 2012-13 is estimated at 5.1 per cent of GDP. The reduction in deficit has been estimated without compromising on allocations for developmental expenditure.

6.8 MODEL QUESTIONS

(a) Questions each needs answer in 2-3 sentences (2 Marks each)

1. Who does present Union Budget in India?
2. Name any two parts of budget.
3. Mention any two trends of Union Budget.
4. What are the major revenue receipts of Central Government?
5. Write on capital receipts of Central Government.
6. Name any two central direct taxes.
7. Mention any two central indirect taxes.
8. Name any two central non-tax revenue sources.
9. Why Central Government is more important than State in collection of taxes?
10. State any two heads of Central Government expenditure.
11. Write any two trends of Central Government expenditure.
12. Give any two reasons for increasing central expenditure.
13. State any two components of central public debt.
14. Mention any two reasons for growing central debt.
15. Why central internal debt is increasing?
16. Name any two limitations of central public debt.
17. Name any two role of public borrowing.
18. State the factors determining problems of public debts.
19. Give any two effects of public borrowing on Indian economy.
20. State the meaning of deficit financing in India.

21. Name any two methods of financing fiscal deficit in India.
22. Mention any two role of deficit financing in India.
23. State any two merits of deficit financing in India.
24. Mention any two demerits of deficit financing in India.
25. Write any two objectives of Indian fiscal policy.
26. State any two tools of Indian fiscal policy.
27. Name any two merits of Indian fiscal policy.
28. Name any two demerits of Indian fiscal policy.

(b) Questions each needs short-note type answer (5 Marks each)

1. Give a brief account of Revenue Budget Model of India.
2. Write a note on Capital Budget Model of India.
3. Discuss in brief the revenue receipts of Central Government.
4. Write a short-note on trends in Central Government revenue.
5. Explain in brief the heads of central revenue expenditure.
6. Write a note on trends in Central Government expenditure.
7. Analyse briefly the reasons of increase in Central Government expenditure.
8. Discuss in brief the components of Indian public debt.
9. Write a note on trends in Indian public debt.
10. Write note on causes for increase in Indian public debt.
11. Discuss in brief the role and limitation of Indian public borrowing.
12. Discuss briefly the problems of Indian public debt.
13. Narrate in brief the effects of Indian public debt.
14. Write a note on Indian public debt policy.
15. Give a brief account on Indian deficit financing.
16. Write a note on role of deficit financing in India.
17. Discuss in brief the merits and demerits of Indian deficit financing.

18. Analyse in brief classical concept of fiscal policy.
19. Explain in brief the objectives and methods of deficit budgeting.
20. Write a note on role and effects of deficit budgeting.
21. Analyse in brief the role of India fiscal policy.
22. Evaluate Indian fiscal policy.

(c) Questions each needs essay type/long answer (10/15 Marks each)

1. Explain critically Union Budget of India 2012-13.
2. Discuss the various sources and trends of revenue of Central Government.
3. Explain the various heads and trends of central expenditure.
4. Elucidate the reasons for increasing central expenditure.
5. Explain the components and magnitude of Indian public debt.
6. Discuss the magnitudes of Indian public debt, give reasons for its increase.
7. Analyse the role, limitations and problems of Indian public borrowing.
8. Explain the various effects of public debt on Indian Economy.
9. Discuss role and various methods of deficit financing in India.
10. Critically evaluate deficit financing in India.
11. What is Indian fiscal policy? Explain its objectives and evaluation.

Glossary

Ad Valorem Tax: It is a tax which is levied as a percentage of the value of a community.

Budget: Budget is a financial statement that shows the anticipated income and expenditure of the coming financial year.

Capital Budget: Capital budget consist of capital receipts and payment.

Capital Levy: Tax on wealth or property.

Dead Weight Debt: The other name of unproductive debt which does not add to the productive capacity of the country.

Debt Conversion: Conversion of high rated debt into low-rated debt.

Depression: Period of heavy unemployment and stagnation of business activity.

Digressive Tax: The people with higher income do not make a due sacrifice in the form tax to the government. The burden of tax imposed on them is relatively less. This will happen when a tax is only mildly progressive.

Direct Tax: Direct tax is really paid by a person on whom it is legally imposed. It means the impact and the incidence of a tax is on the same person.

External Debt: It refers to the loans taken from foreign government, foreign nationals and international institutions.

Fee: Fee is also a compulsory payment made by those who obtain a definite service in return from the government. For example, License fee, Education fee.

Federal: It is system adopted in India for resources sharing between state and Central Government (Decentralization of authorities).

Fine Tuning: This involves maintaining a steady rate of economic growth through using fiscal policy. However, this has proved quite difficult to achieve precisely.

Fiscal Policy: It refers to the government taxation and expenditure policies to influence the level of economic activities at the macro-economic level.

Grant-in-aid: It means the transfer of resources from the center to the state government to bridge the gap between revenues and expenditure of the state.

Growth with Stability: Growth speaks about a continuous increase in the national income or physical output of a country. Stability means regulating the prices. Controlling inflation and deflation is the main objective of stability.

Indirect Tax: The tax imposed on one person, but paid partly or wholly by another is known as indirect tax. The indirect tax is shifted or passed on to another person. Here the impact and incidence of a tax are on different persons.

Injections (J): This is an increase of expenditure into the circular flow, it includes government spending (G), Exports (X) and Investment (I).

Internal Debt: It refers to the public loan floated within the country.

Impact of a Tax: It is the immediate money burden of the tax. It means the person who initially pays the tax to the government bears the impact of a tax.

Liquid Assets: Those assets which can be converted into cash within a very short period.

Police State: Police states were concerned with defending the country from foreign aggression and maintenance of law and order within the State.

Price: When the public enterprises sell a commodity or render a service, impose charges on those who avail the services or buy these commodities. Such charges are called as price.

For example the goods and services supplied by the post offices, price on telephone services, railway and bus fare, etc., are few examples of price.

Progressive Tax: The rate or percentage of the tax rises as the taxable income increases. It means "higher the income, higher the rate or percentage of tax".

Proportional Tax: The percentage of the tax for all the taxpayers remains the same irrespective of the size of their income.

Public Debt: It refers to loans raised by a government within the country or outside the country.

Public Expenditure: It is the expenditure incurred by public authorities of Central, State and Local Governments for the economic and social welfare of their citizens.

Public Revenue: The government collected from citizens of particular country.

Public Utility Services: Supply of water, electricity, transport services, etc., is known as public utility services.

Regressive Tax : A tax is said to be regressive when the tax burden falls more heavily on the poor than the rich. It is the opposite of a progressive tax.

Refunding: Issuing of new bonds or securities by the government in order to repay the old matured debt.

Repudiation of debt: Government refuses to pay interest as well as the principal of public debt.

Revenue Budget: It consists of revenue receipts of the government and expenditure is met from this revenue.

Sinking Fund: A fund established by the government for the further repayment of public debt.

Social Services: Providing education, public health measures, medical, etc., are called as social services.

Special Assets: The assets the government creates the tangible goods for the benefit of common people of the country.

Surplus Budget: It means, the anticipatory revenue exceeds expenditure, and occurred imbalance in the budget.

Tax: Tax is a compulsory contribution made by individuals and institutions to the government exchequer and it is meant for the general purposes of the government.

Tax Incidence: The final resting place of the tax burden. The incidence of tax falls on the person who cannot shift it any further.

Taxable Capacity : The extent to which the people can be taxed without producing undesirable repercussions on the economy.

Withdrawals (W): This is leakages from the circular flow of income. It includes: Net Savings (S) + Net Taxes (T) + Net Imports (M).

Bibliography

Alesina, Alberto, 1990, *A Positive Theory of Budget Deficits and Government Debt*.

Alesina, Alberto and Roberto Perotti, 1994, *The Political Economy of Budget Deficits*.

Alesina, Alberto and Guido Tabellini, 1990, *A Positive Theory of Fiscal Deficits and Government Debt*.

Barman, Kiran, *Indian's Public Debt and Policy since Independence*.

Barro, Robert J., 1974, *Are Government Bonds Net Wealth?*.

Barro, Robert J., 1979, "On the Determination of the Public Debt", *Journal of Political Economy*, 87(5), 940-71.

Barro, Robert J. and Vittorio Grilli, 1994, *European Macroeconomics*, Hampshire and London: The Macmillan Press Ltd.

Blanchard, Olivier, Jean-Claude Chouraqui, Robert P. Hagemann and Nicola Sartor, 1990, *The Sustainability of Fiscal Policy: New Answers to an Old Question*.

Buchanan, James M., 1987, "Public Debt", *The New Palgrave Dictionary of Modern Economics*.

Buiter, Willem H., 1985, "A Guide to Public Sector Debt and Deficits", *Economic Policy*, 1, 13-81.

Buiter, Willem H. and Ujrit R. Patel, 1992, *Debt, Deficits and Inflation: An Application to the Public Finances of India*.

Cauvery, R. and Others, 2000, *Public Finance* (chapters 8 and 10) (fiscal policy), S. Chand & Company Ltd., New Delhi.

Chandra, Dalays, *External Debt of the Government of India.*

Corsetti, Giancarlo, 1991, "Testing for Solvency of the Public Sector: An Application to Italy", *Economic Notes* by Moute dei Paschi di Siena, 20(3), 581-99.

Domar, Evsey D., 1944, "The 'Burden of the Debt' and the National Income", *American Economic Review*, 34, 798-827.

Easterly, William and Klaus Schmidt-Hebel, 1994, "Fiscal Adjustment and Macroeconomic Performance: A Synthesis" in William Easterly, Carlos Alfredo Rodriguez and Klaus Schmidt-Hebbel, eds., *Public Sector Deficits and Macroeconomic Performance*, Oxford University Press, World Bank.

Gordon, Robert J., 1993, *Macroeconomics*, 6th edition HarperCollins College Publishers.

Guidotti, Pablo E. and Manmohan S. Kumar, 1991, "Domestic Public Debt of Externally Indebted Countries", *IMF Occasional Paper.*

Hugh, Dalton, *Principles of Public Finance* (chapters 21, 22 and 23), Allied Publishers (Pvt) Ltd., Bombay.

Lekhi, R.K., 1999, *Public Finance*, Kalyani Publishers, Ludhiana.

Modak, S.K., 1978, "Public Finance", Seth Publishers, Bombay.

Pigou, A.C., "A Study of Public Finance".

Prest, A.R., *Public Finance in Theory and Practice.*

Richard, A. Musgrave, "In the Theory of Public Finance".

Roubini, Nouriel and Jeffrey D. Sachs, 1989, "Government Spending and Budget Deficits in the Industrial Countries", *Economic Policy*, No. 8, 99-133.

Roubini, Nouriel and Jeffrey D. Sachs, 1989, "Political and Economic Determinants of Budget Deficits in the Industrial Democracies", *European Economic Review*, 33, 903-38.

Sargent, Thomas J. and Neil Wallace, 1981, "Some Unpleasant Monetarist Arithmetic", *Federal Reserve Bank of Minneapolis Quarterly Review*, 1-17.

Spaventa, Luigi, 1987, "The Growth of Public Debt; Sustainability, Fiscal Rules and Monetary Rules", *IMF Staff Papers*, 34(2), 374-99.

Steekantradha, B.S., *Public Debt and Economic Development in India*.

Taylor, Phillip, *The Economics of Public Finance*.

Tyagi, B.P., 2000-01, *Public Finance*, Jai Prakash Nath & Co.

Von Hagen, Jurgen, 1990, "A Note on the Empirical Effectiveness of Formal Fiscal Restraints", *Sonder for Schungsbereich* (SFB) 303, 1-20.

Wilcox, David W., 1989, "The Sustainability of Government Deficits: Implications of the Present-Value Borrowing Constraint", *Journal of Money, Credit and Banking*, 21(3), 291-306.